THE BARTERING MINDSET

A Mostly Forgotten Framework for Mastering Your Next Negotiation

We use money to solve our everyday problems, and it generally works well. Despite its economic benefits, however, money has a psychological downside: it trains us to think about negotiations narrow-mindedly, leading us to negotiate badly. Suggesting that we need a non-monetary mindset to negotiate better, Brian C. Gunia shows us how to look outside the monetary economy – to the bartering economies of the past, where people traded what they had for what they needed. Moreover, he argues that because of the economic difficulties associated with bartering, barterers had to use a more sophisticated form of negotiation – a strategic approach that can make us master negotiators today.

This book immerses readers in the assumptions that barterers typically make, collectively referred to as the "bartering mindset," and then demonstrates how to apply this mindset to modern, monetary negotiations. *The Bartering Mindset* concludes that our individual, organizational, and social problems fester for a predictable reason: we apply a monetary mindset to our negotiations, leading to suboptimal thinking, counterproductive behaviors, and disappointing outcomes. By offering the bartering mindset as an alternative, this book will help people negotiate better and thrive.

BRIAN C. GUNIA is an associate professor at the Carey Business School, Johns Hopkins University.

T0327095

BRIAN C. GUNIA

THE BARTERING MINDSET

A Mostly Forgotten
Framework for
Mastering Your
Next Negotiation

UNIVERSITY OF TORONTO PRESS
Toronto   Buffalo   London

© University of Toronto Press 2019
Rotman-UTP Publishing
Toronto Buffalo London
utorontopress.com
Printed and bound by CPI Group (UK) Ltd, Croydon, CR0 4YY

Reprinted in paperback 2022

ISBN 978-1-4875-0096-2 (cloth)   ISBN 978-1-4875-1217-0 (EPUB)
ISBN 978-1-4875-4846-9 (paper)   ISBN 978-1-4875-1216-3 (PDF)

Publication cataloguing information is available from Library and Archives Canada.

We wish to acknowledge the land on which the University of Toronto Press operates. This land is the traditional territory of the Wendat, the Anishnaabeg, the Haudenosaunee, the Métis, and the Mississaugas of the Credit First Nation.

University of Toronto Press acknowledges the financial assistance to its publishing program of the Canada Council for the Arts and the Ontario Arts Council, an agency of the Government of Ontario.

Canada Council   Conseil des Arts
for the Arts   du Canada

ONTARIO ARTS COUNCIL
CONSEIL DES ARTS DE L'ONTARIO

an Ontario government agency
un organisme du gouvernement de l'Ontario

Funded by the   Financé par le
Government   gouvernement
of Canada   du Canada

Canadä

*I dedicate this book to my two daughters, Vivian and Bridget.
May the bartering mindset help you find opportunities in
the conflicts and challenges that life inevitably presents.*

CONTENTS

Acknowledgments   ix

1 The Limits of the Monetary Mindset   3

2 The Bartering Mindset   29

3 Step 1: Deeply and Broadly Define Your Needs
  and Offerings   54

4 Steps 2–3: Map Out the Full Range of Transaction Partners
  and the Full Range of Their Possible Needs and Offerings   82

5 Step 4: Anticipate the Most Powerful Set of Partnerships
  across the Market   104

6 Step 5: Cultivate the Most Powerful Set of Partnerships
  across the Market   136

7 Integrating the Bartering and Monetary Mindsets   157

8 Objections to the Bartering Mindset   182

9 Conclusions and Applications   201

Notes   217

Index   229

ACKNOWLEDGMENTS

This book is the by-product of an extended and extensive collaboration, often with people who were no more aware of a book collaboration than I was. In other words, its ideas originate in countless and often casual interactions spread across my academic career, many that predated the book and others that at least ostensibly had nothing to do with it. Accordingly, any credit for the book's strengths should be dispersed broadly – much more broadly, even, than the people mentioned below. (Any blame for its errors, in turn, should be directed squarely at me.)

In particular, I would like to acknowledge and thank my three doctoral advisors at the Kellogg School of Management – Keith Murnighan, Jeanne Brett, and Adam Galinsky. You collectively taught me to think big without losing focus. Many of the ideas in this book are yours as much as mine.

In addition, I would like to thank my many negotiation students over the years, at both Northwestern University and Johns Hopkins University. It was your reflections on countless negotiation simulations – along with my own difficulty in intelligibly explaining integrative negotiation to you – that ultimately led me to the bartering mindset.

Much credit is due to my collaborators on negotiation research projects – you know who you are! Each of you has pushed me to broaden and deepen my own thinking about negotiation, without which I could not have completed this project (or many others). Thank you.

In addition, several people were kind enough to talk through the book's specific ideas with me. Your questions, comments, and quizzical looks all found a way into the book. A special thanks to Jeff Gish, David Loschelder, and Roman Trötschel.

Several others were kind enough to read through the whole book and offer their detailed comments and suggestions. These include three anonymous reviewers, Jeanne Brett, Mona Mensmann, Amy Pei, and Tom Allen. Each of you, in your own way, has dramatically improved the work. Reading through it, I hope you can spot your fingerprints!

A big and sincere thanks to University of Toronto Press and especially Jennifer DiDomenico, who saw early promise in the work and shepherded this first-time book author through a thicket of considerations and decisions. Thank you for your consistent support and consistently helpful feedback.

Last but certainly not least, I'd like to thank my immediate family: Betsy, Vivian, and Bridget; Mom, Dad, Amy, and Abby. Though we talk about negotiations less often than the others mentioned above, we've negotiated no less often – typically to everyone's benefit. More importantly, your constant and unwavering support have been a consistent source of inspiration and strength. Thank you.

THE BARTERING MINDSET

A Mostly Forgotten Framework for Mastering Your Next Negotiation

THE LIMITS OF THE
MONETARY MINDSET

On 9 April 2017, shortly before the departure of United Flight 3411, passenger David Dao was forcibly dragged from his seat, up the aisle, and off the flight by airport authorities – kicking, screaming, and bloodied.[1] Other passengers captured the soon-to-be viral video on their phones, imploring the authorities to stop their seemingly brutal treatment. As the world watched, the backstory slowly emerged.

United had determined, after fully boarding the flight, that they needed to put four crew members into passengers' seats. They offered passengers monetary incentives to take a later flight, and three accepted the offer. But the airline needed a fourth. In the absence of any takers, they randomly selected Dao, a doctor trying to return home. Learning of his selection, Dao became increasingly agitated, mentioning his ailing patients and refusing to leave the flight. From there, the situation escalated and culminated in his forcible removal and subsequent hospitalization.

In the wake of these events, United's troubles only multiplied. The viral video sparked worldwide outrage and condemnation on social media, especially on the Chinese website Weibo, where it attracted 210 million views within two days (a major problem, considering the airline's strategic focus on Asia). Incensed passengers around the world called for a boycott, and the company's stock initially took a $1 billion hit. United's CEO seemed to make matters worse, first by saying they had "re-accommodated" Dao and then by blaming the passenger for his belligerence even while praising the company's measured response.

The focal issue in this story was the disputed seat, not the monetary incentives offered to passengers. Nevertheless, the story embodies what this book will call the monetary mindset: an I-win-you-lose way of looking at the world that originates, at least in part, in our daily monetary transactions. United's stance embodied the monetary mindset in that its decision-makers saw themselves as occupying one side of an adversarial relationship with one other party, Dao, who wanted the opposite of what they wanted. Thus United saw no alternative to a show of force or a forced compromise on the monetary incentives. United's behavior and the world's reaction reveal the monetary mindset's shortcomings. This book will describe a mindset that can serve everyone better, helping us solve our own problems and meet our own needs much more effectively: the bartering mindset. By the end of the book, you should be able to devise a solution to the seat dispute that does not involve anyone's forcible removal.

But first, let's consider the mindset we already have: Think about a typical weekday, and count the number of times you at least implicitly use money. How many monetary transactions do you engage in, be they with cash, credit, or check? Maybe you buy gas in the morning, lunch at work, or an on-demand movie at home. Maybe somebody else pays you a salary or some other form of income. And even if you don't engage in any explicit monetary transactions, isn't money all around you – in the ads on the web, the bills in your mailbox, and the back of your mind when your kids leave the lights on? Whether we know it or consciously consider it, money is all around us. For most of us, monetary transactions are ubiquitous.[2]

And monetary transactions are ubiquitous for a good reason: they help us satisfy our needs and thereby solve our problems. Fundamentally, we use money to meet our unmet needs and help other people meet theirs. When you needed fuel, sustenance, or evening entertainment, didn't money help you obtain them? When somebody else needed your skill set or services, didn't they pay you for that reason? Anytime we need something from someone or someone needs something from us – and regardless of whether that someone is a person or an organization – engaging in a monetary transaction is an obvious and omnipresent way of obtaining it, albeit not the only way.[3]

Even before the days of Adam Smith, the economic benefits of monetary transactions and the surrounding monetary economy were well established:[4] buying lunch with the same resource your employer just provided makes life easy. Indeed, monetary transactions are ubiquitous *because* they allow us to solve our problems so efficiently. For example, if we had to scrounge around for something to trade with the cafeteria manager whenever we wanted lunch, we would undoubtedly live in a hungrier, poorer, and less pleasant world. So the economic benefits of monetary transactions and the surrounding monetary economy are not in question.

Yet an economic analysis of the monetary economy says little about its psychological effects. This book starts from the premise that the ubiquity of monetary transactions has an adverse psychological effect: it trains us to make a particular set of assumptions whenever we have a problem – assumptions that essentially portray our own needs as directly opposed to somebody else's. Assumptions that I call the "monetary mindset." Satisfactory as that mindset may be for satisfying our everyday needs efficiently, it serves us poorly when we apply it to our biggest problems and most pressing needs. Steeped as we are in the monetary economy, though, most of us do just that. In sum, while money is not the only way we solve our problems, it's such a ubiquitous and useful solution that it steeps us in a particular mindset – a mindset that can backfire when applied to bigger and more consequential problems: individual, organizational, and social.

The Monetary Mindset

A mindset is a way of seeing the world. It's *how* we think, not *what* we think.[5] More formally, a mindset is "a psychological orientation that affects the selection, encoding, and retrieval of information; as a result, mindsets drive evaluations, actions, and responses."[6] As this definition suggests, mindsets matter because they color the way we see the world around us – how we evaluate our situations, as well as how we act within or respond to them. In general, individuals can adopt mindsets repeatedly (using similar patterns of thinking across many situations)[7] or temporarily (adopting particular patterns of thinking in particular situations).[8]

The idea that money can at least temporarily put us into a particular mindset is well established in psychology.[9] For example, physical contact with or subliminal exposure to money (versus neutral objects) inclines people to think about themselves as relatively more independent or even self-interested, which can help them try harder and persist longer on challenging independent tasks. But it also makes them less caring, warm, and generous, and it inclines them to cheat and steal. Similar effects emerge across many cultures and in children as young as three, who cannot even consciously comprehend the purpose of money.[10] Consistent with these findings, people who presumably consider money and monetary transactions often – economics majors – tend to anticipate self-interested behavior from others and act in a relatively self-interested fashion themselves.[11] This last finding is particularly notable, as it suggests money can activate a chronic and not just a temporary mode of thinking. Temporary or repeated exposure to money and related concepts, it seems, tends to make people self-focused and potentially unethical.

In addition, exposure to money changes the way that people think about solving problems, both individual and societal. In particular, money elicits "a market-pricing orientation" toward the world,[12] in which people endorse competition among self-interested actors as the appropriate way of solving individual and societal problems.[13] Rather than supporting the more collaborative, cooperative, and egalitarian approaches to problem-solving that they might adopt in a family or community setting, people exposed to money tend to support free-market competition among self-interested parties, even if it results in inequality.

In other words, exposure to money leads people to apply the relatively competitive, self-interested lens associated with monetary transactions to a much broader set of problems – even problems that don't explicitly involve money. Expanding on this research, the current book suggests that our chronic and daily experience with monetary transactions trains us to see most of our own problems through a monetary lens. Repeated exposure to money, in other words, trains us to adopt a specific mindset when solving problems in coordination with other people. In particular, whenever we need something from someone else, I suggest we tend to make five assumptions, which are fully appropriate for monetary transactions and collectively constitute the monetary mindset:

1 I will be on one side of a transaction (for example, the buyer or seller).
2 I will interact with one party (for example, the seller or buyer).
3 I want one thing (for example, a low price), and they want the opposite (for example, a high price).
4 The only way for me to get a better deal is for the other party to get a worse deal.
5 I can avoid conflict by compromising.

Most of us never consider these assumptions consciously, much less verbalize them. Yet they're consistent with the psychological research above, painting a competitive and individualistic picture of people and their social surroundings. In addition, a little reflection verifies that most of us readily adopt the five assumptions when satisfying our everyday needs. Think back to a recent gas purchase. When filling your car, weren't you obviously operating as a buyer, not a seller? And weren't you obviously dealing with just one seller, a particular station? And wasn't it obvious that you'd prefer a low price and they'd prefer a high price – and that a better price for you would mean a worse price for the station, making it necessary to compromise on the posted price? Knowingly or not, you were using the monetary mindset.

And the monetary mindset efficiently resolved your need for gas. Indeed, for most of our everyday needs – gas, lunch, or a movie – there's no reason to think differently. The potential upside of somehow negotiating a better deal is negligible. Put on your bargaining hat, and you might find a way to save a whopping fifty cents on gas, for example. But the potential downside is sizable, since you'll probably waste much more than fifty cents' worth of time devising and executing the optimal negotiation strategy. For most of our everyday needs, we gain less by negotiating the best possible deal than we lose by spending time devising and executing the best possible strategy. So satisfying our everyday needs through the monetary mindset makes good economic sense.

Yet a little reflection reveals that most of us don't restrict the monetary mindset to our mundane problems and everyday needs. Our daily experience with money leads us to apply the mindset to much bigger problems and more important needs: a car to consume the gas, a raise to buy the lunch, or a home to host the on-demand movie, for example. Encountering these critical needs less often, few of us know exactly how to approach them – which assumptions to make. Absent any priors, and seeing that many of these big and important needs also involve money, chances are we apply the monetary mindset we know so well.

Consider or imagine a recent car purchase. In making the purchase, wasn't it obvious that you were acting as the buyer, not the seller? And also that there was just one party on the other side, a particular salesperson? And that he or she wanted a high price (preferably the sticker price), whereas you'd prefer something lower? And that only one of you could win this particular battle, necessitating some sort of compromise? I've certainly made those assumptions myself. If you have too, you've been using the monetary mindset to satisfy a very important need.

Unfortunately, none of the five assumptions was particularly accurate. You were not just on one side of the table, but both: you were probably selling your trade-in, or at least a lot of hard-earned money. You didn't have one counterpart, but many: all of the other dealers in town and on the web, as well as anyone else selling his or her car. And while you and this particular salesperson probably had opposing preferences on price, both of you probably cared about other issues too (for example, features, financing plan, future business). Chances are, your preferences on all of the issues were not completely opposed; an agreement on some of them (for example, a sunroof) might have benefitted you both, or at least benefitted one of you more than it hurt the other. That being the case, a compromise in the sense that most people use it – meeting in the middle on a single issue like price – was neither necessary nor desirable. You could've probably devised a trade-off to make you both happier, making a simple compromise on price suboptimal. Rather than splitting the difference on price, for example, you might've paid a bit more for the beloved sunroof (or the salesperson might've accepted a bit less in exchange for dealer financing, etc.). Neither your assumption about the need to compromise nor the other four assumptions were particularly accurate or helpful.

Indeed, applied to your need for a car, the five assumptions of the monetary mindset were just plain harmful. Having made them, the likely outcome was a low price for your trade-in, a high price for your new car, a suboptimal set of features, and the absence of a desirable financing plan or discount. In short: an unhappy outcome, and an unhappy customer. The monetary mindset wasn't

particularly helpful – it actually burned you (both) badly.[14] In this
way, the monetary mindset produces poor solutions to many of our
problems, costing everyone dearly. But why, when the same mindset
was so accurate for our everyday needs like a tank of gas?

Well, technically, it wasn't so accurate for that need either. Going
back to your fuel fill-up, you were technically doing more than buying gas. From the station's perspective, you were also potentially
"selling" your future business and referrals. Your community probably features at least a few gas stations, after all, and this one would
probably prefer a steady stream of future fill-ups at their pumps to
an additional fifty cents right now. So might you. Accordingly, a
discussion about the station's loyalty program could've saved you
money right now in exchange for future business – which is more
like a trade-off than a compromise. So the five assumptions of the
monetary mindset weren't really right for this everyday need either.
It just wasn't worth your time and brain cells to consider them
more deeply.

In other words, it didn't really matter whether you got the best
possible deal on gas. But the bigger the need, the more you stand to
gain from a great deal – and lose from a bad one. The extra few hours
and brain cells spent devising and executing an optimal car-buying
strategy, for example, will probably cost you far less than the massive savings obtained. For our biggest and most important needs,
it's well worth our time to consider our mindset carefully. Unfortunately, the confluence of our daily monetary transactions with the
fact that our biggest problems tend to involve money causes most of
us – myself included – to mindlessly apply the monetary mindset.

The problem gets more serious still when we realize that the monetary mindset is hardly restricted to our personal problems. It also
surfaces in some of our most serious organizational and political
problems. Most businesspeople can easily recall a situation when
they couldn't get a colleague to cooperate. Can you? Is it possible
your uncooperative counterpart (or even you) was making one or

more of the monetary mindset's five assumptions – perhaps assuming you wanted the opposite of the one thing someone else did, without asking? The United Airlines story at the start of the chapter, the collapse of mortgage-backed securities, the wasteland of underperforming mergers and acquisitions, the seeming deterioration in customer service across industries: look hard enough, and I think you'll see traces of the monetary mindset in all of these diverse and multiply determined examples. In particular, I think you'll see many people assuming that many problems involve two parties with strictly opposed preferences – one winner and one loser. The monetary mindset – a competitive, fixed-pie way of seeing the world – infuses our organizational lives, in addition to our personal ones.

And, as anyone who pays attention to politics can tell you, it infuses our political lives too. Consider the impasse between Mexican President Enrique Peña Nieto and U.S. President Donald Trump over the financing of a border wall.[15] Mr Trump was elected on the back of a promise that Mexico would pay for the construction of a border wall, a claim that Mr Peña Nieto flatly rejected when Mr Trump took office. In retrospect, it seems clear that each man saw himself as occupying one side of a conflict with one other party who wanted the opposite of the one thing he wanted (assumptions 1–3). Mr Trump wanted Mr Nieto to pay; Mr Nieto wanted just the opposite. In addition, unless one of them found a way to win the battle at the other's expense, it seems clear they would eventually have to compromise, if only to avoid an overt conflict (assumptions 4–5).

But in reality, both parties had many demands other than financing for a wall, in addition to many other potential enticements to offer – from trade, to law enforcement, to immigration policy (opposing assumption 1). Both were implicitly negotiating with many parties – Mr Trump with Mexican legislators, the American public, and the states involved in a border wall, and Mr Peña Nieto with the U.S. Congress, Mexican public, and Mexicans residing in the United States, for example (opposing assumption 2). While the parties' preferences on wall financing were probably opposed, they had a common interest in many issues, such as maintaining robust trade (opposing assumption 3). Had either party introduced these issues into the discussion, both would've realized that neither had to "win" at the other's expense (opposing assumption 4), or else compromise on a mutually dissatisfactory compromise involving the wall (opposing assumption 5). Rather, both might've made progress on multiple issues of vital importance to both countries. The monetary mindset was alive and well in this important political problem. And unfortunately it's just one of countless examples.

In sum, we as individuals, managers and leaders, and members of the body politic don't use the monetary mindset just to satisfy our everyday needs. We use it to satisfy needs that are much too big and important for it to handle. As a result, we either bear the costs of poor solutions ourselves or battle the people around us in an unpleasant attempt to offload the costs onto them. Across the personal, organizational, or political spheres, then, it should come as no surprise that we see such a proliferation of dissention, distrust, and discord – ultimately leaving many of our most important needs unsatisfied and problems unresolved. Nor should it surprise us that the problems that are solved hinge on tenuous and tentative compromises, reflecting so little of the creativity otherwise brimming across our societies – and usually leaving all sides unhappy. Nice as the word sounds, *compromise* is not the ideal in our most important negotiations – it's a disappointing way-station on the road between conflict and real solutions, a solution that ultimately makes no one happy.[16]

Pick a major political issue in any nation over the last ten years: chances are, it's still festering or at least teetering on the brink of a tenuous compromise. Watch any cable news channel: chances are, you'll see seething dissatisfaction with our social and political stalemates. To be sure, these issues have numerous and manifold causes – too many to enumerate or even count, let alone cover in a single book. But take a close look at any of these issues and I bet you'll see traces of the monetary mindset – especially the idea that we and our preferences are always opposed to our monolithic opponents and theirs. So appropriate for our everyday needs, the monetary mindset is simply unequipped to satisfy our most important needs as individuals, managers or leaders, and members of the body politic.

The Monetary Mindset in Negotiation

So maybe you're convinced that the monetary mindset is unhelpful for solving our biggest problems and meeting our most important needs. But why? What is it about the mindset that results in suboptimal outcomes? The answer involves negotiation.

Whether we realize it or not, any situation in which we need someone else's cooperation to satisfy our needs is actually a negotiation.[17] Whether it's fuel, food, or a new car we need – and whether we think we're "negotiating" or not – most of us negotiate every day, several times a day. One of the fundamental contentions of this book, though, is that the monetary mindset prompts an unproductive set of negotiation behaviors. And while these behaviors have trivial consequences for everyday problems like the lack of fuel or food, they have tremendous consequences for big and important problems like the lack of a car. In short, the monetary mindset fails us by prompting us to negotiate poorly, and poor negotiation behaviors have especially serious consequences for big problems. Understanding this issue requires a brief journey into the intriguing world of negotiation research.

The last fifty years or more have seen a groundswell of negotiation research. From the beginning, this research has emphasized that people can engage in two fundamentally different types of negotiation behaviors: distributive behaviors and integrative behaviors. Distributive behaviors are competitive maneuvers like making the first offer, engaging in persuasion, and cultivating a strong alternative. Integrative behaviors are cooperative maneuvers like building trust, exchanging information, and focusing on interests instead of positions.[18]

Distributive and integrative behaviors rest on very different assumptions, represent very different approaches, and have very different purposes. People engage in distributive behaviors because they assume that they and their counterpart are both seeking to claim the largest possible portion of a single, fixed resource (that is, a "pie") like money. In other words, they assume that the resources under discussion cannot change and simply need to be divided, suggesting that their primary interest consists of getting a better deal at the other party's expense.[19] So they act distributively to claim the biggest possible slice of the fixed pie for themselves. And it often works: people who make the first offer, for example, consistently obtain a larger slice of the pie, that is, a final price that benefits themselves more than their counterparts.[20]

Conversely, people engage in integrative behaviors because they suspect the pie is smaller than it could be – that the parties could identify more, mutually beneficial resources to divide if they tried. In other words, they assume that the resources under consideration need to be grown in addition to divided, meaning that they and their counterpart have some interests in common – or at least not entirely in conflict.[21] So they act integratively to maximize the size of the pie before anyone takes a slice. Far from naive altruism, integrative behaviors reflect enlightened self-interest, as even a small slice of a big pie is often bigger than a big slice of a small pie. Indeed, in the absence of integrative behaviors, the pie is often so small that the parties can't find a viable deal at all. And integrative behaviors tend to work: negotiators who make the effort to build trust, for example, tend to initiate an information exchange that breaks impasses and generates a bigger profit for both sides.[22]

Neither set of negotiation behaviors is sufficient on its own. Negotiators need to engage in both distributive and integrative behaviors to succeed.[23] Yet engaging in both sets of behaviors is far from easy, as each makes the other more difficult, and people often find distributive behaviors too tempting to resist. If their counterpart acts distributively (for instance, by making an aggressive first offer), many people react distributively just to protect themselves; as one example, they might make an aggressive counteroffer. And if their counterpart acts integratively (for instance, by sharing information), many people act distributively out of temptation; as one example, they might use shared information against the other party in an aggressive counteroffer. This situation creates a "negotiator's dilemma," in which both negotiators spiral toward distributive behavior, even though both would benefit from additional integrative behavior.[24] The result is a proliferation of distributive behaviors and disappointing outcomes.

Against this backdrop, more than fifty years of negotiation research and writing have consistently urged negotiators to go beyond their distributive impulses by engaging in much more integrative behavior.[25] Indeed, the overwhelming majority of articles have concluded that distributive behaviors, though necessary and appealing, are completely inadequate for achieving advantageous outcomes. For example, the foundational book on negotiations – *Getting to Yes* – along with the decades of research it inspired have been making that point persuasively since the 1980s. Unfortunately, as the 2013 *Forbes* article "Negotiators Still Aren't Getting to Yes" argued, "It didn't work."[26] In other words, decades of encouragement to act more integratively have not changed the fact that most negotiators still rely much more heavily on distributive behaviors, achieving consistently poor outcomes. In particular, individuals do not necessarily transfer integrative negotiation skills from negotiation courses into the real world,[27] the assumptions underlying distributive negotiation have clearly persisted into twenty-first century negotiations,[28] and conflicts in business, politics, and international relations are hardly abating.

But why? Why does the world continue to find integrative negotiation so difficult?

This book offers one reason. The mindset that people chronically
adopt because of their routine reliance on money – the monetary
mindset – strongly inclines them toward distributive behaviors, as
indicated by evidence presented in the next chapter and throughout.
Looking back at the five assumptions of the monetary mindset, you'll
see that they line up nicely with the assumptions that promote distributive negotiation behavior. The monetary mindset paints a competitive, adversarial, fixed-pie view of the world: a view that it's "my way
or your way," that two negotiators' interests are strictly opposed, that
whatever's good for one is bad for the other. And this view stimulates
distributive negotiation behavior. Given the ubiquity of money and
thus the ubiquity of the monetary mindset, it should surprise no one
that distributive negotiation continues to hold such appeal.

Thankfully, distributive negotiation is harmless enough for our
everyday needs, where the benefits of optimal negotiation strategies
are low. When used to satisfy our biggest and most important needs,
however, the monetary mindset and its associated implications for
negotiation hold dire repercussions. Individuals envision themselves
on one side of a transaction, opposing one other party who wants
the opposite of the one thing they want. They act competitively if not
aggressively, trying to win if they can but compromise, disappoint-
ingly, if they must. In other words, they see themselves as combatants
seeking to claim the biggest possible portion of a fixed pie, not collaborators seeking to maximize everyone's interests at the same time.
Fifty years or more of negotiation research have labelled this approach
"distributive" and shown that it doesn't really work, at least not on its
own. And when the stakes are high, the consequences are dire.

So what kind of mindset might support integrative behaviors?
Unfortunately, most of us just don't have one. And that's just the
problem. That's why *Getting to Yes* and the research it inspired "didn't
work," according to *Forbes* – why even the best negotiation courses

Figure 1.1 Mindsets and Negotiation Behaviors

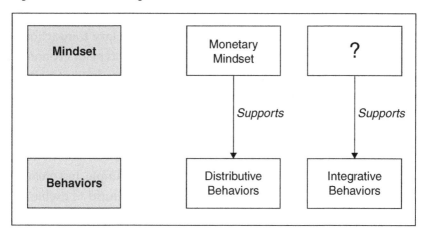

or the most successful negotiation experiences still don't result in much sustained integrative behavior in the real world. That's why most of us, myself included, still find it extremely hard to act integratively in most negotiations. Absent a mindset that supports integrative behavior, we fall back on the mindset we have – the monetary mindset – along with all of the distributive behaviors it stimulates. In short, the monetary mindset fails us for our biggest problems and most important needs because it strongly inclines us toward an insufficient and often counterproductive set of distributive negotiation behaviors. The negotiation behaviors we really need to display – integrative behaviors – require a very different mindset, and most of us just don't have one. Figure 1.1 illustrates the situation.

The Bartering Mindset

We need a better mindset. Our most important personal, professional, and political problems depend on it. They demand a more productive way of thinking about the world – a complementary way of understanding our problems that makes integrative negotiation behaviors at least possible, if not probable. Since the monetary mindset comes, at least in part, from our chronic monetary transactions, we need to look elsewhere – that is, to a different type of economic transaction. In particular, we need to take a closer look at bartering: a form of economic exchange in which people directly trade the goods or services they have for the goods or services they need.[29]

Where in the world (quite literally) does bartering occur – or did it? Bartering certainly still occurs in certain corners of the modern world. The rise of the "sharing economy,"[30] for example, has created a variety of opportunities for people around the world to exchange their goods or services directly through couch sharing, food swapping, and time banking. Consider the Couchsurfing website,[31] which allows people to sleep on strangers' couches but also strongly encourages them to share their own couches later. Similarly, participants at food swapping events make and trade food through bilateral exchanges. Most interestingly, time-banking services allow members to directly or indirectly exchange their time. So a contractor might perform five hours of home repair for an accountant. The accountant could then "repay" the time by preparing the contractor's taxes – or someone else's. If the latter, then the time bank would owe the contractor five hours of another party's time.

Bartering also persists in a variety of other circumstances that have little to do with the sharing economy.[32] For example, some individuals or businesses barter today to reduce their tax bills or circumvent trade restrictions (sometimes on questionable legal grounds). In addition, businesses often barter as part of their cross-border transactions, frequently at the insistence of foreign governments, while governments often barter with each other, particularly when exchanging defense technologies. And bartering still flourishes among individuals who lack cash – for instance, in developing economies or countries with unstable currencies and/or recessionary conditions; recent examples include Spain, Greece, and Argentina.

Most familiar to many people is the bartering that still occurs in family or community settings, even in developed Western economies. We've all bartered by agreeing to help a friend move in exchange for a subsequent six-pack, for example, and our kids barter almost automatically when they exchange their Christmas presents with siblings. Particularly in close-knit and/or rural corners of the developed economies, community members may barter routinely within the confines of the community – for example, by shoveling a neighbor's snow now in explicit or implicit anticipation of the neighbor mowing their lawn occasionally in the summer. Bartering is far from dead to the modern world.

And yet, as implied by the subtitle of this book, it's far from the norm either. Most people buying this book necessarily live in a modern monetary economy. And in modern monetary economies, most people necessarily engage in far fewer bartering than monetary transactions daily, and far fewer bartering transactions than their ancestors did in the distant past.[33] Indeed, while bartering was once the predominant form of economic exchange around the world,[34] only a relatively small number of geographically isolated groups like the Lhomi of Nepal appear to use bartering as their primary mode of economic exchange today.[35] In sum, bartering as a predominant form of economic exchange was much more prevalent in the past (hence my predominant use of the past tense). And it's in that sense that bartering is "mostly forgotten" today.

The historical trend away from bartering, along with the economic benefits of the monetary economy, have long led economists and commentators to regard bartering economies as "primitive."[36] An 1894 book on money, for example, introduced bartering by saying, "Before the appearance of money in the world, exchanges of commodities were made in a very crude way."[37] A more recent article indicated that barter is "associated with a marginal, primitive world defined by the absence of such things as money."[38] And a recent book indicated, "Before money there was barter, a slow and uncertain method of exchange. One party might not want what the other offers, or the offers may not have equivalent values. Money, however, is a reliably valuable, divisible, and portable form of wealth."[39]

Accurate as this economic portrayal of bartering may be, it says little about the psychology of bartering. In contrast to the "primitive" hypothesis, the confluence of anthropological, psychological, and negotiation evidence underlying this book suggests that the difficulties of bartering economies actually required their inhabitants to use a highly sophisticated mindset to satisfy their needs: the bartering mindset. Economically primitive as bartering may be, I hope you'll walk away understanding that it rests on remarkably sophisticated psychology.

The idea that the psychology of bartering differs markedly has precedent: anthropologists like Caroline Humphrey have noted that "barter ... is radically different from the monetary mentality."[40] In addition, the psychological research on money that I've described often contrasts the effects of handling money with the effects of handling objects like those traded in a bartering economy (for example, buttons). It shows that people who handle objects often feel more connected, interdependent, and egalitarian, displaying more warmth and generosity.[41] This evidence hints at the idea that bartering may lead people to think differently.

Still we know little about what the differences might be or how they might relate to any of our modern problems and associated negotiations. This book seeks to uncover the features of the bartering mindset, arguing that it's not just different from the monetary mindset – it's better for the purpose of engaging in integrative negotiation behaviors. Since most of us barter so irregularly, I portray the bartering mindset as mostly *forgotten*. Since most of us still barter on occasion, though, I also portray it as *mostly* (rather than completely) forgotten. And it's a good thing we haven't forgotten it completely, as we'll need to remember the psychology of bartering to understand and apply it to the modern, monetary world.

Objectives and Non-Objectives of This Book

Let me be as clear as possible on what this book is trying to do – and not do. Starting with its non-objectives, this book will not encourage you to barter more! Nor will it teach you how to barter more effectively. Why? First, several popular primers (for example, *No Cash? No Problem!*)[42] already do both; one even offers ninety-three "inside secrets" on bartering. Second, since you're reading the current book, you probably live in a modern monetary economy. And whether you like it or not, many of your most important problems and pressing needs probably still involve money. Thus, I don't see a purely bartering-based approach, bereft of any monetary considerations, as particularly realistic – or helpful.

So this book will not try to inject more bartering activities into the monetary world. Just as important, it will not try to inject more money into the bartering world. The fact that you helped your friend move for a six-pack, that your kids exchanged their Christmas presents, or that you ploughed your neighbor's driveway – all without the expectation of money – is fully appropriate in the associated family or community settings. To ask your friend, your kids, or your neighbor to pull out their wallets would be downright inappropriate.

So what will the book actually do? Its primary purpose is to help you master your modern negotiations, many of which inevitably involve money. I will not encourage you to spend your negotiations bartering. But I will encourage and meticulously train you to apply the bartering *mindset* – the way that people in the full-blown bartering economies of the past prototypically *thought* about their problems – to your modern negotiations, even the ones involving money. By the end of the book, you should be fully equipped to master your modern negotiations by remembering a mostly forgotten mindset. Put differently, you'll find yourself starting to devise better solutions to big problems like United's seat dilemma, your own need for a new car, and even the Mexican-U.S. border wall dispute – solutions that don't involve everyone walking away in dissatisfaction or disgust. By the end of the book, I hope you'll agree that our predecessors' way of thinking is just as relevant for the modern world – and potentially even more useful than our own monetary mindsets.

In sum, this book seeks to resurrect the bartering mindset for the modern reader, reminding you of its essential features and training you to use it in your modern negotiations. Ultimately, the message is simple: An "old" way of thinking can help us master our "new" and often money-laden negotiations. Or, put differently: bartering offers a better metaphor for negotiation than money. Through numerous practical examples and exercises, the book will immerse you in the bartering mindset, helping you to translate it for the monetary world. By the end I think you'll find yourself equipped to engage in a diverse set of integrative negotiation behaviors – some new, some known. Indeed, if the book succeeds, you'll see yourself using numerous new strategies that improve your negotiation outcomes. At the end of the process, though, you'll also find yourself deploying some of the same integrative negotiation behaviors that books like *Getting to Yes* and numerous negotiation articles have recommended. The key difference? You'll actually have the right mindset to use them. In other words, your new mentality should allow you to display those behaviors *in practice*, not just in theory, effectively replacing the unhelpful question mark in figure 1.1 with the bartering mindset. My sincere hope, then, is that *Forbes* may someday update their 2013 article about *Getting to Yes* with another article indicating that "thanks to the bartering mindset, it did work."

Organization of This Book

Let's walk through the organization of the book so you know what to expect. To immerse you in the bartering mindset, chapter 2 will define bartering and walk you through a thought experiment about a man named Keith living in an idealized bartering economy, as portrayed by a combination of anthropological research and economic theory. This process will reveal the five key assumptions of the bartering mindset, which contrast sharply with the five assumptions of the monetary mindset. Finally, chapter 2 will link the assumptions of the bartering mindset to a five-step process you can follow to translate that mindset for, and apply it to, the modern world.

Using an extended example about a struggling small business, chapters 3–6 will then walk you through the five-step process in detail, offering a tangible template to help you satisfy the needs in your own life. Chapter 7 will round out our discussion about applying the bartering mindset by addressing a critical detail: how to integrate it with the monetary mindset that comes so naturally – and that will certainly come naturally to your negotiation counterparts. Chapter 8 will then seek to answer some important questions that you might still have about the bartering mindset – nagging issues that might prevent you from embracing it completely. Chapter 9 concludes with a brief summary and set of scenarios intended to test your knowledge of the bartering mindset, reveal its immediate relevance, and help you start applying it right away.

A couple of important notes before commencing the journey. First, to get the most out of this book, I would encourage you to actively engage with the exercises and examples. For example, chapters 1–7 end with a mini-case about job negotiations; to benefit from this book (and your next job negotiation), I would suggest you actively engage with the example, especially by answering the questions I pose. In addition, in the chapters using the extended example about the struggling small business (3–7), I would ask you to imagine yourself as the protagonist, making the same kinds of choices he or she must make along the way. Doing so will not only make the book a lot more fun; it will also train you to implement the mindset. In sum, tempting as it might be to skip portions of the book or passively consume it, I would encourage you to be an active consumer. The more active your engagement with the bartering mindset, the more complete your immersion in a new way of thinking – and the more thoroughly you'll be able to deploy it in the modern world.

Will it be worth your time? Persist through the book, and I think it will. By the end you'll be better able to engage in integrative negotiation – and thus better able to satisfy your biggest needs and solve your most important problems. In the process, and as a side benefit, you'll also learn to do some things that many negotiation books tend to gloss over: methodically prepare for your negotiations, manage multiparty negotiations, creatively engage with the world to find value where there was none, and treat negotiation as a proactive form of problem-solving.

In sum, I know you'll find the book useful. And I suspect you'll realize in the process that, as economically primitive as bartering may be, the bartering mindset is anything but. As a direct result I think you'll leave with both the desire and the ability to make that mindset your primary approach for satisfying your most important needs – becoming a master negotiator by deploying a mostly forgotten mindset.

Summary of Key Points from This Chapter

1 In the modern monetary economy, most of us engage in frequent monetary transactions to satisfy our needs and solve our problems.
2 Our chronic monetary transactions immerse us in a monetary mindset, which we apply to many of our problems.
3 But when the stakes are high, the monetary mindset produces poor outcomes, exacerbating personal, organizational, and political problems.
4 That is because the satisfaction of high-stakes needs requires negotiation, and the monetary mindset encourages purely

distributive negotiation behaviors, which are insufficient and often counterproductive.

5 Bartering activities and the bartering mindset that permeates them can prepare us to engage in the integrative behaviors necessary for success in modern negotiations.

Exercise: Job Negotiation and the Monetary Mindset

This and the following six chapters conclude with a mini-exercise that will help you move beyond the monetary mindset and master the bartering mindset in your own life. A few notes before commencing the journey. The example concerns your current job and especially your perceived need for a salary bump. Given the direct focus on money, this may seem like a strange setting to explore the bartering mindset. But since the goal is applying the bartering mindset to money-laden negotiations rather than bartering per se, this is exactly the right setting!

In addition, since the book will be useful only if you can apply the bartering mindset to your own life, I'd encourage you to actively engage with the exercise by connecting it to your own experiences and circumstances – even if money at work is not your most pressing problem. Please use your imagination! And finally, please know that you'll have to stick with me for a series of chapters to get the most out of the example. Since most people approach such problems simplistically – and especially by applying the monetary mindset – we'll first go down the rabbit hole that inevitably engulfs them. But over a series of chapters (and especially by the sixth or seventh), I think you'll see the benefits of a different mode of thinking – the bartering mindset. In particular, I think you'll find yourself learning to understand your own situation, the external world, and the options that can usefully unite you with the external world. So please stick with me! And now, without further ado, let's get started.

Think about your current job – the real job that you, the reader, really have right now. Are you completely satisfied with your paycheck? Perhaps your pay is passable, but I'd guess that you could probably use a few more dollars. Who couldn't? Although your real-life dissatisfaction might not be so serious as to demand immediate action, please imagine – for the purpose of the exercise – that it was. In other words, please imagine that you thought the real pay in your real job just had to get better. If you felt that way in real life, what would you do? Please take a moment and consider your likely course of action.

Now I'll admit that I can't see inside your head. But I'm guessing you would probably do the same thing as most people: most would request a meeting with their boss, present the relevant facts, and ask for a raise. Suspecting their boss would prefer to award little or no raise, they might pad their initial request a bit and justify it a lot, preparing to settle on a smaller amount if they had to. But if their boss declined to award any kind of a raise, well, then many people might consider dusting off their résumés. Is that basically what you would do? Before I started to study negotiation, that is basically what I would've done. So I'm guessing you would do too.

Supposing you'd follow this approach, here are three important questions to consider:

1 How does this approach relate to the monetary mindset, if at all?
2 Which assumptions of the monetary mindset does it involve, if any?
3 What might be wrong with these initial assumptions?

Please take a moment to review the five assumptions of the monetary mindset and devise your own answers to these questions before proceeding.

Remembering that you're not alone in adopting the above approach, how does this approach relate to the monetary mindset and its five assumptions (questions 1–2)? I'd say your approach clearly reflects the mindset and all five assumptions. First, in adopting this stance, you assumed you were on one side of the transaction, asking for something (a raise) but focusing less attention on what you were offering or could offer (assumption 1). At this point, at least, you assumed that there was only one party on the other side of the table (your boss; assumption 2) and that this person preferred the opposite of the one thing you wanted (little or no raise instead of a big one; assumption 3). Accordingly, your approach involved aggressively staking out your own need for a big raise (assumption 4) but preparing to compromise on a middling raise if necessary (assumption 5). This approach, quite natural for most of us, given our daily monetary experiences, is fully consistent with the monetary mindset.

But what, if anything, was wrong with these assumptions in this case (question 3)? To answer that question, please think about your own job. In the context of your actual job in real life, is it really money you want, or money for the sake of something else? And couldn't you potentially offer a whole bunch of things in exchange for a salary increase (assumption 1) – to assume more responsibilities, more travel, or another role, for example? Or even to accept your current pay if the company covered your commuting costs? (Just examples – please supply your own.) In addition, in real life, isn't it possible that obtaining more money might require you to talk to more people than just your boss (assumption 2) – HR, others in the company who might value your skill set, people at other organizations, a bank willing to offer you a loan, even people who would pay you for your unique expertise in the form of a consulting arrangement? And in real life, wouldn't you and your boss both care about a multitude of issues in addition to your raw salary (assumption 3) – your ability to work at home, the proportion of your paycheck awarded via performance-based pay, time off, responsibilities, or career trajectory? If so, then isn't it possible that both of you could've walked away happier at the same time (assumption 4) by surfacing solutions that satisfied you both? Perhaps your boss could've easily paid you more if you agreed to travel more? If so, wouldn't you want to forget the middling salary compromise (assumption 5) in favor of a big raise coupled with an opportunity to fulfill your lifelong dreams of travelling?

Although I don't know your individual circumstances and am confident the specifics vary, I hope that actively considering the assumptions in the context of your real life highlights the inadequacy of the monetary mindset – the fact that the monetary mindset's five assumptions don't hold water if you consider them closely. Of course you probably didn't think to question these assumptions before reading this chapter, and possibly before reading the previous paragraph. Who would? Virtually no one, since we live in the modern monetary economy. Yet I hope you're now wondering how well the monetary mindset serves you – whether it actually helps you identify the best solutions to your most important problems. If not, then I hope you're motivated to find a better mindset. That's exactly what we'll do in the next chapter. And by the end of chapter 7 you won't be fighting with your boss over a middling raise at all. You'll be exchanging sophisticated multi-issue proposals over virtual work and a re-imagined set of travel responsibilities, even while applying for a Costco membership and considering an apartment-sharing arrangement. If that sounds crazy, I hope you're intrigued to read on.

2

THE BARTERING MINDSET

In 2005 Kyle MacDonald decided that something had to change.[1] An unemployed writer living with his girlfriend, he was tired of moping around her Montreal apartment – and she was tired of his moping. But how could he fix the situation without the hint of a job?

Fortunately, in the midst of Kyle's gloomy reverie, he remembered a childhood game called "Bigger and Better." The rules were simple: Start with something small like a button or pencil, knock on some doors, and find someone willing to trade for something bigger and better. Then keep trading, in hopes of eventually ending up with something really valuable. Considering his dismal prospects, why not try it again now? What did he really have to lose by trading the first thing he saw – the one red paperclip on the desk – for something bigger and better, then repeating the process in hopes of obtaining something much more valuable? Crazy as it might sound, could he even eventually trade for something as substantial as a place to live? Thus began Kyle's year-long adventure encompassing fourteen trades and culminating in his own house in Kipling, Saskatchewan.

Within minutes of Kyle's initial offer to trade one red paperclip on craigslist, he heard from several interested parties, including two women willing to trade a pen that looked and wobbled like a fish. After considering a variety of less interesting offers, Kyle decided to make the trade. And it seems that all parties were satisfied – Kyle because he acquired something more interesting than a paperclip and the women because they could now organize their papers and tell a very interesting story.

With growing confidence, Kyle traded for a ceramic doorknob, then a camping stove, then a thousand-watt generator, even while building a website for his increasingly famous project. But the project hit a snag with the generator, as it seemed that none of his newfound followers really wanted one. But the protracted process of offloading the generator (eventually for a beer keg with a neon sign) taught Kyle an important lesson: he had to consider not just the value *he* attached to a particular item, but the value his potential trading partners would. With that lesson, the beer keg / sign, and the names of several interested parties (many offering and asking for numerous items) in hand, he made the following series of trades:

- Snowmobile
- Trip to Yahk, British Columbia
- Large van
- Recording contract
- One year rent-free in a Phoenix apartment
- One afternoon with Alice Cooper

At this point Kyle's project was obviously taking off. But his followers were stunned by his next move: the decision to trade the afternoon with Alice Cooper for a motorized, KISS-themed snow globe. Why would anyone do that? Because the actor Corbin Bernsen had already promised him a role in a Hollywood movie in exchange for something sufficiently interesting, and Kyle's research had surfaced Bernsen's avid interest in snow globes. The generator experience had served him well, even if few of his followers could fully appreciate it. Finally, with the snow globe in Bernsen's hands and the movie role in his, he could realize his dream by trading the role for a two-story farmhouse in Kipling.

Kyle's amazing story epitomizes what we will call the bartering mindset. In each trade he was both offering and receiving something of value. He interacted with many parties before executing any given trade, especially his ultimate trade for a house. Many of these parties brought many needs and offerings to the table. None of his trades seemed to reflect unilateral "wins" or even compromises; strange as some of them were, they all benefitted both sides in a big way, sometimes by design (for example, the snow globe). Whether or not Kyle was actually using the bartering mindset, his story epitomizes its central features.

While most of us can easily understand the monetary mindset, which infuses our daily thinking, the bartering mindset comes less naturally. Even if we can understand how Kyle offered and received something as part of each trade, for example, it's harder to see how that translates to our own monetary lives. In what sense do we stand on both sides of a monetary transaction? Since we inhabit a thoroughly monetary world, it's challenging to square Kyle's story and the bartering mindset it epitomizes with our own experiences. Thus we'll have to step away from our own monetary experiences to understand the bartering mindset.

Though we could probably do that by thinking about the situations in which we still barter, we're necessarily limited by our experiences. Maybe you haven't bartered very often (or successfully)? And even if you've bartered frequently with gusto, you're probably still steeped in the monetary economy, meaning that your bartering has likely reflected at least some aspects of the monetary mindset. Instead of thinking about our past experiences, then, what we need is to consider a common story that presents the bartering mindset in pure form. Thus we'll use this chapter to step into a full-blown bartering economy and the mind of one of its inhabitants, trying to see the world through a barterer's eyes. In particular we'll conduct a thought experiment, trying to understand (or remember) what it "feels like" to barter routinely. Having done that, we'll all be better equipped to understand how the bartering mindset can improve our own monetary lives. And, just as a reminder, that's the ultimate goal. After this chapter we won't be talking about bartering per se all that often. We'll be trying to apply the bartering *mindset* to our modern negotiations, many of which involve money.

Bartering Economies and the Bartering Mindset

As noted in the last chapter, individuals around the world still barter for a variety of reasons, but full-fledged bartering economies are quite rare.[2] Perhaps as a result, our knowledge about the psychology of bartering is necessarily limited and sparse. The knowledge that we have tends to come from anthropological studies of the remaining bartering economies (for example, the Lhomi of Nepal), along with economic theories of bartering. In this chapter we'll combine anthropological and economic perspectives on bartering to construct an idealized bartering economy: an economy that represents the prototypical features of the once-prevalent bartering economies (rather than any specific society). Mentally steeped in that economy, we'll conduct a thought experiment in which we consider what one specific person is probably thinking as he barters. This thought experiment admittedly integrates the evidence with our own logic and imagination. But it's far from a flight of fancy, as revealed by evidence at the end of the chapter.

Before we attempt to construct a historically representative picture of a bartering economy and its inhabitants, though, let's acknowledge two ways we'll intentionally deviate from the historical record. First, to maintain focus, we'll describe an economy that relies entirely on bartering. This is consistent with the economic view that bartering preceded or even led to a society's widespread adoption of money, with commonly bartered goods like silver becoming early media of exchange.[3] Yet it differs from the anthropological findings that

(1) bartering and money typically coexisted for extended periods, and (2) no pure bartering economy has yet been identified.[4] Thus the pure bartering economy we'll describe may represent an abstraction.

Second, we'll describe an economy in which friends, family, and community members get together regularly in a fixed location to barter – arrangements typical of many bartering societies.[5] We will not focus on a second historical form of bartering in which adversarial groups bartered ad hoc (for example, when European explorers arrived at Polynesian islands and traded with their inhabitants) – arrangements that sometimes led to manipulation and subjugation.[6] While acknowledging rather than minimizing this second form of bartering, we'll focus on the first and more benign form in hopes of becoming better negotiators today.

With that background in hand, let's construct a picture of a bartering economy: a form of economic organization in which people directly exchanged the goods and services they had for the goods and services they needed. In other words, barterers gave "what was not wanted directly for that which was wanted."[7] In one sense, bartering trades in these economies were simpler than modern monetary transactions: bartering trades satisfied a trader's needs immediately, whereas today's monetary transactions require the person receiving the money to engage in a second transaction.[8] In a broader sense, though, bartering trades are typically considered much more complex than monetary transactions, since the former require a "double coincidence of wants": a situation in which each of two parties simultaneously wants exactly what the other party has and has exactly what the other party wants.[9] In other words, both parties to a bartering trade must experience the trade as "balanced" (what you get is at least as valuable as what you give) and "excess demand reducing" (what you get makes you better off).[10]

As implied by the word *coincidence*, that doesn't happen too often or easily. To see for yourself, think of a good or service you need right now. Got one? Then think of a specific person in your own life who will offer you just that in exchange for a specific good or service (not money) that you're currently willing to offer. Can you think of someone? Maybe so, but it's probably much easier to think of someone who would provide whatever you needed if you paid them enough money. Hence the difficulty of bartering. The double coincidence of wants typically presents a daunting challenge. Thus, while certain conditions (credit, trading for the purpose of future trades, organized markets) can make bartering a bit easier, particularly by minimizing the costs of finding a partner,[11] bartering trades are undoubtedly more difficult than monetary transactions. That is bartering's major economic disadvantage and the primary reason that many economists have labelled it "primitive."[12]

But a close look at the anthropological research on bartering, which is less concerned with the efficiency of bartering and more concerned with how cultures barter, tells a very different story.[13] This research suggests that the challenges associated with bartering and its associated double coincidence of wants may actually carry a psychological upside. In particular, anthropological studies suggest that the difficulties of bartering may have compelled the members of bartering economies to think more broadly and creatively to solve their problems. If they didn't, their basic needs – water, food, clothing, and the like – would've simply gone unmet.

Drawing from this research, the current book makes a simple argument: *because of* rather than in spite of the difficulties of bartering, the members of bartering economies tended to use a more sophisticated and ultimately more productive form of problem-solving than we do. This contention does not imply that individuals in bartering economies were inherently smarter or more creative than we are. If they were, there would be no point in distilling their thinking for our own lives. It simply implies that we can learn from our predecessors, even if they used an economically "primitive" approach.

In sum, I suggest that bartering economies and the associated bartering activities had the positive psychological effect of broadening the way that people thought about solving their problems and

Table 2.1 Monetary versus Bartering Mindsets

Assumptions of the monetary mindset	Assumptions of the bartering mindset
I will be on one side of a transaction	I will be on both sides of a transaction
I will interact with one party	I will interact with multiple parties
I want one thing, and they want the opposite	Everyone has many possible needs and offerings
The only way for me to get a better deal is for the other party to get a worse deal	The only way for me to get a great deal is for other parties to get a great deal too
I can avoid conflict by compromising	I can avoid conflict by trusting enough to trade

meeting their needs. In particular, and consistent with anthropological research on bartering,[14] the members of bartering economies likely made the five assumptions on the right side of table 2.1 when they sought to satisfy their needs through barter.

Collectively the assumptions on the right side constitute the bartering mindset. As you can see, they differ quite markedly from the assumptions of the monetary mindset, offering a truly different way of thinking. Thus we will treat the bartering mindset as an alternative to the monetary mindset, albeit an alternative that we will ultimately merge with the monetary mindset in chapter 7.

To immerse ourselves in the bartering mindset, let's now step into the mind of a farmer named Keith, living in an idealized bartering economy. Let me warn you that I'll make Keith's thoughts extremely explicit to explain his mindset clearly. But I'm not suggesting that Keith or anyone else in a bartering economy thought so explicitly or systematically. Indeed, the members of bartering economies probably ruminated on their bartering mindsets about as often as we ruminate on our monetary mindsets. But the bartering mindset nevertheless guided people's behavior then, just as the monetary mindset guides our behavior now. To reiterate, the point of this exercise is not to make you barter like Keith (or inject our own monetary thinking into Keith's bartering world). It's to immerse you in a bartering mindset that can improve your modern and often money-laden negotiations, which we'll do in the next few chapters.

A Farmer Named Keith

Nestled away in a far-flung prairie, in a time and place where bartering prevailed, lived a farmer named Keith and his family. The family
farm, though far from bountiful, nevertheless produced a consistent
crop of corn and barley, along with a regular supply of milk and
eggs. Their lifestyle, though far from prosperous, was nevertheless
stable, as the farm met many of their needs and produced enough
surplus to trade in the nearby market. While days found the family
working the farm, nights found them happily gathered around the
fireplace listening to Keith read stories, as he had since an educated
cousin taught him to read.

This simple, pastoral picture characterized most of the family's
time together, and they had no reason to expect anything different
this year. Unfortunately, winter came early. Although they had har-
vested their crops by the time the temperature dropped, they had
not yet prepared for the cold season. Without firewood and warm
clothes – and without having sealed the cracks in their cabin walls
and gotten some medical attention for a daughter's sprained ankle –
the winter was looking unbearable and potentially dangerous.

Against this troubling backdrop, Keith and his horse set out for
the biweekly market in the nearest town, which he visited whenever
he needed to trade. With a wagonload of corn, barley, milk, and eggs
in tow, Keith started to consider his upcoming trades. What was he
implicitly thinking as he made the chilly walk?

Bartering mindset assumption 1: I will be on both sides of a transaction.
In pondering his upcoming trades, Keith probably assumed that
his goal was to satisfy his family's needs by "purchasing" things
like firewood and medical attention for his daughter. In a bartering economy, though, Keith was not assuming he'd purchase any
of these goods or services with money. Instead, he was assuming
he'd have to "sell" the goods in his wagon. Otherwise, why was the
horse pulling them, and why would anyone bother to help him? Put

simply, Keith was implicitly assuming he would be on both sides of the upcoming transactions, acting as both a "buyer" who receives and a "seller" who provides valuable goods and services.[15]

Reflecting on his prior experiences, though, Keith probably realized that this process wouldn't be easy. Prior efforts at bartering would've taught him how hard it is to identify a double coincidence of wants, particularly if he arrived at the market without a crystal-clear understanding of his own needs and his offerings. If he didn't understand his own situation comprehensively, how could he explain it to anyone else? With that worrisome reminder, Keith probably tried to make sure he truly understood the family's needs – what exactly did they need and why exactly did they need it (was the firewood for warmth, cooking, or both)? And did they need anything else (to retrieve that plough from the ditch, perhaps)? In addition to whatever the family needed immediately, would he perhaps need to acquire something purely to acquire something else later (having experienced how these "pass-through" trades can make the double coincidence slightly less coincidental)?[16] Without knowing it, Keith probably tried to understand the family's needs both deeply and broadly.

And the same goes for their offerings (the value he was bringing to the "table" on their behalf). Having experienced the necessity of knowing and explaining what he could offer in utmost clarity and detail, Keith probably tried to make sure he knew what was so great about the particular commodities he was offering – hadn't the bookseller previously noted how delicious his eggs were? Having experienced the difficulties of a critical transaction partner who didn't want anything in his wagon, he probably also considered what else he might offer. Hadn't he previously offered to help people with less educated cousins read or write letters? Keith might've even considered whether others would want his items to make their own pass-through trades, having witnessed many traders "buying" his corn for that reason in the past. In sum, Keith probably sought to understand the family's offerings, like their needs, both deeply and broadly. In so doing, he probably saw his confidence start to rise. "I'm not just going and begging for help," he may have thought. "I'm also bringing valuable goods and services to the market."

In sum, on the long, chilly walk to the market, Keith probably assumed he'd be acting as both a buyer and a seller. But past difficulties in doing that probably reminded him to consider his family's needs and offerings carefully, understanding them both broadly and deeply – a process that probably boosted his confidence by reminding him that others needed his offerings as much as the reverse. Just in time, as he was just now cresting the hill high above the market. What was Keith implicitly thinking as he descended toward it?

Bartering mindset assumption 2: I will interact with multiple parties. Spotting the market, Keith probably remembered just how many people were typically there. Always busy, today's prematurely wintry market was probably teeming. Watching the frenetic activity below, Keith probably remembered that he always traded with multiple people. This was mostly by necessity, as few people could provide both the firewood and medical attention his family needed, and even fewer would provide them in exchange for his barley and letter-writing skills, for example. Such was the difficulty of the double coincidence of wants. Since he always came to market with such a diverse set of needs and offerings, he always had to consider and ultimately trade with many counterparts.

Over the years he had also probably learned that trading with multiple people tended to benefit him. On a previous visit he was struggling to convince any of the available doctors to accept his produce in exchange for medical attention – all they needed was iron for their instruments, which he definitely didn't have. But then it occurred to him to trade corn with the blacksmith for iron, then iron with the doctor for medical attention – and it worked! Keith had then seen the tailor struggling to write a letter and realized he could turn his own literacy into some warm clothes. Remembering such experiences while watching the frenetic market below, Keith probably understood that interacting with multiple people created new opportunities.

In sum, while approaching the market, Keith was probably struck by the large number of people, which reminded him that he usually engaged with multiple partners. Out of necessity or opportunity, this multi-partner approach was just the way that most people bartered. And now, having reached the bottom of the hill and hitched his horse, Keith prepared to explore the market. What was he implicitly thinking as he began to walk around?

Bartering mindset assumption 3: Everyone has many possible needs and offerings. As Keith began to explore the bustling market, he probably remembered that he had to analyze the possibilities before approaching anyone. Even if he couldn't understand other people's needs and offerings completely before talking to them, Keith probably knew that getting an initial sense of everyone else's needs and offerings was far better than either of the alternatives: talking to everyone (far too time-consuming and risky, particularly if it annoyed the partners he ultimately rejected) or randomly selecting his partners (unlikely to surmount the double coincidence of wants). So Keith probably kept walking and resisted the urge to start talking.

In the course of his walk Keith probably noted the diversity of products and services on offer. There was the doctor with a line of patients (human and otherwise), apparently suffering various maladies. And there was the tailor stacking an overwhelming array of mittens, coats, and hats. Come to think of it, the strapping tailor looked strong. Would he consider helping with the plough? Listening to other people's conversations and inspecting the written and drawn signs affixed to their stalls, Keith probably also noted the diversity of products and services that people were requesting. The doctor's sign, for example, suggested he needed some repairs to his instruments, a set of medicinal herbs, and another horse. On a previous visit, he had asked Keith for eggshells, apparently to draw infections from the skin. Might he need more now? The tailor, in turn, was telling someone he needed some barley and work on his wagon. Is it possible he needed another letter written?

In observing all these diverse needs and offerings, Keith probably noted that almost everyone in this bartering economy needed several goods and services, as he did. Observing each party's array of needs and offerings, Keith probably remembered that his seemingly dire situation was far from unique. Everyone in the market faced essentially the same situation.[17] Finally, as Keith observed other people's needs and offerings, he may have realized that he hadn't remembered all of his own. Seeing the blacksmith, he now remembered a few broken tools; seeing a neighbor struggling to fit her dried food into a single wagon, he wondered whether he could offer some space in his own.

In sum, as Keith walked around the market, he probably observed everyone's numerous needs and offerings, coming up with a few initial trading ideas and concluding that everyone was on essentially the same footing. At the same time, he probably noted that he had a few additional needs and offerings of his own. Through this slow and cumbersome yet unavoidable and ultimately beneficial process, Keith started to understand the market thoroughly. Surmounting a double coincidence of wants required nothing less. Having taken the measure of the market, Keith was now ready to plan some specific trades. What was he implicitly thinking as he did?

Bartering mindset assumption 4: The only way for me to get a great deal is for other parties to get a great deal too. Having observed a panoply of needs and offerings, Keith probably identified at least a few people who desperately needed things he considered worthless. He would just as soon throw away a cartload of barley, but a bunch of people listed a few bundles as their primary need. Conversely, he probably observed several people being extraordinarily cavalier with items he desperately needed. Considering his shivering family and frostbitten fingers, how could the tailor tear up that pile of slightly discolored mittens?[18]

In observing the very different values that people apparently attached to the items like barley or mittens, Keith was noting a critical feature of bartering economies: the absence of market prices.

There was no "going rate" for these items or any others; people assigned their own personal values to the goods or services, in accordance with their individual needs.[19] Indeed, the members of this market didn't even think in terms of prices – they thought in terms of personal priorities. Yet Keith probably knew that differing personal priorities and values, attached to a wide array of goods and services, represented an opportunity rather than a hindrance. Far from impeding anyone's ability to trade, a diversity of commodities that people valued differently – the fact that others needed his abundant barley and he needed their abundant mittens – made trades possible in the first place. If everyone needed nothing but barley, who would trade with whom? Diverse needs and offerings afforded the only hope of surmounting a double coincidence of wants.[20]

In observing the array of goods with varying values, Keith probably felt increasingly confident he could satisfy his own needs, if only he could satisfy other people's needs. In other words, he probably realized that he wouldn't have to satisfy his own needs at anyone else's expense. Quite the contrary, he probably understood that he could satisfy his own needs only if he used his own offerings to satisfy other people's needs. The tailor could surely provide mittens and might help with Keith's plough, but only if Keith provided barley and perhaps some letter-writing assistance. The doctor could surely treat his daughter's sprained ankle, but only if Keith provided some eggshells or iron (the latter compliments of the blacksmith). Come to think of it, would the artist ever consider sealing the cracks in the family's cabin with her sculpting clay? Perhaps, since he overheard her asking for some eggs and corn.

Despite the double coincidence of wants, this process probably helped Keith identify several parties who could satisfy his needs rather easily, if only he satisfied theirs (easily too, he would hope). At the same time, he probably identified some parties who either couldn't satisfy his needs or whose needs he couldn't satisfy – at least not now. With their focus on fancy pursuits of little interest to

Keith's simple family (luxurious furniture, wine, jewelry), the cosmopolitan traders from the city could probably do little for Keith. Conversely, with comparable cartloads of produce, the other farmers probably wouldn't benefit from his offerings.

In sum, Keith probably identified some partners who presented the possibility of highly beneficial trades: parties like the tailor, doctor, and artist. Without ever using the term, he had identified parties who might form the basis of a power partnership: an agreement that could potentially meet both parties' needs extensively and inexpensively. And what could be better than getting what he wanted and also getting rid of what he didn't? Implicitly appreciating the possibility of power partnerships, Keith may have even started to enjoy himself.

But Keith probably didn't stop after identifying some potential power partnerships. Past difficulty with the double coincidence of wants had probably taught him that he needed to take it one step further, considering his potential trades *as a set*. In other words, Keith probably knew that he needed to consider the relationships between his potential partnerships, assessing all partners and associated trades holistically before spending time and social capital on any actual negotiations. So perhaps Keith compared a potentially powerful partnership with the artist (who would probably request only a small number of eggs and few ears of corn to seal his cabin cracks) with a similar arrangement involving the carpenter. But a long line at the carpenter's stall suggested he would request much more to seal the same cracks. Since a partnership with the carpenter seemed to offer an imperfect substitute for a partnership with the artist, he may have decided to pursue the latter instead. In addition, he may have realized that no one but the doctor could properly treat his daughter. So he'd better find a way to partner with the doctor.

In sum, before initiating any negotiations, Keith probably sought to identify the *set* of trades that would satisfy the largest number of his family's most important needs at the lowest possible expense. This involved passing on some partners to capitalize on powerful trades with others, as well as making sure he included certain partners in the final set. Ultimately Keith implicitly understood that meeting his needs in a bartering economy meant piecing together a powerful set of solutions across a wide array of partners – not just making one trade with one person (nor trading with everyone and anyone). Having whittled the market down to a potentially powerful set of partners, Keith was finally ready to talk to them. What was he implicitly thinking as he did?

Bartering mindset assumption 5: I can avoid conflict by trusting enough to trade. Up to this point, Keith had walked around the market and observed the goods and services that people were outwardly offering (via their wares) or requesting (via their conversations and signs). On the basis of his experiences in the market, he had also done a little guesswork about the other things that people might offer (for example, plough assistance from the tailor) or need (such as eggshells for the doctor). This process had left him with an educated guess about the parties offering power partnerships – as well as the most powerful set of partnerships. But he hadn't actually talked to others about their respective needs and offerings.

This approach was by design, as his experiences had taught him that he could never surmount the double coincidence of wants without understanding the market in his own mind first. Still he'd obviously have to talk to others to confirm, refute, or expand on his initial intuitions. Thus Keith probably realized it was time to strike up some conversations, the point being to exchange some honest information that could capitalize on potential power partnerships. To do that, Keith probably understood that he'd have to trust his conversation partners at least enough to allude to his own needs and offerings and ask about theirs.[21] If he didn't, how could he ever hope to discover a trade that surmounted the double coincidence of wants? Keith probably knew that trust was a necessary precursor to any bartering trade. And he probably felt reasonably comfortable extending some trust, since he knew many of these traders personally. And even if he didn't, he knew the community would look none too fondly on a dishonest trader.[22]

With those thoughts in mind, Keith probably approached potentially powerful partners and began exchanging information about their respective needs and offerings. In so doing, he probably connected their needs to his own offerings. In talking to the doctor, for example, Keith may have learned that the doctor just ran out of eggs and eggshells but didn't need any more iron. In talking to the tailor, perhaps he discovered that the tailor didn't need any letters written but had just received and needed a stack of letters read. And in talking to the artist he may have confirmed that she needed some eggs and corn for consumption but also learned that she was thinking of trying her hand at corn husk dolls. Since he was already offering eggs and corn and could easily offer eggshells, letter-reading, and corn husks, these insights probably refined Keith's understanding of his partners' needs and showed him he could satisfy even more of these needs than expected.

Even while learning about his counterparts' needs, Keith probably conveyed critical information about his own needs and connected them to his counterparts' offerings. Openly and honestly alluding to his daughter's sprained ankle, for example, he may have learned that the doctor had planned to visit a neighbor in a few days and could easily check on his daughter. Mentioning the plough, maybe the tailor volunteered his services. Telling the artist about his draughty cabin, which was especially chilly in the absence of firewood, perhaps he confirmed that she was happy to seal his cabin with sculpting clay but also learned the she had a bunch of long-fallen branches on her own property. Would he like to haul them off as free firewood? In sum, Keith probably confirmed some of his initial intuitions about power partnerships but also surfaced some interesting and unexpected possibilities.

At the same time Keith may have discovered that some of his partnerships were less powerful than expected, or simply infeasible.

Perhaps the bookseller was requesting all of his delicious eggs in exchange for some intriguing new books. Though Keith and his family loved books, his daughter needed medical attention more than they needed a good read – and the doctor needed his eggs. So Keith may have determined he had to pass on a trade with the bookseller to accommodate a trade with the doctor.

These realizations probably helped Keith confirm the most powerful set of partnerships available. Partnerships with parties like the doctor, tailor, and artist were clearly powerful, while the bookseller might not have made the final cut. Reflecting on the ultimate set of power partnerships, the concept of compromise probably didn't feature prominently in Keith's thinking. Since trading involved the exchange of two or more discrete goods or services, and since the double coincidence of wants required all trades to be mutually beneficial, neither he nor anyone else probably thought in terms of "meeting in the middle." Meeting in the middle on what issue exactly? Rather, all including Keith probably thought about how they could most easily trade to satisfy everyone's most important needs at the same time. Of course he'd eventually have to figure out how much barley he would offer in exchange for mittens, for example, but experience had taught him that he wasn't yet ready to do that. The bartering mindset had led him down a long and winding but exceptionally beneficial road.

Comparing the Bartering and Monetary Mindsets

Reflecting on Keith's story, the differences between his bartering mindset and our own monetary mindset become clear. First, with a monetary mindset, we approach our transactions as a buyer or seller, but not both (for example, as a buyer of gas for our car). But Keith approached the market knowing he would have to act as both in each of his transactions (for example, by buying medical care even while selling his eggs). Second, we typically see each of our own transaction partners as separate and independent – the gas station as having nothing to do with our employer. But Keith understood that he would have to engage with many interrelated parties at the same time (for example, the doctor and tailor) – each helping to satisfy a certain subset of his interrelated needs.

Third, we typically see each of our transaction partners as wanting the opposite of the one thing we want – the gas station wanting a high price instead of our preference for a low one. But Keith realized that everyone both wanted and could offer many different things – the artist wanting his corn and husks while sealing and warming his cabin. Finally, we tend to assume that the only alternative to conflict is compromise (for example, by settling on the gas station's posted price). But compromise didn't make much sense to Keith since he knew he could make himself supremely happy (by obtaining clothing, medical care, etc.) only if he did the same for others (by providing eggshells, letter-writing, etc.). Doing so was simply the sole way of surmounting the double coincidence of wants. The bartering mindset offers a very different way of thinking, and the way that the rest of the book will advise you to think in your next negotiation.

Implementing the Bartering Mindset Today

But implementing that advice is harder than it sounds: while the bartering mindset presumably worked well in a bartering economy, most of us don't live in one. What if we tried to apply the bartering mindset by fueling up our car, then offering to pay the station attendant with a trunk-load of corn? Even if he really loved corn, he would probably respond with a call to the police. Since most of us don't live in a bartering economy, we can't just plop the bartering mindset into our own world. We need to distil the essence of each assumption comprising the bartering mindset – the general insights that apply to our own monetary economy in addition to a bartering economy. In

Table 2.2 The Bartering Mindset and a Five-Step Process for Implementing It Today

Assumptions of the bartering mindset	Five-step process for implementing the bartering mindset today
I will be on both sides of a transaction	1. Deeply and broadly define your needs and offerings
I will interact with multiple parties	2. Map out the full range of transaction partners
Everyone has many possible needs and offerings	3. Map out the full range of their possible needs and offerings
The only way for me to get a great deal is for other parties to get a great deal too	4. Anticipate the most powerful set of partnerships across the market
I can avoid conflict by trusting enough to trade	5. Cultivate the most powerful set of partnerships across the market

other words, we need to translate the bartering mindset for a monetary world, ideally in a way that allows us to act on its insights.

Thus the rest of this book will take the five assumptions of the bartering mindset and translate them into a five-step process that you can implement in the modern world – and especially in your own negotiations, which often involve money. Table 2.2 presents the five steps, next to the underlying assumptions.

The first step involves understanding yourself. The second and third steps involve understanding your prospective partners. And the fourth and fifth steps involve understanding the partnerships that can bring you and the rest of the world together. The next few chapters of this book will bring the five-step process to life through an extended example. By the end I think you'll find yourself thinking and acting like Kyle MacDonald, finding unexpected value in your own red paperclips.

Evidence for the Bartering Mindset

Now that we have discussed the monetary and bartering mindsets, I'd like to present the results of a sample research study that tests the link between money and the monetary mindset, as well as bartering and the bartering mindset. Note that this is but one of several studies I have run (and am running) on the topic, and it's meant to be illustrative rather than comprehensive. While I will present the study and its results briefly and non-technically, some readers will undoubtedly be more interested than others. If you are one of the less-interested readers, please feel free to skip this section – provided you take my word that the results are supportive! If interested, please read on.

I conducted an online survey of 206 adults from across the United States. About 48 per cent were women, and their average age was about thirty-four. Respondents were asked to "imagine that you have a problem: The faucet in your shower is leaking. This wastes a huge amount of water and creates an annoying, around-the-clock 'dripping' sound." The next screen then presented one of three conclusions to the scenario. A third of the participants read the monetary version of the scenario, which said, "Many people in your area only do plumbing work in exchange for cash – they fix your shower, and you give them cash. Please take a moment and think very carefully about what kind of cash you might pay for plumbing work." Another third of the participants read the bartering version of the scenario, which said, "Many people in your area do plumbing work in exchange for goods and services – they fix your shower, and you either give them something you have, or you do some service for them. Please take a moment and think very carefully about what kinds of goods or services you might exchange for plumbing work." The remainder of the participants read a neutral (control) version of the scenario that used parallel language but didn't say anything about payment for the plumbing work: "There are many people in your area who do plumbing work – they could fix your shower. Please take a moment and think very carefully about all of the steps involved in the completion of plumbing work." After reading one of these three scenarios, respondents wrote a paragraph detailing their thoughts.

Figure 2.1 Adoption of the Bartering Mindset as a Function of Scenario Read

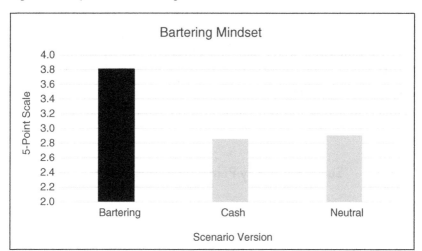

Next respondents answered five questions about whether the monetary versus the bartering mindset applied to their upcoming plumbing work. For example, they completed a five-point scale to indicate how much they agreed that: 1 = I will be acting only as a buyer to 5 = I will be acting as both a buyer and a seller. In other words, the scales represented a continuum between the monetary and bartering mindsets. Respondents concluded the survey by answering some demographic questions.

In support of the arguments in this book, respondents who read the bartering version of the scenario generally endorsed the bartering mindset significantly more than respondents who read the money or neutral version. In fact, the responses of people who read the latter two versions were statistically indistinguishable, and that makes sense, since people in the neutral condition (who received no information about payment) likely presumed they would pay with money, as anyone in a monetary economy would. Averaging across participants' responses to the five questions produces a graph like figure 2.1.

As you can see, these results provide evidence that monetary transactions elicit the monetary mindset, while bartering transactions elicit the bartering mindset. Other studies that I have run or am now running come to the same conclusion. Thus while our journey into Keith's world required us to integrate anthropological and economic thinking with our own logic and imagination, accumulating evidence portrays the journey as far from a flight of fancy.

Summary of Key Points from This Chapter

1 The best way to understand the bartering mindset is to step into the mind of someone in a full-blown bartering economy.
2 The fundamental requirement for a bartering trade is a double coincidence of wants, in which each of two parties needs exactly what the other is offering and is offering whatever the other needs.
3 As a result of the double coincidence of wants, individuals in a bartering economy had to make a set of assumptions very different from ours – assumptions that amount to a broader and more creative form of problem-solving.
4 To apply those assumptions to the modern world, we need to develop and apply a five-step process.
5 Evidence supports the link between monetary transactions and the monetary mindset, as well as bartering transactions and the bartering mindset.

Exercise: Job Negotiation and the Bartering Mindset

Chapter 1 presented the introduction to an exercise spanning several chapters. I asked you to think about your real job, imagining that you considered your current pay inadequate. Next, I asked what you'd do about it in real life, and we decided that you, like most people, would probably ask your boss for a raise – an approach fully consistent with the five assumptions of the monetary mindset. The exercise concluded by exploring some potential inaccuracies of those assumptions when applied to your real job.

In leading you down the rabbit hole that most people encounter when applying the monetary mindset to a big problem, I asked for your patience, promising that we'd reveal an alternative and much more beneficial approach over a series of chapters. Well, the current chapter introduced the alternative approach – the bartering mindset. So let's now consider, in general terms, how the bartering mindset might relate to the job exercise. While this chapter won't discuss the nuts and bolts of the bartering mindset in action – that is, the five-step process you'd use to apply it in real life – the chapter will start to illustrate the bartering mindset's markedly different assumptions. So please think back to the job situation described in the last chapter, imagining again that you consider the current salary in your real job inadequate. Next, please review the five assumptions of the bartering mindset (table 2.1). What would it mean to make each assumption in the context of your real job? Please jot down your own answers before reviewing mine.

Using the monetary mindset, you originally assumed that you were requesting a raise but thought less about why or what you might be offering in exchange. Using assumption 1 of the bartering mindset, in contrast, you'd assume you're on both sides of the transaction. On the asking side, you'd consider why exactly you need a salary increase, as well as what else you might need to do to solve the underlying problem. On the offering side, you'd realize you're bringing multiple sources of value or at least potential value to the table. Most obviously, you're offering your track record of high-quality contributions to the organization. As noted in chapter 1, you might also consider offering other "out-of-the-box" sources of value like the willingness to travel, assume more responsibilities, or reconfigure your pay structure. Whether these specific examples apply to your own circumstances, the point is that assumption 1 leads you to ponder not just what you're demanding but also issues like why, and what you're offering or could offer.

Using the monetary mindset, you originally assumed that the salary discussion involved only your boss. Using assumption 2 of the bartering mindset, you would assume that getting more money might require you to talk to other people inside or outside of the organization. Critically, you'd then spend some time thinking about who these parties are. As noted in chapter 1, some examples include HR, others in the company who might value your skill set, people at other organizations, the loan department at your local bank, and people who would pay you for consulting services. Can you think of anyone else who might help you solve a salary problem in real life? If so, assumption 2 would urge you to note them, even if you're not yet sure about their relevance.

Using the monetary mindset, you originally assumed that you wanted only a big raise, and your boss wanted only a small raise (or none at all). Using assumption 3 of the bartering mindset, you'd assume that both you and your boss (as well as all other relevant parties) have many needs and potential resources to offer. As suggested in chapter 1, your boss might offer you the option to work at home, performance-based pay, time off, enhanced responsibilities, or an accelerated career trajectory. In real life, would any of these possibilities meet your needs? What else might your real boss offer? And what might your real boss need that you're not currently offering? Meeting one of your boss's unmet needs would undoubtedly make your requests at least a little more palatable. And with the bartering mindset you wouldn't just stop with yourself and your boss. You'd assume the other parties identified in the last paragraph also have an array of needs and offerings, and you'd consider what they are. If you were considering a higher-paying opportunity in another department of the organization, for example, what might the head of that department need from you, and what could you offer?

Using the monetary mindset, you originally assumed that there was little point in understanding your needs or your boss's needs further. Under assumption 4 of the bartering mindset, you'd assume you have to. Indeed, you'd assume that eventually you must convey your needs not just to your boss but to anyone and everyone who might help you solve the problem – a full set of potentially powerful partners. And you'd also assume that eventually you have to learn their needs. In addition, you'd assume that eventually you must discuss each party's prospective offerings, identifying solutions that fully satisfy both parties. Thus you'd steel yourself for a longer and more involved set of discussions with a wider range of parties – but discussions almost certain to yield better solutions. The point is simply that preparing yourself to exchange information about respective needs and offerings with a wider range of parties opens up new frontiers for your consideration.

Finally, under the monetary mindset, you assumed that you'd ultimately have to compromise on a middling raise. Under assumption 5 of the bartering mindset, you'd make no such assumption. Instead, you'd assume that you can have exactly what you want most if you trust other parties enough to surface trade-offs that could do the same for them. In other words, you wouldn't settle for a compromise or even really consider one, as you'd spend your time figuring out how to make yourself and several other people happy. If that were possible, wouldn't it be illogical to seek a compromise that barely satisfies anyone?

As you can see from the exercise, the bartering mindset involves a very different mode of thinking – and one that necessarily feels less natural for anyone living in a modern monetary economy. Indeed, no one would expect a "mostly forgotten" mindset to come easily. But the next few chapters will help you remember it and apply it quite naturally to your own life.

STEP 1: DEEPLY AND BROADLY DEFINE YOUR NEEDS AND OFFERINGS

By the middle of 1787 the fledgling American nation – if anyone could actually call it that – was facing considerable trouble.[1] The Articles of Confederation, which protected state sovereignty by vesting little power in the national government, seemed far too weak to handle the demands of a diverse and expanding nation. Accordingly the founding fathers assembled in Philadelphia for a Constitutional Convention, the goal being a universally agreeable revision of the articles. But the subsequent debate, on the scope and details of the revision, nearly derailed the fledgling nation.

At first, two competing proposals were floated. The Virginia Plan called for a sharp break with the articles in which the states would send multiple representatives to a bicameral legislature, in proportion to their populations. Populous states like Virginia typically preferred the plan, as it afforded them the bulk of the power, while less populous states generally loathed it. The New Jersey Plan, in contrast, proposed a minor revision of the articles in which each state would get one vote in a unicameral legislature. Smaller states like New Jersey generally preferred the plan, as it put them on equal footing, while many populous states opposed it. How could anyone reconcile the two opposing proposals and resolve the mounting tension?

The representatives of the smaller states, embodied by Connecticut's Roger Sherman, knew what they'd ultimately need to see from any viable reconciliation plan: a solution that protected their sovereignty and prevented the big states from trampling their interests. And their proposal – the "Connecticut Compromise"[2] – also demonstrated a keen awareness of the specific conditions they'd need the big states to meet: equal representation in at least one legislative chamber (currently called the Senate) and certain powers allocated to that chamber – notably, longer terms and the ability to preside over impeachment proceedings. If the big states could meet these demands, the small states were also quite clear about what they could offer: fundamentally to approve a proposal that would unify rather than further divide the nation. More broadly they were willing to create a second chamber based on proportional representation (now the House of Representatives), reserving the important power to originate spending bills for that chamber. Collectively, these terms – the Senate and House in combination – averted disaster and gave rise to a new nation.

As in any example, the details are more complicated: some rapidly growing small states in the South supported proportional representation, for example. And the Compromise included a detestable proposal to count slaves as three-fifths of a person, a detail no one would hold up as a positive example of anything. Neither ignoring nor endorsing these aspects of the story, however, I would nevertheless suggest that its broader outlines epitomize the first step of the bartering mindset: to deeply and broadly define your needs and offerings. The small states knew what they fundamentally needed from the big states, and what they specifically needed the big states to do. And they knew what they could fundamentally offer the big states in return, as well as the specific concessions they were willing to make.

In short, even if America's founding fathers knew nothing about the bartering mindset, their story nicely illustrates the first step involved in implementing that mindset, as well as the potentially enormous importance of doing so. With the Connecticut Compromise as a backdrop, this chapter will discuss the first step and describe how to implement it in the modern world. The next four chapters will discuss the remaining steps and how to integrate them with the monetary mindset.

The Café Story: Setting the Stage

To aid in the translation from a bartering economy like Keith's to a monetary world like ours, this and the next few chapters will use an extended example about a struggling small business – a café, based loosely on a Baltimore-area business I know well. While the example will take us deep inside the bartering mindset, the stories at the start of each chapter (for example, the Constitutional Convention) will reconnect us with the real world. And while the café example focuses on a small business, it's actually a metaphor for a challenge we all face from time to time: thriving or at least surviving in a resource-constrained world. So even if you don't identify with the surface-level features of the story, I think you'll identify with the underlying problem of staying financially afloat.

As you read the story, I'd implore you to imagine yourself as the protagonist, carefully considering the questions I pose and attempting to apply the bartering mindset when I ask you to. Keep in mind that your answers will not always align with mine. That's fine! It suggests you're considering the mindset on your own terms, which is so much better than not considering it at all. So please immerse yourself in the example, making the problem and subsequent process your own, even if you disagree with the details. By doing that you'll see yourself systematically adopting the bartering mindset.

I'd also ask you, while reading, to remember what we're fundamentally trying to do here: provide a method for thinking about and eventually solving your most pressing modern problems through negotiation. We're not trying to change the way you think about or approach your minor problems, for which monetary solutions probably work fine. And we're not trying to convince you to barter in negotiations per se – that being less than fully feasible in a monetary economy. This background is critical, as it heads off some likely concerns: for example, that the following steps would take too long in the "real world," or that the recommended method isn't "realistic." For serious problems – like the need for a new house, job, car, business deal, or organizational strategy – you don't have the time *not* to adopt something like the following steps. And the fact that most of us can't barter our way through negotiations is exactly the point – the very reason we're spending so much time unpacking the five steps of the bartering mindset for potentially money-laden negotiations (like the one in the story).

A final word of preparation: as you step through the story and apply the bartering mindset, you'll encounter three "alter egos": Monty, Getty, and Bart. You can think of them as little people who show up on your shoulders and urge you, with the best of intentions, to adopt their counsel. Monty gives voice to the monetary mindset, consistently encouraging you to see the world like a money problem, that is, through a competitive and distributive lens. As you'll see by chapter 7, Monty's perspective can eventually inform your thinking, but it's woefully counterproductive on its own. Getty, in turn, gives voice to the principles articulated in *Getting to Yes*, implemented in most negotiation classes, and embodied in decades of negotiation research:[3] that you should mostly reject distributive thinking and just act integratively. In keeping with that perspective, Getty consistently urges you to do things like separating the people from the problem and/or focusing on interests instead of positions, for example. Valuable as this advice may be in the abstract, the next few chapters suggest it's consistently premature: Getty repeatedly advises you to act integratively before you're mentally prepared to do so.

Figure 3.1 Alter Egos, Mindsets, and Negotiation Behaviors

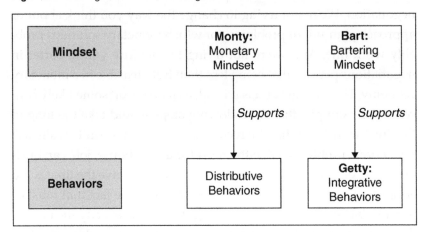

Hence the need for the bartering mindset, as embodied by Bart – a third alter ego who will quickly critique Monty's and Getty's recommendations, then step out of the way to let the rest of the chapter flesh out his recommendations. With Bart's bartering mindset firmly in hand, we'll eventually reconcile with Getty and the recommendation to act integratively (in chapter 6) as well as Monty and the recommendation to think distributively (in chapter 7). Figure 3.1 updates the first figure from chapter 1 to include the bartering mindset and relevant alter egos.

One final note: to reinforce Monty's and Getty's differences relative to Bart, I'll occasionally attach some adjectives to their names: "distributive-minded Monty" and "integrative go-getter Getty." Despite these silly sounding names and the characters' personification as little people on your shoulders who lead you down the occasional rabbit hole, my goal is not to poke fun at either of them (or Bart). Quite the contrary, as all three perspectives will eventually inform your thinking. I employ these characters and labels merely to draw out the differences between existing negotiation approaches and the bartering mindset.

The Café Story

For the last three years, you've owned a small café in a small town. Located in a historic post office building, the business specializes in caffeinated drinks, breakfast pastries, and delicious breads. In the time since you founded it, the business has proven reasonably stable, though not particularly profitable. It now employs a handful of servers and kitchen staff, enjoying a growing reputation as *the* place for a coffee or small breakfast. All in all, you're proud of what you've accomplished and contributed to the town, and you certainly like working for yourself.

With the benefit of experience, though, you're starting to see some writing on the wall. It's becoming clear you need to cut costs. Having done everything under your control to operate more efficiently – dimming lights, turning down the air conditioner, reducing your own salary, etc. – your bills continue to escalate. For example, ingredient and labor prices continue to rise faster than the yeast in your bread, and your landlord just mentioned a rent increase. Everyone seems to want more money! You simply can't keep absorbing such rapidly rising expenses. Facing a particularly empty bank account one morning, you sit down to consider your options. And, wouldn't you know it, there's Monty on your shoulder! At this point, let me pause and ask you – the reader – what Monty would probably advise. In other words, how would someone with a monetary mindset think about this situation? Please stop and consider that question.

Monty would probably start by reiterating that the problem is really all about money. "You've obviously got a cost problem!" Monty might say. Accordingly, Monty would probably direct your attention to one of the annoying parties driving your cost increases. "That no-good landlord," Monty might say. "You always pay your bills on time and go out of your way to take care of her property, and now all she wants is more of your money! Go out and give her a piece of your mind instead: ask her to cut you a break, make an aggressive counter-offer, threaten to leave. Compromise only if you have to!" Monty, in other words, would prompt you to adopt the monetary mindset, which might eventually lead you to engage in distributive negotiation behavior, competitively seeking to claim a larger portion of someone else's fixed pie.

Although this approach might buy you a bit of short-term breathing room, research is unequivocal: the benefits of distributive thinking and behavior are limited and fleeting.[4] If you succeed at claiming value, you probably won't claim much. How much of a discount will your landlord really offer? In a competitive market replete with razor-thin margins, not much. And then there's the very real possibility that you won't reach an agreement at all, as distributive approaches are known to drive people away from the table. If your counterpart does leave the table – if you can't find a deal with the landlord, for example – you'd better have another, more affordable, and equally attractive place to run your business, and it better be cheap to move. And then there's the remote possibility that you'll actually succeed in claiming a big portion of the landlord's fixed pie. As well as that works now, how will she feel about the process? Not particularly good. Her lingering dissatisfaction is likely to motivate aggressive demands in your next negotiation, if she lets you have one. But chances are, she won't: she'll probably start looking for a more agreeable tenant. Since none of these possibilities is particularly attractive, distributive-minded Monty's monetary mindset and the behaviors it eventually triggers are far from optimal.

In light of these disadvantages, you might decide to shoo Monty off your shoulder. And particularly if you've read *Getting to Yes*, taken a negotiation class, or read any negotiation research, Getty would probably appear immediately. What would Getty probably advise? Please stop and consider that too.

Getty would probably start by verifying that you rid yourself of Monty. Are Monty and the monetary mindset truly gone? Good. With Monty in hiding, Getty would probably urge you to pick a promising counterpart, any promising counterpart, and start focusing on your respective interests rather than anyone's positions or personalities. For example, Getty might prompt you to select and initiate a conversation with your wheat supplier, after which you might try to build some trust and exchange the information necessary to convey your underlying interests and/or understand theirs. Then, rather than demanding a lower wheat price, you'd try to find a creative way of reconciling your core interest – say in protecting yourself against seasonal price spikes – with the supplier's. Getty, in other words, would probably urge you to display an immediate set of integrative negotiation behaviors with any potentially promising counterpart.

Although Getty's counsel certainly seems more promising than Monty's, you'd probably encounter a couple of challenges in trying to implement it. First, since you haven't yet considered whether you need anything other than price protection, your conversation may come to a quick end if the supplier has no interest in offering such protection. Second, since you haven't yet considered what you could offer in exchange for price protection, you won't feel very emboldened to demand it. Indeed, your request will probably strike the supplier as quite meek, and you'll probably have to back down in the face of scoffing. Finally, you'll face the very real possibility that the wheat supplier, selected randomly from a limited list of counterparts, isn't the best party to deal with in the first place. Since you haven't considered the wider range of parties who could help to meet your needs or the wider range of parties whose needs you could help to meet, you haven't identified the most promising partners, nor certainly the most promising *set* of partners. If you did, you might well discover that other parties offer better solutions.

In short, in leading you to select a single counterpart and launch into integrative negotiation, Getty has prompted you to roll the proverbial dice, hoping that this one person somehow has exactly what you need and needs exactly what you have. Sound familiar? Our old friend, the double coincidence of wants. But unlike Keith, you (following Getty's advice) haven't followed the sophisticated process required to surmount it. Integrative go-getter Getty has led you down the integrative path prematurely.

So away with Getty, you might say, only to see the final alter ego, Bart, popping up on your shoulder. And what would Bart say? That you and I and anyone else with a complex and important problem need to do much more before we start "negotiating." In particular, Bart would suggest you start the whole process differently: by telling Monty and Getty to cool their jets while you critically consider your own needs and offerings, not to mention others'. Only then would you "negotiate" in the traditional sense of the word. In return for this extended process, Bart would promise a much larger and more durable set of solutions. "I'll take you to a place where you're not fighting a particular landlord over rent, nor hoping a particular wheat supplier happens to want what you have and have what you want," Bart might say. "In the not-so-distant future, you'll be thinking about solving your problem by talking to employees about management training programs, your landlord about employee retention, the grocery store and a farmers' market about expanding your customer base, some local artists about hosting their art shows, the soup kitchen about donations, and a real estate agent about subletting. And these are just examples." Sounds crazy now, but let's spend the next few chapters unpacking Bart's premonition.

The Café Story: Your Needs

So what would Bart, following the first step of the bartering mindset, actually advise? First, Bart would suggest you return to your basic assumptions about your own needs. The story started with your perceived need to cut costs. But is cost-cutting your *real* need? And are lower costs *all* you need? Since you wouldn't need lower costs if you had higher revenues, nor would lower costs help if your revenues were declining, the likely answer to both questions is no. Far from an anomaly, this is an exceedingly common situation, particularly under the guidance of Monty: the needs we initially perceive are neither as deep[5] nor as broad as our true needs.

So the bartering mindset first requires you to define your needs both deeply and broadly. Defining your needs deeply means understanding *why* you need whatever it is you think you need – that is, what underlying need you're really trying to satisfy. Getty pointed you in the right direction by urging you to consider one real concern underlying your perceived concern – managing seasonal price spikes. Defining your needs broadly, in turn, means understanding *all* of them – that is, all the specific things you might need to do to satisfy the underlying need. Neither Monty nor Getty really prompted you to consider your needs broadly. But that's exactly what Bart would suggest. And it's exactly what Keith did by thinking through his family's winter requirements and all of the specific trades necessary to satisfy them. And it's exactly what the small states did by insisting on their sovereignty and making several specific requests to guarantee it. In short, deeply and broadly defining your needs is the proper place to start the café story. But how?

Well, let's first define your needs *deeply*. The easiest way to do that is to take what you think you need and simply ask, "Why?" Since you think you need to reduce costs, just ask yourself that question: "Why do I need to reduce costs?" Perhaps it sounds silly to ask such a self-evident question, but consider what happens when you do. You get an entirely different and automatically deeper need: "Because I need to ensure the café remains viable," you might say to yourself. So the simplest and most effective way to achieve a deeper understanding of your needs is to take your perceived need and ask why.

But is your new and deeper need deep enough? Maybe yes, maybe no. You could theoretically continue asking yourself "why" for a long time. Asking yourself why you need to ensure business viability, for example, you might decide you need to secure your family's long-term financial outlook. Asking why you need to secure their outlook, you might start thinking about your children's need to attend an excellent college. And you could continue this line of questioning for a long time – presumably until you got to a "final good," that is, a need that is good in and of itself, like "happiness" or "contentment."[6]

So you could theoretically ask a whole lot of why questions culminating in a supremely deep need. Since few people facing serious problems have the time to ponder their deepest and most enduring needs in life, however, it's important to determine how deep is deep enough. An easy albeit imperfect way to do that is to start with the need you initially perceived (cost-cutting), then continue asking why until you reach a need that seems utterly impossible to satisfy right now. Thus, you might determine you could cut costs and possibly (though not easily) find a way to ensure business viability. But protecting your family's long-term financial outlook? Since that depends on a whole host of contingencies outside your control (for example, your spouse's employment, children's health, etc.), you probably can't achieve it right now. Thus, you'd never ask the why question leading to the college need; instead, you'd conclude that the need just before financial outlook is "deep enough" – that ensuring business viability is a sufficiently deep need to try to satisfy right now. And that's typical: your deep need lies somewhere (one or two layers) beneath your perceived need, but not too far.[7]

Having defined your need deeply, I'd recommend starting to collect your thoughts in a diagram called a logic tree.[8] Useful for many purposes, your logic tree will help you keep track of your needs, which will very soon expand. Placing the perceived need on the right and any deeper underlying needs on the left, yours would currently look very simple (see figure 3.2).

Figure 3.2 Logic Tree Version 1

You've just defined your needs deeply, but the bartering mindset also calls on you to define them broadly. As noted, a broad definition of your needs is an understanding of everything you might need to do to satisfy your underlying need – in this case, to ensure business viability. Cutting costs is certainly one such to-do, but is it the only one? By starting to think about revenue, you already know it's not.

There are really two ways to define your needs broadly: a deductive approach and an inductive approach. The deductive approach involves logically deducing the types of things any business owner can do to ensure the viability of a business. In thinking through this issue, the goal is a logical list of categories – the *types* of things a business owner needs to do. And these categories should meet two important criteria: mutually exclusive and collectively exhaustive (MECE).[9] *Mutually exclusive* means the categories don't overlap; *collectively exhaustive* means they don't have gaps – that is, they cover all possibilities: in this case, all major drivers of business viability. To come up with such categories, I'd suggest using your general knowledge of business (supplemented, perhaps, by a textbook or the internet) to answer the following "how" question: "How does a business owner ensure the viability of a business?" At this point, I'd encourage you to actually stop and think about that.

Well, you already know one way a business owner does that: by reducing costs. And you've already started thinking about another: by increasing revenues. Just like that, you have two major categories of steps a business owner might need to take. Are they mutually exclusive? Since costs and revenues represent two separate sections of an income statement, they certainly seem so. And what about collectively exhaustive? Does a business owner need to do anything else to ensure viability? Well, the two categories seem much more exhaustive than the one you started with, especially since low costs and high revenues represent the Business 101 definition of a viable enterprise.

But just in case they're not, I'd recommend trying the inductive approach to defining your needs broadly. Whereas the deductive approach focused on business owners and businesses in general, the inductive approach focuses on you and your particular café. In other words, it involves reflecting on your own experiences with this specific café and asking a slightly different "how" question: "How could I ensure the viability of this specific café?" In response to this inductive question, you'd reflect on your experiences with this specific business and probably produce a laundry list of possibilities. And many of the entries on that list – attracting new customers, reducing ingredient costs, etc. – would probably fall neatly into the revenue or cost categories already identified. That's great, as it suggests your deductive categories were spot-on.

On the basis of your experiences with this specific café, though, you might arrive at a few needs that didn't pop out of the deductive approach. And herein lies the value of trying both the deductive and inductive approaches, as they tend to produce complementary answers. For example, the inductive approach might help you to realize that the viability of this particular café depends not just on revenues and costs but on the health of the surrounding community, which teeters between blight, crime, and poverty on the one hand and growth, development, and vitality on the other. Although the community's health has implications for revenues and costs, let's imagine you personally see it as a mutually exclusive category, since the community's health really represents an existential threat to the café more than an entry on its income statement. No matter how high your revenues or low your costs, will you want to own a business in a dangerous place, and will your employees want to work there? Maybe not.

Identifying a new and mutually exclusive category suggests that your initial categories were not collectively exhaustive. Here you might

Figure 3.3 Logic Tree Version 2

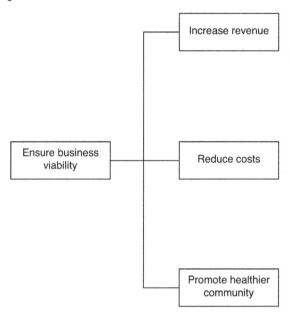

realize that you need to do more than reducing costs and increasing revenue. You need to do what you can to promote the health of the surrounding community. Having achieved this broader definition of your needs, I'd suggest expanding your logic tree like figure 3.3.

As depicted in the logic tree, you've now achieved a deep and broad definition of your needs: I need to ensure the viability of the café by increasing revenue, reducing costs, and/or a promoting a healthier community. This definition is deep because it focuses on the underlying need (viability) rather than the initially perceived but surface-level need (cost-cutting). And it's broad because it identifies a set of MECE categories capturing the steps you might need to take to satisfy the underlying need. Ideally you'd want to meet all three broad categories of needs. But note the "and/or" in your need definition, which signifies that you will ultimately determine which specific needs must be met to satisfy the underlying need.

Will lower costs and higher revenues suffice for business viability, or must the community improve too? Ultimately, you'll have
to decide.

You've come a long way, but you can go even further if you wish.
While you're at it, why not try to expand the logic tree further by
asking more "how" questions, this time of your three categories?
For example: "How does any business owner increase revenues?"
and "How could I increase the revenues of this specific café?" Making sure all of the needs you surface in each category (for example,
all items listed under "increase revenue") are MECE, you might
expand your logic tree to look something like figure 3.4.

Perhaps you can now see the power of these "how" questions,
asked as many times as you wish. Indeed, you could actually continue
this exercise indefinitely, asking as many rounds of "how" questions
as you wish, adding more and more boxes to the right, and surfacing
increasingly granular needs. Indeed, if you ask enough "how" questions, you'll realize something interesting: you're now finding needs
that count as such only because they serve other needs (similar to
Keith acquiring iron to trade for medical care). For example, you
might discover you need to insulate the café's windows, not because
it directly serves any of your own needs but because it increases
customers' comfort, which might convince them to stay longer and
buy more food. When it comes to asking "how" questions, you're
bounded only by time and imagination.

But even if you asked only one or two rounds of "how" questions,
the importance of defining your needs both deeply and broadly
becomes apparent. Had you not done that – had you assumed that
cost-cutting was your only and true need – you would've missed
the revenue and community needs completely, along with all the
more specific needs you just identified. And that's exactly what happens when we try to satisfy our perceived need, as Monty generally
advises, before defining our needs deeply and broadly. We understand neither the underlying need nor most of the specific things we
might need to do to satisfy it, setting ourselves up for near-certain

Figure 3.4 Logic Tree Version 3

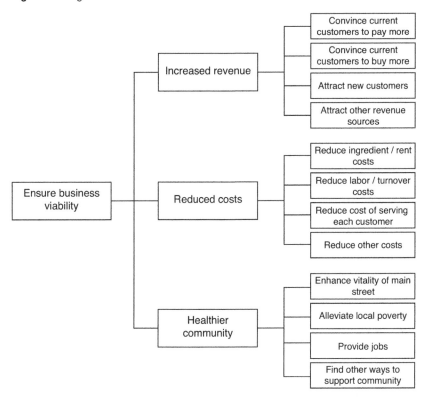

disappointment. Following Getty's advice, we might at least try to define our perceived need deeply, for example, by appreciating that our cost-cutting need really reflects our underlying need to ensure business viability. At least in my reading of *Getting to Yes* and the research it inspired, however, we're unlikely to systematically broaden our needs, meaning that we ultimately stand to miss out on a great many partners and potential solutions.

In sum, by deeply and broadly defining your needs, you've identified a plethora of needs you didn't know you had: many more than the one identified by Monty. And, by broadening those needs further, you've paved the way for an abundance of solutions: many more than the distributive pie-slicing approach prompted by Monty's monetary mindset. And many more than the one win-win solution that might, with a stroke of luck, emerge from Getty's advice to negotiate integratively and immediately. Can you now see how the small states, in determining what they fundamentally needed from the big states and specifically needed them to do, were implicitly defining their needs deeply and broadly?

By defining your needs deeply and broadly before "negotiating" in the traditional sense, you've come a long way in the café story. In particular, you've paved the way to consider a surprisingly wide variety of partners and potential solutions. And, with that, Monty and Getty would both almost certainly advise you to start negotiating.

The Café Story: Your Offerings

Unfortunately, from Bart's perspective, you're still not ready to start negotiating. You still understand only half of yourself: what you need from the world. The bartering mindset implores you to understand the other half too: what you're willing to offer. In particular, Bart would prompt you to understand the value your café already offers the world – or could. Think about it in the same terms that Keith did: If you're not clear on what you're offering, how could you make it clear to anyone else? And if you couldn't make it clear to others, why would they want to help? Only out of the goodness of their hearts. So we now pick up the café story in search of your offerings: the features of the café that other members of the market already find, or might find, valuable for satisfying their own needs. Step 1 of the bartering mindset involves focusing on your offerings to your current transaction partners – the parties who currently interact with the café in some way (for example, customers, employees, suppliers). Step 2 (next chapter) considers your offerings to the wider world.

Much like your needs, your goal is to define your offerings both deeply and broadly. But those terms have slightly different meanings for offerings. Defining your offerings deeply means truly understanding the value the café is providing to your transaction partners – what they currently appreciate about the café (versus competitors). Defining your offerings broadly means envisioning all of the value the café *could* provide to your partners – what they *might* value about the café if only you thought to offer it. Keith was essentially completing those steps by considering both the goods and services he was already offering (such as corn) and the goods and services he could offer if necessary (for example, his reading skills). So were the small states in the Constitutional Convention by holding out the prospect of an agreement, as well as several specific concessions (for example, the creation of a House of Representatives). And defining your own offerings deeply and broadly is where you should go in the café story.

Now, before we do that, a clear caveat is in order: Since you haven't yet talked to anyone about your problem, defining your offerings at this stage will not be easy nor precise. How can you know what you're offering – and particularly what you could offer – without asking whether anyone needs it? Indeed, understanding your offerings at this stage amounts to little more than an educated guess. And yet an educated guess about your offerings is so much better than no guess at all, as it immediately enables you (like Keith and the founding fathers) to approach the world with confidence and even with negotiating power.

Indeed, research suggests that knowing what you bring to the table before you get there – and knowing that it's more than your hat in hand – can afford substantial negotiating power.[10] By reminding you that other people depend on you as much as you depend on them, developing an awareness of your contribution to a negotiation can quite literally pay. Thus I'd advise you to spend some serious time thinking through your offerings, even at this early stage and even if your recent financial concerns have made you question whether the café offers anything valuable at all.

So let's now define your offerings deeply, understanding what your transaction partners already value about your café versus competitors. The first step, of course, is figuring out who those transaction partners are: What types of people interact with the café in some way? Customers, employees, suppliers, others? Having identified your current transaction partners, why not start the process of deeply understanding the café's offerings by questioning yourself – that is, by wracking your own brain about the features of the café that these partners appreciate? What value do *you* think the café provides relative to its competitors? What do *you* think the world most appreciates about it? Perhaps you think your customers particularly value its tasty pastries, welcoming atmosphere, or friendly and attentive employees. Perhaps you think the friendly and attentive employees value the chance to develop a relationship with customers, and your suppliers the consistent business. Using this process, you should seek to develop the longest list possible – even if your list of offerings sounds silly, speculative, or boastful. You can always cull the list later.

Given your own blinders, I'd also advise you to casually ask a few of your current transaction partners what *they* most value. Chances are, they'll identify a few beloved features you hadn't yet considered. Perhaps your customers appreciate your reliable Wi-Fi versus the library's spotty service, and your bottomless cups of coffee versus Starbucks' charge-by-the-cup policy? Perhaps your landlord appreciates the timeliness of your rent payments? In addition, as a means of determining what your partners *might* like about the café, you might consider what they *don't*. Finally, I'd advise you to solicit the reactions of a few people who aren't really transaction partners in the traditional sense – friends, family, random passers-by – what value they see in the café. Without the burden of an existing economic relationship, they may provide the freshest and most honest perspective.

Collectively, the answers to such questions should produce a deep definition of your offerings. Having considered the café's value from several perspectives, you should now have a deep awareness of what your partners already value. While defining your offerings deeply, though, you might've happened on some opportunities to offer even more value. For example, you might've started wondering whether current customers would appreciate special holiday dishes or the opportunity to upgrade to a higher-speed wireless service. Hence the need to define the café's offerings broadly in addition to deeply, considering the value it *could* offer its transaction partners in addition to the value it already offers. In other words, you also want to envision the café's unrealized potential, devising creative, out-of-the box ways that the café could satisfy your partners' potentially unmet needs.

In doing so, you might follow a similar process, asking yourself, "What else could this café reasonably offer my partners?" Or your existing partners, "What else could the café do to satisfy you even more?" Or friends, family, and passers-by, "What else do you think would make the café even better?" These questions are likely to prompt speculative but intriguing answers. Maybe you've been meaning to do something with the unused space in the back of the café and now see the possibility of subletting it, potentially to a supplier. Maybe you've been wondering what to do with all of those still-fresh pastries at the end of the morning rush. Would your employees like to choose one? Collectively, such questions should substantially broaden your understanding of your offerings.

Just in case all this deepening and broadening seems a bit tedious, let's step back to reflect on what you've been doing and how it accords with negotiation research. By thinking about all of your partners and what you now offer them or could, you've effectively been trying to climb inside the heads of your potential negotiation counterparts. In other words, you've been engaging in perspective-taking, formally defined as "the cognitive capacity to

Table 3.1 List of Offerings

Customers	Tasty pastries
	Welcoming atmosphere
	Friendly and attentive employees
	Reliable Wi-Fi
	Bottomless cups of coffee
	Holiday dishes
	Upgrades to high-speed Wi-Fi
Employees	Ability to develop a relationship with customers
	Free pastries
Suppliers	Steady stream of business
	Extra space in back as a subleased unit
Landlord	Timeliness of rent payments

consider the world from another individual's viewpoint."[11] What's my negotiation counterpart likely to value? What makes the other side tick?

Research suggests that negotiators who attempt to take their counterparts' perspectives even before meeting them ultimately grow bigger pies and take bigger bites. Indeed, it suggests that perspective-taking negotiators not only outperform negotiators who do no such thing; they also out-perform negotiators who adopt a popular alternative: empathy, or "the ability to connect emotionally with another individual." In short, taking the time to climb inside your counterpart's head represents a supremely useful exercise – even before meeting said counterpart and even if the process results in highly speculative answers. Effortful as it might seem, deeply and broadly defining your offerings before approaching the market is an exercise well worth doing.

Returning to the café story, then, you'll now have a long list of offerings, some of which you've probably understood for a long time but some you're considering anew. For example, your list might include items like those in table 3.1, organized according to the party who values or might value them.

Table 3.2 Your Needs and Offerings

Your needs	Your offerings
Ensure the viability of the café by:	• Customers
• Increasing revenue	○ Tasty pastries
○ Convince current customers to pay more	○ Welcoming atmosphere
○ Convince current customers to buy more	○ Friendly and attentive employees
○ Attract new customers	○ Reliable Wi-Fi
○ Attract other revenue sources	○ Bottomless cups of coffee
• Reducing costs	○ Holiday dishes
○ Reduce ingredient / rent costs	○ Upgrades to high-speed Wi-Fi
○ Reduce labor / turnover costs	○ Advertising on bulletin board
○ Reduce cost of serving each customer	• Employees
○ Reduce other costs	○ Ability to develop a relationship with customers
• Promoting a healthier community	
○ Enhance vitality of Main Street	○ Free pastries
○ Alleviate local poverty	• Suppliers
○ Provide jobs	○ Steady stream of business
○ Find other ways to support community	○ Extra space in back as a subleased unit
	• Landlord
	○ Timeliness of rent payments

This list represents a first cut at your offerings – what the café offers or could offer to its current partners. You've come an awfully long way. Still, it might be helpful to spend just a bit more time thinking critically about the list. Did you leave anything off? Which potential offerings seem most valuable? Most speculative? Reflecting on the list, for example, you might remember the big bulletin board that usually remains empty. Would enterprising customers value the board for advertising their own small businesses? Wasted space has just become an offering. Add it to the list!

Overall, you now have a deep and broad definition of your needs and offerings. At this point, I'd suggest organizing your thoughts in a chart like table 3.2.

With a table like this in hand, you're well on your way to an excellent solution. Congratulations! But before we move on, let's stop and compare what you've done against Monty's or Getty's advice (to construe the world in distributive terms or just start negotiating integratively). Having applied the bartering mindset, how much better do you understand your needs? You've verified the need for cost-cutting but now understand your deeper need for business viability. And precisely because you know your deep need, you also know what else you might need to do – raise revenue and promote a healthier community. Separately and independently of what you need and need to do, you also understand your offerings a whole lot better. And you should, because neither Monty nor Getty would have prompted you to consider your offerings. Having adopted the bartering mindset by considering your offerings carefully, you've now devised a strong set of reasons for the market to take you seriously. With your offerings as well as your hat in hand, I hope you see your confidence growing.

In sum, with the help of the bartering mindset, you now see that your real needs are much broader and deeper than your perceived needs. And your offerings are much broader and deeper than you ever imagined. You now know you're on both sides of the transaction, bringing a deep and broad set of offerings to the world in addition to making demands of the world. Like Keith in the previous chapter or the small states in this one, you're already in a much better negotiating position – and you haven't even started "negotiating" in anything like the traditional sense.

Time to move on! In particular, and now that you understand yourself better, it's time to come to grips with the external world. Which segment of the world might satisfy your broad and deep needs or demand your broad and deep offerings? We'll grapple with that question in the next chapter, then seek to winnow the world to the most promising partners thereafter.

Step 1 of the Bartering Mindset:
Key Questions to Ask Yourself

- Why do I need [my perceived need]?
  - o Answer(s) indicate my deep need.
- How do people like me generally satisfy [my deep need]? How could I, specifically, satisfy [my deep need]?
  - o Answers indicate my broader set of needs.
- What value do I provide to my current transaction partners?
  - o Answer indicates my deep offerings.
- What value could I provide to my current transaction partners?
  - o Answer indicates my broader set of offerings.

Summary of Key Points from This Chapter

1 The bartering mindset involves deeply and broadly defining your needs.
2 Deeply defining your needs means understanding the underlying need you're trying to satisfy; broadly defining them means understanding the MECE set of ways you might go about satisfying your underlying need.
3 The bartering mindset involves deeply and broadly defining your offerings.
4 Deeply defining your offerings means truly understanding the value you're already providing your partners; broadly defining them means understanding the value you could potentially offer your partners.
5 Ultimately, the bartering mindset involves understanding yourself much more thoroughly than you otherwise would have.

Exercise: Job Negotiation and Step 1
of the Bartering Mindset

In the last two chapters we've discussed how you might go about solving a problem in your real life: insufficient income. In the first chapter we reviewed how you might think about the problem through the monetary mindset. In the second we considered how you'd think about it through the bartering mindset. And now, finally, we're ready to apply the bartering mindset's first step: deeply and broadly defining your needs and offerings. In so doing, we'll start to ask you – the reader – to take an even more active role in applying the mindset to your own life. Remember: it's a process that will continue to play out over the coming chapters.

So, without further ado, let's try to apply the first step to your real job. Imagining again that the pay in your real job was insufficient, let's try to deeply define your need for money. How would you do that? Applying the guidance in this chapter, you'd first ask "why." As in, "Why do I need more money?" And you'd keep asking why until you reached a need that you just can't satisfy right now. So please try it for yourself: supposing you needed more money in your real job, please ask why a few times and see what happens.

So what happened? I'd guess your why questions prompted some soul-searching that produced some pretty interesting answers. Do you need more money to cover commuting costs? Make a big purchase? Save for your children's education? Keep up with inflation? Whatever your answer, and whether you arrived at it after your first why or your seventh, asking why is an interesting and essential exercise that immediately increases the likelihood of eventually satisfying your real need – and solving your real problem. At this point I'd suggest filling in a logic tree, placing your original need on the right and as many why boxes as necessary along the left. Figure 3.5 is an example in which your first "why" question produced a deep need.

Figure 3.5 Example of Your Logic Tree, Version 1

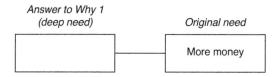

OK, so now let's take your deep need – the one on the left – and broaden it. How would you do that? In accordance with the advice above, you'd ask yourself just that question: "How?" Namely, how do people generally go about satisfying that need (deductive approach)? And how would I, in my own life, go about it (inductive approach)? Please ask yourself those questions.

So what did you come up with? Answers will certainly vary, but maybe an example will help. Imagine you realized you need more money to cover escalating commuting costs – a need you deemed deep enough for now. Between escalating fuel expenses, frequent maintenance on your car, and punitive parking fees, the cost of driving from a far-flung suburb is simply unsustainable. What would you need to do to solve that problem? Getting a raise is certainly one option. But what about working from home more often, changing jobs inside or outside the company, getting a bank loan, buying a more fuel-efficient car, or signing up for a Costco membership to avail yourself of discount gas? Whatever your individual need and whatever answers your "how" questions produced, I hope you can see the power of this approach. Regardless, I'd now suggest expanding your logic tree. Continuing with the logic tree in figure 3.5, you might fill in a tree that looks like figure 3.6, with the options you just surfaced in your own life (analogous to working from home, changing jobs, etc.) in the "broad need" boxes.

OK, so now you've defined your needs both deeply and broadly. Halfway there! Remember the other half? You still need to define

Figure 3.6 Example of Your Logic Tree, Version 2

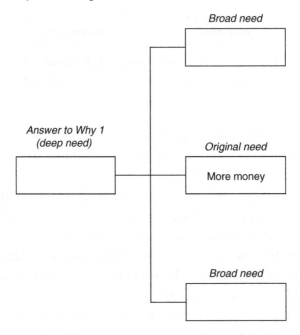

your offerings. As noted above, the first step is defining your offerings deeply, noting all the value you're currently offering the people with whom you routinely interact – and who might help to solve your problem. Since your initial inclination was to seek a raise, I'd start by considering the person who would have to approve that request – your boss. What kind of value do you provide your boss? What do you do better than any of your colleagues? What does your boss most appreciate about you? What would your boss miss about you if you left? Please think about it and even make yourself a list. Maybe your boss particularly appreciates your reliably error-free reports or your sharply analytical mind and irrepressibly positive attitude? And what do the other relevant parties value – for example, the people in other departments who might hire you or even the loan officer at your local bank?

Next, you'd want to define your offerings broadly by asking what value you *could* provide to such parties. Perhaps your boss recently lamented the need to travel so much – could you bear some of the burden? Perhaps a contact in another department is about to post for a particularly interesting position – and one in which you'd particularly excel? Again, these are just examples, and yours will widely vary. But the point is to think about the people you're already dealing with and carefully examine what you're currently offering them or could offer, suspending humility momentarily to consider what you do or could do particularly well. I think you'll agree that this exercise – while tentative and potentially difficult or embarrassing – is interesting and exciting because it points toward some new ideas that start to make your money problem seem less problematic. And it'll at least temporarily inflate your ego. With your list of needs and offerings (broad and deep) in hand, you're ready to identify the wider range of people who might satisfy your needs and benefit from your offerings. That's exactly where we're going in the next chapter, after which we'll decide which potential partnerships hold the most promise.

STEPS 2–3: MAP OUT THE FULL RANGE OF TRANSACTION PARTNERS AND THE FULL RANGE OF THEIR POSSIBLE NEEDS AND OFFERINGS

In November 2016 the Colombian Congress approved a landmark peace accord with the Revolutionary Armed Forces of Colombia, commonly known as FARC.[1] Supporters hoped the deal would mark an end to more than fifty years of violence, which had claimed more than 200,000 lives. The agreement also represented a breakthrough for President Juan Manuel Santos, who won the Nobel Peace Prize for his efforts – and especially his persistence after Colombian voters rejected the initial version of the deal for being too "soft" on FARC.

In brokering a new version of the deal, Santos had to think very carefully about all of the parties whose support he ultimately needed, and particularly what they might need in exchange for their support. He'd obviously need the support of FARC's leaders and members, who had refused to return to the table if he threatened to try them for war crimes. Thus the revised deal included no such threat. But he still needed at least some support from his political opponents – and got it by promising to try FARC leaders in front of a special court. Santos no longer needed the direct support of Colombian voters, as he found a way to bypass them by letting Congress approve the deal. But he still needed their indirect support, especially by helping former FARC members transition into society and paying the deal's multi-billion-dollar price tag. Thus the deal included several nods to popular discontent; for example, it sought to curb FARC members' influence by prohibiting them from running for office in conflict zones. Finally, Santos needed support from less obvious corners of society, notably the drug traffickers whose land could be seized to make way for the land redistribution demanded by FARC.

Importantly, Santos also needed the support of several parties outside of Colombia. He needed the United States to follow through on President Barack Obama's promise to provide $450 million in foreign aid, despite the subsequent election of Donald Trump. He needed the United Nations to supervise the disarmament process. Broadly speaking, he needed international support and legitimacy; indeed, the Nobel Committee's decision was arguably motivated, in part, by the desire to bolster his credibility in the longer term. Although his offerings to other world powers in exchange for their support are mostly shrouded from public view, a study of the long and complicated relationship between Colombia and the United States, for example, suggests that there was probably some quid pro quo.

At the time of this writing, the durability of the deal remains unclear. Voters may elect a political opponent who scraps it. Some of the deal's current requirements – that drug traffickers willingly sacrifice their land, for example – may prove impossible to implement. The United States may curtail or eliminate the promised foreign aid, as President Trump has publicly suggested. Indeed, in an environment this volatile and complex, precious little is certain.

Still, this example nicely illustrates the second and third step of the bartering mindset, which collectively suggest that the best negotiators not only understand themselves and their own needs and offerings. They also develop an understanding of the world around them: particularly the full range of people who are or might become partners, and *their* needs and offerings. By thoroughly considering both themselves and their social surroundings before embarking on a "negotiation" in the traditional sense, they stand a much better chance of succeeding once they do. In Santos's case, for example, a deal would've probably been impossible if he hadn't studied and sought to satisfy the full suite of interested parties. With the Colombian peace deal as a backdrop, the current chapter will discuss the interrelated second and third steps of the bartering mindset in the context of the café story, providing straightforward guidance to help you map out the full landscape of partners, needs, and offerings in your own life.

The Café Story: Setting the Stage

By the end of the last chapter, you – the owner of the struggling café – had already come a long way. Going far beyond your initial worries about the café's costs, you achieved a deep and broad understanding of your own needs: deep because you understood why you needed to cut costs (to ensure business viability), and broad because you understood what else you needed to do (increase revenue and promote a healthier community). In addition, you achieved a deep and broad understanding of your own offerings: deep because you understood why your current transaction partners currently value your café, and broad because you understood what else they might be convinced to value about it. This legwork left you well-equipped for an eventual negotiation. And at the thought of a "negotiation," Monty would probably appear again on your shoulder. Knowing that you've already come to understand yourself quite well, what would Monty probably advise you to do? Please consider.

At this stage, Monty would probably focus your attention on the demands you might place on one of the parties from the last chapter, probably the party who could offer the biggest discount or revenue boost. "You thought a lot about your landlord and the fact she should appreciate your timely rent payments," Monty might say. "Why not demand a discount in exchange? Could you at least ask her to freeze your rent instead of raising it?" Anticipating the landlord's skepticism, Monty might urge you to think of your offerings as ammo: "You know, not all tenants in town submit their payments on time like you do. Could you threaten to saddle her with someone less reliable if she doesn't accede to your demand?" In short, Monty would probably reiterate the initial advice to focus on a single monetary issue, but might now emphasize the possibility of turning your offerings into levers or threats for claiming value. For all of the reasons mentioned right after Monty's advice in the last chapter, though, this approach and the behavior it stimulates still represent a poor strategy. What if the landlord happens to know someone quite reliable and quite willing to move into the café's space, thereby calling your bluff? Even if she doesn't, what are the chances this one maneuver will solve your overall problem? With these thoughts in mind, you might dispatch distributive-minded Monty again, only to have Getty reappear on the other shoulder. What would Getty probably advise?

Getty, like Monty, would probably urge you to approach one of the parties implicitly identified in the last chapter. But Getty, being action-focused, would probably spend less time putting you into a particular mindset. Instead, Getty would probably encourage you to initiate an integrative negotiation, particularly with someone whose interests complement your own – someone who could cut your costs, bolster your revenue, or help you to support the community in exchange for one of your offerings. "Since the landlord seems to appreciate your timeliness," Getty might whisper, "go offer to prepay your rent each month in exchange for a rent freeze." Approaching the landlord and proposing that trade-off, how would the landlord respond? Pretty well, if she happened to find cash at the beginning of the month significantly more attractive than cash at the end – in which case you would've taken a positive step on costs. But you haven't done anything to deal with revenue or the community. And then there's the non-negligible chance the landlord won't really care whether you pay at the beginning or end of the month, in which case she'd probably say,

"Thanks but no thanks." And then what? Since you haven't even solved your cost problem and have little sense of what else the landlord might need or be willing to offer, integrative go-getter Getty has left you without many options, jumping the proverbial gun again. Accordingly, you might bid Getty goodbye and ask for Bart's perspective.

And what would Bart suggest? Bart might reach down from your shoulder to give you a congratulatory pat on the back. "Great job understanding yourself so well!" he might say. Still, Bart might remind you that you know comparatively little about your transaction partners: "Who all could you work with, and what might they need or offer?" So Bart would again prompt you to put the brakes on "negotiating," urging you to understand your partners better first, via steps 2–3 of the bartering mindset.

Now, astute readers will realize that you're not totally clueless about your transaction partners. Since you couldn't have understood your own offerings, current or potential, without at least a cursory thought to the current partners who value them, you already started to grapple with the external world in the last chapter. Still, your understanding of the external world is severely limited in several ways, some of which we'll consider later in this chapter. Here suffice it to say that your understanding is limited by its exclusive focus on your *current* transaction partners – current customers, employees, and suppliers, for example. You haven't yet considered the rest of the world – the many other parties who could become potential transaction partners by helping to satisfy your needs (or whose needs you could help to satisfy).

Without understanding the rest of the world or at least the rest of the market, as Keith did while peering down on the market and then starting to explore it, you're severely limiting your possible solutions, essentially shooting yourself in the foot. Unfortunately a lot of research and writing on negotiation focuses exclusively on one or two current partners, potentially leading to a proliferation of wounded feet.[2] An important exception is the book *3-D Negotiation*, which does suggest that negotiators must attempt to ascertain the proper partners before negotiating – an insight on which the current book builds.[3]

Now, understanding yourself is a whole lot easier than understanding your transaction partners. Compared to your comprehensive access to your own thoughts and feelings, you know little about your partners. In addition, understanding your current transaction partners is a whole lot easier than understanding your potential partners. Considering your frequent interactions with current partners, you know comparably little about the many amorphous parties who could potentially become partners. Still, the second and third steps of the bartering mindset call on you to make an educated guess – an attempt to anticipate additional partners and their situations before ever approaching them. In the process you'll vastly expand your own solution set, keeping your own feet intact. But you'll also avoid the futility of talking to everyone and anyone, or a randomly selected partner unlikely to offer a good solution.

At this point, astute readers will also realize that we're talking, again, about perspective-taking.[4] In the previous chapter, you took the perspective of your current partners, climbing into their minds to consider what they currently value or might. In this chapter you'll actually do two more types of perspective-taking: First you'll determine who else might think about your café if they only knew about it. Second you'll determine what your partners' thoughts might be. In this way you'll engage in a much more extensive form of perspective-taking than research typically considers. Going beyond the existing advice, you'll effectively take the world's perspective, deciding which minds to explore before diving into them. Table 4.1 details what we did in the offerings section of the last chapter and what we're about to do now.

Table 4.1 Comparison of Chapters 3 and 4

	To current partners (chapter 3)	To new partners (chapter 4)
What you're currently offering	Deeply define your offerings	New partners who might value your current offerings
What you could offer	Broadly define your offerings	New partners who might value new offerings

The Café Story: New Potential Partners

Having considered your current partners in the last chapter, let's set out in search of some new partners – additional parties who might meet your needs, if only you met theirs (step 2 of the bartering mindset). How could you possibly identify such people?

Well, if the goal is to meet your own needs – and let's assume it is – you might as well start by remembering what those needs are. So let's start by reviewing the needs articulated in the last chapter, then asking who might help to fulfill them. You previously decided that you need to "ensure the viability of the café by increasing revenue, reducing costs, and/or promoting a healthier community." Indeed, your last logic tree defined your needs even more broadly than that, but let's keep it simple. The beauty of defining your needs broadly as well as deeply is that the broad part – everything after the "by" – provides clues about other potential partners. Just as you asked "why" to define your needs deeply and "how" to define them broadly, you can now ask "who" to discover some additional partners. As in "Who else might help me increase revenue, reduce costs, and/or promote a healthier community?" Before reading my own answers, please place yourself back into the mind of the café owner and come up with some preliminary ideas – parties who could do that in the real world. Be creative! The goal is to come up with as many potential partners as possible.

So who made the list? The possibilities are limitless, but here are some realistic examples. Who else might help me to ...

- *Increase revenue?* The nearby movie theater, by referring movie-goers for a post-movie coffee. The grocery store, by selling the café's goods to a broader market. The radio station, by attracting new customers through advertising.
- *Reduce costs?* Local farmers, by minimizing transportation, trading, and storage costs. Politicians, by providing tax or fee relief. Artists, by decorating the walls and thus relieving the café of the need to pay for decorations.
- *Promote a healthier community?* The local soup kitchen, by working to alleviate poverty. The politicians again, by creating an economic opportunity zone. Police officers, by keeping a close eye on Main Street.

These are just examples, but they illustrate a critical milestone in implementing steps 2 and 3 of the bartering mindset. Consider what you just did: used your own needs to creatively define some additional parties who might fulfill them (for example, the movie theater). And by indicating what they could actually do to fulfill your needs (for example, referring customers), you began to define these parties' potential offerings. For example, the grocery store could contribute to your revenue need by acquainting additional customers with your products (essentially a pass-through trade in which they buy your pastries to sell to customers). In sum, you've come to understand a great deal about the external world simply by thinking more deeply about your own needs. You're well on your way to mapping out the external world.

But your impressive list of possible partners, growing by the minute, is just the beginning. You have another readily available resource to use in expanding your list of partners. Any idea what it is? Your own offerings! In addition to listing your needs in the last chapter, you detailed what you already offer and could offer to your current partners (for example, tasty pastries, subleased unit, timely rent payments). Isn't it at least conceivable that other, previously unimagined parties might be interested in the same offerings? I think it's at least conceivable. So just as Keith must've done when he saw and approached the market, you can now go back to your offerings (table 3.2) and ask another "who" question: "Who else might value my tasty pastries" (for example)? Before reviewing my ideas, please formulate a few such questions of your own and propose some plausible answers.

Again, the possibilities are limitless. But here are few additional parties who might value your current and potential offerings in the real world. Who else might value my ...

- *Tasty pastries?* Residents of nearby towns (which are basically food deserts)
- *Coffee?* Organizers of the weekly farmers' market, held in the morning but currently lacking any caffeine
- *Still-fresh pastries at the end of the morning?* Homeless community members not currently served by the soup kitchen
- *Subleased unit?* A local real estate agent who recently mentioned she wanted to establish her own office
- *Holiday dishes?* Local residents who don't usually visit your café because they have to leave early to beat the morning rush

Again, these are just examples, but they illustrate another critical milestone in implementing steps 2 and 3 of the bartering mindset. Quite the opposite of what you did before (using your own needs to identify other parties and their offerings), you've now used your own offerings to define some other parties and their needs. The residents of nearby towns, you realized, might need your tasty pastries just as much as the residents of your own town do. You're rapidly coming to grips with the external world.

Still it's worth pausing to make sure you haven't missed any potential partners. "How many possible partners can I possibly handle?" you're asking. And you're right. You can't and won't negotiate with the whole wide world; you'll eventually pick the most promising subset. But you'll never find the best subset at the end unless you develop an exhaustive list at the beginning. So I'd encourage you to go back to your needs and offerings and ask a final "who" question: "Who else might help me to satisfy any of my needs or value any of my offerings?" Given the intensity of your brainstorming, chances are you'll come up with at least one other party. Come to think of it, didn't someone tell you that the local Alcoholics Anonymous (AA) group is struggling to find a meeting space? And wouldn't you be happy to offer the café in service of community health and well-being? Sounds like another potential partner: add them!

Whatever your final list, this process has vastly expanded the possibilities compared to both Monty's and Getty's focus on a single promising partner. In contrast to their guidance to think competitively (Monty) or start negotiating integratively (Getty), you've now attained a bird's-eye view of the market and started to assess the many needs and offerings nestled within it, much like Keith on the hill – and much as Colombia's president must have done while reassessing the possibilities of a peace accord. But much like Keith walking around the market and Santos developing a strategy, you also need to think more carefully about these needs and offerings – and particularly how they relate to your own – before "negotiating." Let's give it a try!

The Café Story: Your Partners' Needs and Offerings

Between the current partners you identified in the last chapter (for example, customers) and the new partners you identified by thinking critically about your needs (such as artists) and offerings (such as residents of nearby towns), you've compiled an impressive list of potential transaction partners. And even without trying, you've also taken initial steps toward mapping out their needs and offerings. As a by-product of understanding what your current partners (chapter 3) and potential partners (chapter 4) value about your offerings, you've begun to map out their needs. For example, you now understand that the residents of your own town as well as the nearby towns probably need your tasty pastries. And as a by-product of understanding how your potential partners might help to meet your needs (chapter 4), you've started to understand their offerings. You now suspect, for example, that local artists might be willing to offer their paintings as decorations.

Thus you've discovered the beautiful symmetry between needs and offerings: your own offerings can satisfy your partners' needs, while your partners' offerings can satisfy your own needs. The bartering mindset has led you to the powerful insight that needs and offerings represent two sides of the same coin. If you take away just one insight, let it be that.

So at this point let's collect your thoughts by listing all the partners you've identified thus far, along with all of their needs and offerings as you currently understand them. Using table 3.2 and the two lists you just compiled, I'd suggest creating something like table 4.2, shortening the entries for brevity.

This table summarizes your current understanding of your partners, along with their needs and offerings. And it's already quite impressive, especially compared to the lone partners Monty or Getty might've called to mind. Still, you don't need a PhD in negotiation studies to see that the chart has some gaps. You haven't yet considered what your current transaction partners (for example, customers) or a set of your potential partners (such as residents of the neighboring towns) are offering or could offer. For another set of potential partners (for example, local farmers), you haven't yet considered what they need. Finally, a little reflection suggests that some of your current entries may not be entirely complete. Don't the police officers also offer revenue in the form of frequent coffee purchases? So the next step in implementing the bartering mindset – step 3 – involves comprehensively filling in the gaps. Once again, the process will amount to a series of educated guesses. But they're guesses well worth making, since the guesswork will eventually

Table 4.2 First Cut at Partners, Needs, and Offerings

	Their needs	Their offerings
Current partners		
Customers	• Tasty pastries • Welcoming atmosphere • Friendly employees • Reliable Wi-Fi • Bottomless coffee • Holiday dishes • Wi-Fi upgrade • Advertising on bulletin board	•
Employees	• Relationship with customers • Free pastries	•
Suppliers	• Steady stream of business • Subleased space	•
Landlord	• Timely rent	•
Potential partners		
Movie theater	•	• Referrals
Grocery store	•	• Sales to broader market
Radio station	•	• Advertising
Farmers	•	• Reduced transportation, trading, and storage costs
Politicians	•	• Tax or fee relief • Economic opportunity zone
Artists	•	• Decorated walls
Soup kitchen	•	• Poverty alleviation
Police officers	•	• Watching Main Street
Neighboring towns	• Tasty food items	•
Farmers' market	• Coffee	•
Homeless individuals	• Free pastries	•
Real estate agent	• Subleased space	•
Residents who leave early	• Holiday dishes	•
AA group	• Meeting space	•

save you time and focus your attention on the most promising set of partners.

Luckily the previous chapter already provided you with the basic tools to anticipate other people's needs and offerings. Suppose you first wanted to make the offerings column as comprehensive as possible. Don't you already have some questions about offerings in your arsenal? In the last chapter, you already asked questions like: "What value *does* my café provide to the world, and what value *could* my café provide to the world?" Although you originally asked such questions to assess your own offerings, why not adapt them to assess your *partners'* offerings? For example, "What value *do* current customers provide to the café?" And "What value *could* current customers potentially to the café?" I would suggest asking those questions of each partner in the chart, even if you already think you understand everyone quite well. Asking such questions, I think you'll find you could understand them better still.

And you can do even more to round out the offerings column: for the partners with needs already listed (for example, current customers), you can (and should!) use those needs as a lever to come up with additional offerings. For example, if customers really need your tasty pastries, is it possible they might need even tastier pastries that happen to sell for a higher margin? If customers really want to advertise on your bulletin board, would they be willing to offer some money? Irrespective of the answers, such questions are certainly worth asking. Indeed, by asking systematic questions and thinking critically about each of your partners' offerings, you'll achieve a much more sophisticated understanding of the role they might play in the café's long-term viability – that is, in satisfying your deep need. At this point, I'd suggest you give it a try by updating the offerings column of the previous chart.

Doing so might produce an updated chart like the one shown in table 4.3, with italics indicating items that were added or changed versus the last version. Please review these items, in particular, to see how your thinking has evolved.

Wow! Notice how much more sophisticated and interesting these possibilities are starting to sound. Revenue from art shows? Employees from the soup kitchen? Who would've thunk it? Neither

Table 4.3 Filling In Your Partners' Offerings

	Their needs	Their offerings
Current partners		
Customers	• Tasty pastries • Welcoming atmosphere • Friendly employees • Reliable Wi-Fi • Bottomless coffee • Holiday dishes • Wi-Fi upgrade • Advertising on bulletin board	• *Current spending at the café* • *Current referrals* • *New spending at the café* • *New fees (e.g., for Wi-Fi upgrade or coffee refills)* • *New referrals* • *Purchase of higher-margin food* • *Advertising revenue*
Employees	• Relationship with customers • Free pastries	• *Friendly and responsive service* • *Commitment to working at the café*
Suppliers	• Steady stream of business • Subleased space	• *Ingredients* • *Volume discounts* • *Subleasing revenue*
Landlord	• Timely rent	• *Building* • *Rent relief* • *Approval for subleasing*
Potential partners		
Movie theater	•	• *Referrals* • *On-screen advertising*
Grocery store	•	• Sales to broader market • *Sign about café in window*
Radio station	•	• *Paid advertising* • *Free advertising during fund drive*
Farmers	•	• Reduced transportation, trading, and storage costs • *Fresher ingredients* • *Differentiation through local sourcing* • *Goodwill with the community*
Politicians	•	• Tax or fee relief • Economic opportunity zone • *Current spending at the café* • *New spending at the café*
Artists	•	• Decorated walls • *New revenue from art shows, etc.* • *Differentiation through local art*
Soup kitchen	•	• Poverty alleviation • *Tax break from donations* • *Clients trying to escape homelessness by working as employees* • *Goodwill in the community*

(Continued)

Table 4.3 (Continued)

	Their needs	Their offerings
Police officers	•	• Watching Main Street • *Current spending at the café* • *New spending at the café*
Neighboring towns	• Tasty food items	• *New revenue*
Farmers' market	• Coffee	• *New revenue* • *Free advertising*
Homeless individuals	• Free pastries	• *Potential employees*
Real estate agent	• Subleased space	• *Subleasing revenue* • *New revenue from client meetings*
Residents who leave early	• Holiday dishes	• *New revenue*
AA group	• Meeting space	• *Supporting health of community* • *Food purchases during meetings*

Monty nor Getty, most likely. In addition, notice how this process has helped you to refine the offerings that were already there. You already knew the radio station could provide paid advertising, for example, but by thinking about that offering carefully, you realized that they might do it for free if you catered their fund drive ("Thank you to Café X for providing lunch during our fund drive!"). Accordingly, you've split the original offering in two. With that you've mapped out your partners' offerings.

Finally, it's time to map out their needs. Again you already have some questions about needs in your arsenal, don't you? Using the deductive approach, didn't you already ask what any café owner needs to do to ensure a business's viability? Using the inductive approach, didn't you already reflect on this particular café and ask what you need to do to ensure its viability? These questions helped you ascertain your own needs, but why not adapt them to assess your *partners'* needs, asking questions like "What does a local farmer usually need from a café?" (deductive), and "What do the local farmers in this area need from my café?" (inductive).

Again I'd suggest asking those questions of every partner in the chart, even if you already think you understand them well. By asking systematic questions, I think you'll find that you could understand them better still. In addition, and just like the procedure you followed to complete the offerings column, I'd suggest using your partners' offerings as a lever for refining or adding to their needs. If artists would eagerly offer their paintings as decorations, doesn't that suggest a need for public recognition or broader exposure? By thinking critically about your partners' needs in addition to their offerings, you'll achieve a much more sophisticated appreciation for the ways you could ultimately obtain their offerings (and thus meet your needs). Again, I'd suggest you give it a try by updating the needs column of the chart.

Doing so might produce something like table 4.4, with italics connoting changes or additions versus the last version. Again, please review these items to see the progression in your thinking.

Wow again! You've now compiled a truly impressive list of partners, needs, and offerings. The latest list adds several new needs: you've incorporated your landlord's passing comment that she needs some new managers to help run her thriving property business, and your employees' oft-noted appetite for career advancement. (Hmm, could you satisfy both needs at the same time?) In addition, the latest list refines the needs that were already there. Thinking about the nearby residents' need for food, you realized you might satisfy it with a food truck. In contrast to Monty's implication that any particular counterpart has a single-minded focus on a single issue (typically money), this process has reminded you that everyone has a wide range of needs. In contrast to Getty's implication that we should approach a promising party and identify a complementary interest, this process has reminded you that identifying potential partners and anticipating their full suite of needs and offerings deserves careful attention itself. Very interesting indeed.

These are the hallmarks of the bartering mindset. You – like Keith in chapter 2 and Santos at the start of this chapter – have now achieved a much better understanding of the external world, particularly the many parties who might help to satisfy your needs if

Table 4.4 Filling In Your Partners' Needs

	Their needs	Their offerings
Current partners		
Customers	• Tasty pastries • *Even tastier (higher margin) pastries* • Welcoming atmosphere • Friendly employees • Reliable Wi-Fi • Bottomless coffee • Holiday dishes • Wi-Fi upgrade • Advertising on bulletin board • *Lots of plugs* • *Recognition for their loyalty* • *Catering for special events*	• Current spending at the café • Current referrals • New spending at the café • New fees (e.g., for Wi-Fi upgrade or coffee refills) • New referrals • Purchase of higher-margin food • Advertising revenue
Employees	• Relationship with customers • Free pastries • *Advancement opportunities* • *Part-time option for education*	• Friendly and responsive service • Commitment to working at the café
Suppliers	• Steady stream of business • Subleased space	• Ingredients • Volume discounts • Subleasing revenue
Landlord	• Timely rent • *Managerial talent to support thriving property business*	• Building • Rent relief • Approval for subleasing
Potential partners		
Movie theater	• *Increased foot traffic*	• Referrals • On-screen advertising
Grocery store	• *Tasty, local food items* • *Prevent erosion of customer base to big box store*	• Sales to broader market • Sign about café in window
Radio station	• *Food for fund drive* • *Exposure via the café's speakers*	• Paid advertising • Free advertising during fund drive
Farmers	• *New revenue* • *Advertising to drive customers to market at farm*	• Reduced transportation, trading, and storage costs • Fresher ingredients • Differentiation through local sourcing • Goodwill with the community
Politicians	• *Political support* • *Advertising* • *Campaign funds* • *Affordable breakfast*	• Tax or fee relief • Economic opportunity zone • Current spending at the café • New spending at the café

	Their needs	Their offerings
Artists	• *Exposure for their work* • *Venue for art shows* • *New revenue*	• Decorated walls • New revenue from art shows, etc. • Differentiation through local art
Soup kitchen	• *Food* • *Monetary donations* • *Employment for clients*	• Poverty alleviation • Tax break from donations • Clients trying to escape homelessness by working as employees • Goodwill in the community
Police officers	• *Discounts*	• Watching Main Street • Current spending at the café • New spending at the café
Neighboring towns	• Tasty food items *(food truck?)*	• New revenue
Farmers' market	• Coffee • *Tasty food items* • *More customers*	• New revenue • Free advertising
Homeless individuals	• Free pastries • *Employment* • *Referrals to soup kitchen*	• Potential employees
Real estate agent	• Subleased space	• Subleasing revenue • New revenue from client meetings
Residents who leave early	• Holiday dishes • *Catering for special events*	• New revenue
AA group	• Meeting space • *Food for meetings*	• Supporting health of community • Food purchases during meetings

only you satisfied theirs. And you, by painstakingly plotting out your partners' offerings and needs, are starting to develop a clear sense of the many possible ways the market could solve your problems. Indeed, you've done all of that from the comfort of your own armchair, without really "negotiating" in the traditional sense.

Reviewing your own work and comparing it to Monty's and Getty's guidance at the start of the chapter, I hope you're impressed by the depth and breadth reflected in table 4.4. And I hope you're struck by the creativity reflected in the entries, even intrigued to see how the underlying possibilities play out – not fearful of a "negotiation." Indeed, the bartering mindset has greatly reduced the need to be apprehensive, as a close examination of the table reveals that a few of the eventual solutions may involve distributive negotiation, but many or most will not – at least not at the beginning. While the bartering mindset does not eliminate Monty's imperative to claim value, as we'll see in chapter 7, it vastly expands the possibilities for creating value – paving the way to adopt Getty's counsel once we're actually prepared to do so. And we're certainly getting closer to that point, having understood ourselves and the external world quite comprehensively. But we're not there yet. We still need to winnow the world to the most promising set of partnerships – a challenge we'll tackle in the next chapter.

Steps 2–3 of the Bartering Mindset: Key Questions to Ask Yourself

- Who else might help me satisfy my [deep and broad needs]? Who else might value my [deep and broad offerings]? Who else might help me to satisfy any of my needs or value any of my offerings?
  o Answers indicate transaction partners.
- What value do [transaction partners] provide to me? What value could [transaction partners] provide to me?
  o Answers indicate transaction partners' offerings.
- What do [transaction partners] generally need from people like me? What do these specific [transaction partners] need from me?
  o Answers indicate transaction partners' needs.

Summary of Key Points from This Chapter

1 Steps 2–3 of the bartering mindset involve trying to understand your transaction partners as well as you understand yourself.

2 Your own needs and offerings provide a starting point for mapping out the full range of partners (step 2).

3 After mapping out the full range of partners, the questions you asked about your own offerings can be adapted to map out the full range of your partners' offerings (step 3).

4 After mapping out your partners' offerings, the questions you asked about your own needs can be adapted to map out the full range of your partners' needs (step 3).

5 Ultimately, these steps will dramatically expand the set of solutions that could satisfy your needs and solve your problems.

Exercise: Job Negotiation and Steps 2–3 of the Bartering Mindset

In the last three chapters we grappled with your realistic need for additional income. Most recently, in chapter 3, we used step 1 of the bartering mindset to map out your needs and offerings. You identified the deep need lurking behind your perceived need for money. Perhaps you needed money to cover escalating commuting costs. Or perhaps you identified something entirely different – and I hope you did, in the process of applying the exercise to your own life. Furthermore, you identified the broad set of needs that might facilitate your deep need; particularly if a requested salary increase doesn't materialize, you might need to request a virtual work arrangement, obtain a loan, buy a fuel-efficient car, or get a Costco membership, for example. At this point you might want to stop and review your own thinking in the last chapter, as we're about to use it as a point of departure for exploring potential partners.

Having understood yourself, steps 2–3 of the bartering mindset involve attempting to understand your transaction partners. Following the guidance in this chapter, where would you start? You might test your understanding by trying to remember the process described in this chapter.

I hope you remember that you can use your own set of needs and offerings to get a handle on the identity of your potential transaction partners (step 2). So at this point, please take one of your broad needs, whatever they happened to be, and ask yourself, "Who else could help me do X?" If one of your broad needs was to move closer to the office, for example, you'd ask something like "Who else could help me move closer?" A friend who already lives close to your office and might appreciate a roommate, or even your own company via their discounted corporate housing program? Next, please take your own set of offerings, whatever they were, and ask yourself, "Who else values my Y?" If one of your offerings was a sharply analytical mind, who else might value that? People in a competing company? Or a completely different industry? Or even the potential clients you could cultivate by starting your own consultancy on the side? However many partners you identify, this exercise will surely lengthen the list.

Halfway there! After listing your current partners (such as your boss) in the last chapter and compiling a long list of potential partners (such as potential clients) in this chapter, it's time to better understand all of your partners' needs and offerings (step 3). Following the guidance in this chapter, can you remember how to do that?

I'm hoping you'll remember to first list out all of your potential partners in a table resembling table 4.2. Even if you didn't remember that, I'd now advise you to construct a table to organize all the transaction partners you identified in the last chapter and this one. Then take the information you've compiled so far and try to map out what you know about their respective needs and offerings. Thanks to the last chapter, you already have a decent handle on your current partners' needs. If you realized in chapter 3 that your boss would value less travel, for example, then the boss obviously needs more time at home. Thanks to the current chapter, you also have at least an initial handle on your potential partners' needs. If you identified individuals who would become consulting clients just to access your sharply analytical mind, then these people probably need to better understand their own business or personal situations. By prompting you to consider who else might satisfy your needs, the current chapter also helped you start to surface your potential partners' offerings. The friend who lives closer to the office, for example, potentially offers a shorter commute (and possibly even lower rent).

All of this information is lurking behind the thinking you've already done; the table just helps you organize it. But step 3 of the bartering mindset involves filling in the gaps. I'd encourage you to do that in your own chart, especially by filling in the offerings column for parties whose needs you already understand (such as your boss) and the needs column for parties whose offerings you already understand (such as your friend). What exactly would your boss offer you if you travelled more? What would your friend ask of you as part of an apartment-sharing arrangement? These are just examples, but the point is not the details: it's to show you how the bartering mindset substantially broadens your thinking. Even more importantly, it's to instill a pattern of thinking that will help you map out the many potential partners who can help you solve your own problems in the real world. With the benefit of this chapter and those that follow, I'm confident you'll be able to do that.

Phew! In the process of seeking to understand your partners and their situations, you might feel a bit fatigued. But I think you'll also see that you now understand the rest of the world a whole lot better. As a direct result, you'll be much better equipped to start engaging with the rest of the world, as we'll do after identifying the best and most powerful set of partnerships in the market. We've come a long way in the job exercise (and café example), but we have some important ground to plough in the form of identifying power partnerships. That's where we're going now.

5

STEP 4: ANTICIPATE THE MOST POWERFUL SET OF PARTNERSHIPS ACROSS THE MARKET

In 1995 Los Angeles lost both of its National Football League (NFL) teams.[1] The Rams headed to St Louis and the Raiders to Oakland. Local football fans were crushed. Over the next few decades, various teams expressed an interest in moving to LA, and various power brokers expressed an interest in having them. But it was not until 2015 that the talks started to bear fruit. In that year, three teams – the St Louis Rams, Oakland Raiders, and San Diego Chargers – expressed serious interest in relocating and attracted the NFL's serious consideration.

The NFL's ambitions were clear: they wanted to attract revenue from the country's second-largest media market, expand their fan base, collect at least one multi-million-dollar relocation fee, and get a new stadium – preferably fancy and financed by one or more teams. In exchange, they were offering to green-light the relocation of those teams – a sure-fire way to anger local leaders and now-devoted fans in St Louis, Oakland, or San Diego, not to mention the LA residents displaced or inconvenienced by a new stadium.

The teams, in turn, had several diverse objectives. The St Louis Rams were probably focused on increasing – maybe even doubling – their value by playing in a much bigger metro area. The Oakland Raiders and San Diego Chargers, who already played in populous regions, were probably less focused on the size of their fan base. Instead, they were probably seeking to play in much better stadiums. Indeed, any LA venue would be better than the aging football/baseball stadiums they used back home. And, truth be told, both were probably willing to use the LA talks as leverage to force the publicly financed replacement of those stadiums.

So the teams had differing needs, and they also offered differing visions of football in LA. The owner of the St Louis Rams had already bought a large tract of land in Inglewood, just west of downtown and east of LAX airport. And he had already announced intentions and received approval to build a $2.7-billion, state-of-the-art stadium there – a facility that could host not only Super Bowls but a variety of other mass-market entertainment options. What's more, the stadium would be surrounded by a premier entertainment district featuring a mall, movie theater, office complex, and luxury apartments – all financed by the owner (with a little help from Goldman Sachs). As another owner noted, the Rams' proposal had the "wow factor." The Oakland Raiders and San Diego Chargers, in contrast, proposed to build and share a more pedestrian, football-focused stadium farther away, on the site of a former waste dump. In addition to the proposal's distinct lack of "wow," it suffered from the NFL's reservations about relocating the Raiders, a team whose brand had (rightly or wrongly) become associated with gangs and violence.

With these considerations and months of persuasive maneuvers by the teams in mind, the NFL owners deliberated and decided in private. Ultimately they decided to approve the St Louis Rams' immediate relocation to a temporary stadium in LA, where the team would play until the Inglewood venue's completion. In addition, they gave the San Diego Chargers a yearlong option to join the Rams in LA and eventually in Inglewood. If the Chargers didn't exercise that option, it would default to the Oakland Raiders. The owners had decided that the immediate relocation of the Rams – given their true intention to move, ability to grow a larger fan base, and willingness to finance a premier venue – could best meet the NFL's needs with minimal disruption or expense. And the Rams' determination to move, as evidenced by their ambitious and preapproved plan, suggested that the team also stood to prosper from the deal.

But the agreement didn't stop with the St Louis Rams. The fact that the NFL owners also offered a stadium-sharing option (first to the San Diego Chargers and then the Oakland Raiders) suggested that the owners considered the various possibilities holistically, arriving at the most beneficial *set* of potential deals. A delayed stadium-sharing deal with another team like the Chargers, they probably surmised, would eventually help to guarantee weekly usage of the stadium and nonstop football attention in LA, while minimizing the disruption associated with two teams' simultaneous relocations. The exclusion of the Oakland Raiders, in turn, suggested that the owners did not consider that team part of the optimal package deal in LA. In retrospect these decisions were prescient, as the Chargers have since exercised the option to move to LA, and the Raiders have negotiated a separate relocation to another populous city without an existing team: Las Vegas.

The relocation process was longer and more complicated than described. And it was largely driven by the NFL owners but did involve some "negotiation" with the teams, which we're not yet ready to do in the café story. Still, the NFL example exemplifies step 4 of the bartering mindset, which focuses on anticipating multiple opportunities for mutually beneficial exchange – *power partnerships*, as we'll call them. By itself, an economic "partnership" simply involves exchanging your offerings for someone else's, presumably to address the needs of at least one party. A standard partnership doesn't necessarily meet the needs of either side well or efficiently. But *power partnerships* do a lot more: they satisfy both parties' needs as extensively and inexpensively as possible. They're powerful in the sense that they multiply everyone's economic opportunities, often exponentially.[2] The NFL story suggests that the owners anticipated a powerful set of partnerships with at least two of the teams, and perhaps all three if they were thinking ahead to Las Vegas.

The dogged and systematic identification of power partnerships is a hallmark of the bartering mindset – and the fourth step in implementing that mindset today. The NFL was essentially plotting out a set of power partnerships as they considered the various possibilities. So was Keith while he walked around the market. And so should you as you pick up the café story. In the context of that story, the current chapter will provide a methodology for anticipating power partnerships, providing straightforward guidance to help you identify the best and most powerful set of partnerships in your own life.

The Café Story: Setting the Stage

By the end of the last chapter, you – the owner of the struggling café – were starting to feel a bit more optimistic about the café's viability, perhaps even excited to see what the future might hold. Moving far beyond your initial inclination to cut costs, you developed a deep and broad understanding of your own needs and offerings, then mapped out a wide range of potential transaction partners and developed an impressive understanding of *their* needs and offerings – all from the comfort of your favorite armchair. Just when you started to feel comfortable, though, Monty would probably reappear on your shoulder. And what would Monty probably say?

"Lucky dog!" Monty would probably say. "You now know exactly what you're offering and exactly who needs it most. What a golden opportunity to make some money!" In response to your quizzical looks, Monty might offer an example: "Take the AA group. They seem pretty desperate for a meeting space, don't they? I mean, the last time you talked to the organizer, he was discouraged by everyone's lack of interest in hosting a group of recovering alcoholics. You could practically march in and ask him for $2000 a month to use the café, and he'd have to say yes!" But setting aside any ethical concerns with Monty's recommendations, you'd probably have the pragmatic concern that it just won't work. Even if the organizer happens to have $2000 a month on hand, he probably won't appreciate the demand or want to spend his entire budget on a meeting space. Still seated in your armchair, then, you might shoo distributive-minded Monty away, only to find Getty on your other shoulder. And what would Getty say?

"Get up! Get out of that armchair already!" Getty might say, growing impatient with all this pre-negotiation deliberation. "Just pick a partner from your table already and propose a trade-off!" Overhearing your conversation with Monty, Getty might pick up on the AA example. "Take the AA group that Monty was mentioning. They meet three nights a week and need both space and food for their meetings. You, my friend, need both a healthy community and a healthy bottom line. Why not offer them the use of the café three nights a week, and keep it open after-hours to supply the food?" And you might approach the organizer to propose just that trade-off. Seeing as you've spent some time thinking carefully about the AA group's needs and offerings, it's possible this proposal would strike a chord – at least a less dissonant chord than the $2000 demand envisioned by Monty. So off you might go, making the trade-off and issuing a big thank you to Getty.

But if you made the deal, you'd probably feel some creeping agitation. Offering your space and pastries after-hours, three nights a week, would certainly meet the group's needs for space and food, but at what cost? You're already suffering from cost overruns, and repeatedly keeping your café humming late into the night is unlikely to help. Meanwhile, the group's use of the café might contribute to community health indirectly, and selling your pastries (at a discount) might bring in a smidgeon more revenue. But how much of a dent will either make in the fundamental problem? Since the AA group has only a couple of members, aren't there other partners you could engage to have a bigger impact on the community, possibly at a lower cost to everyone concerned (for example, the soup kitchen)? And aren't there better ways to increase your revenue while still serving the community (for example, by letting the local struggling artists host a once-a-month art show)? Callous as it might seem, you might realize that there are better ways to help the café and the community at the same time, meaning that you've just spent valuable time hammering out a relatively inconsequential or even counterproductive deal. Since integrative go-getter Getty's solution would still leave you (and probably the AA group) disappointed, you'd have to bid Getty goodbye and turn back to Bart. And what would Bart suggest?

Referring to step 4 of the bartering mindset, Bart would suggest that you still have one critical task to complete before approaching the rest of the world: thinking through the actual trades with each partner to anticipate the most powerful set of partnerships across the market. Why not just head out and assess all that through a series of discussions? Your experience with Getty has just shown why. You'd inevitably end up talking to a lot of people who cannot serve each other's needs particularly well, and that would waste everyone's time and force you to sever some potential partnerships midstream, thereby leaving a bad taste in multiple mouths. "If you randomly selected the AA group and then discovered the limited possibilities," Bart might remind you, "you'd have to tell the organizer as much, at which point he'd probably resent the interaction, or at least the wasted time." In the absence of infinite time and infinite social capital, you have to be more selective about your prospective partners.

In short, Bart would call on you to do just a bit more legwork before approaching potential partners. Recognizing that you won't be able to identify power partnerships with certainty, Bart would urge you to make one more round of educated guesses. "You'll be surprised how much you can figure out on your own," Bart might say, "and thus how much time and social capital you can preserve through solitary analysis."

So let's use the rest of this chapter to introduce a methodology for identifying power partnerships. If you're itching for some negotiation, please scratch the itch by assuring yourself that all this pre-negotiation preparation is firmly grounded in negotiation research,[3] is reminiscent of well-established approaches to stakeholder analysis,[4] and will almost assuredly produce superior outcomes once negotiations commence (in something like the traditional sense, in the next chapter). Much like Keith planning some specific trades or the NFL plotting out the possibilities, let's anticipate the potential trades you might propose to each partner and predict how powerful the underlying partnerships are likely to be.

Specifying Potential Trades

The last chapter left you with a very long list of potential transaction partners, along with their likely needs and offerings (summarized in table 4.4). How could you possibly determine which of the partners on that overwhelming list present the possibility of a power partnership? Well, consider what your long list has already accomplished and what it hasn't. Since you developed your list by specifying current partners, then adding additional parties who might satisfy your needs or desire your offerings, your list has already distilled the whole wide world down to the relevant parties. The parties who made the list – for example, customers, farmers, artists – necessarily need something from and/or could offer something to the café, so they could necessarily inform the final solution.

And you didn't stop after identifying the relevant parties. Remember what you did next? Took an educated guess at what, specifically, each party might need from and offer to the café (for example, by asking, "What do the local farmers in this area need from my café? What value do local farmers provide to the café?"). And here's the real pay-off to that approach: by focusing specifically on what they need *from the café* and offer *to the café*, you're already starting to see the general outlines of a potential trade. Since you suspect that the movie theater needs more foot traffic and might be willing to offer

referrals and on-screen advertising, for example, the fuzzy outlines of a trade are probably coming into focus. Can you see what
it might be? Some information in the café about current showings,
in exchange for a form of referral or advertising? Your thinking has
already come a long way!

But it still has a way to go. Consider where you want to end up:
with a list of trades that satisfy both parties' needs as extensively
and inexpensively as possible – trades that form the basis of power
partnerships. How well would a trade with the movie theater meet
their need for foot traffic or any of your needs? Since you haven't
really specified what you or they (or anyone else) would actually do,
it's hard to anticipate how extensively or inexpensively any trade
would meet anyone's needs – or even which needs would be met.
For example, you can't even guess whether the movie theater promises a power partnership, because you don't understand the benefits
(how "extensively" a trade would meet either party's needs) or costs
(how "inexpensively").

Now, there's obviously a limit to the amount of analysis you can
complete from your armchair – about the movie theater or anyone else.
Some of the information needed to identify power partnerships with
precision will obviously emerge from discussion. You might need to
confirm, for example, whether the movie theater could even offer on-
screen advertising. And while you could theoretically spend your time
estimating the exact costs the movie theater might incur in offering
such advertising, you'd probably find the experience time-consuming
and inefficient. So nothing about the process described here is meant
to downplay or ignore the importance of your eventual negotiations.
To truly adopt step 4 of the bartering mindset, though, you can and
should take an initial stab at three questions for each partner:

1 What might a trade actually look like?
2 How well would it satisfy each of our needs?
3 How costly would it be for each of us to execute?

Taking an educated guess at these final questions will leave you with a clear sense of the parties who present at least the possibility of a power partnership.

So let's tackle the first question. How would you go about specifying trades? Well, it's a lot simpler than it sounds, since much of the relevant information is already lurking behind table 4.4). (If you haven't reviewed the table recently, you might want to take a quick look.) Having reviewed the table, I think you'll find it relatively easy to translate its contents into some specific trades. Right? It's no harder than asking some "how" questions.

Starting with the other parties' offerings (right column), which stand to satisfy your own needs, you'd ask questions like "How could the movie theater's on-screen advertising satisfy my needs?" To answer that question, you might need to review your own needs (table 3.2). Having done so, you'd be able to answer the question by linking it to one or more of your core needs (increased revenue, reduced costs, healthier community) and providing any specific details. For example, "By attracting new customers who bring in additional revenue." With this straightforward answer, you've learned both the need that on-screen advertising could fulfill (increased revenue) and the way that advertising could fulfill that need (new customers). Both insights will eventually help to identify power partnerships. Of course this is just an example of the "how" questions you'd ask of each partner and their offerings.

And the "how" questions don't stop there! Since a power partnership has to satisfy your partner's needs in addition to your own, you'd also ask some "how" questions of the other column in the table – questions like "How could I fulfill the movie theater's need for increased foot traffic?" In this case, you might need to refer back to your own offerings (also in table 3.2). Having done that, you'd probably come up with some intriguing answers. Perhaps you could place some fliers with the theater's current showings on the counter, thereby sending some interested feet in their direction. "Looking for something to do after your coffee? Why not catch a flick at the Cineplex 6?" That idea, though preliminary, offers at least a concrete possibility to evaluate when identifying power partnerships. Again, you'd ask some "how" questions like these of each partner and their needs.

Lest all of these "how" questions seem a bit tedious in the abstract, let's pause and actually try a few. At this point, I'd ask you to take a momentary step back into the mind of the café owner, select a few of the offerings and needs in table 4.4, and actually ask yourself a few of the "how" questions above. How could their offerings fulfill your needs? How could your offerings fulfill theirs? Please pause and give it a try.

Having asked a few of these "how" questions, I'll bet you found the process substantially more interesting and challenging than expected. Boring and mechanical as the "how" questions might seem in the abstract, I'd guess the experience of actually answering them revealed the need for both judgment and ingenuity. This is the fun part! In answering the "how" questions, for example, you may have encountered some offerings that don't readily fit into a trade (for example, current revenue from current customers) or needs you can't readily fulfill (for example, campaign funds for politicians – you're broke). When that happens, you'll have to exercise enough judgment to discard them and move on. In other cases, you may have come up with some trade ideas that don't fit neatly into any one of your needs: does publicizing your sourcing from local farmers increase revenue (by encouraging additional purchases), build a healthier community, or both? It's a judgment call. Finally, you may have found that answering such questions brings out your ingenuity. In particular, you probably found yourself identifying new and intriguing ways that your partners could meet your needs or you could meet theirs (for example, a coupon for the grocery store on your receipts?). Just as Keith realized while meandering in the market, you'll probably realize in these moments that finding ways to creatively offload what you don't want in exchange for getting what you do is actually quite fun.

Now all of these "how" questions will probably produce an overwhelming amount of information that you really need to organize. Luckily you have an obvious tool at hand: an additional table, much like the last but with columns listing the details of potential trades. For example, you might include a column called "How to fulfill my needs with their offerings," which lists the needs your partners' offerings could fulfill and how. And you might include a second column called "How to fulfill their needs with my offerings," listing the offerings that might fulfill your partners' needs and how.[5] At this point, and before reviewing my own entries in such a table, I'd suggest creating at least a portion of a table like that yourself, populating it with your own answers to the "how" questions above.

Having done so, you might get a chart that looks something like table 5.1.

Wow! In the space of a table, you've come up with a wide array of fascinating yet feasible ways to engage a plethora of partners. In other words, you've moved well beyond the entries in table 4.4 by replacing general needs and offerings with actionable and promising trades, which form the basis of potentially powerful partnerships. But you're not quite done. You've successfully answered the first question required to identify power partnerships (what the trades might look like), but not the other two: what are the benefits and costs to both sides? Much as the NFL must've compared the costs and benefits of various relocation plans, you need to assess which partnerships are most promising. Luckily, your previous work should make this part of the process easy and enjoyable.

Table 5.1 Potential Trades

	How to fulfill my needs with their offerings	How to fulfill their needs with my offerings
Customers	**Revenue** • Spend more money as a result of customer loyalty program • Spend more money on holiday dishes and/or catering • Spend more money on higher-margin foods • Pay more in fees for services (e.g., Wi-Fi, bottomless coffee) • Pay to advertise their small businesses • Refer new customers through customer referral program	• Create a customer loyalty program • Offer holiday dishes and/or catering • Offer more diverse menu with higher-margin foods • Provide a high-speed Wi-Fi option • Provide bottomless coffees for a charge • Create study area with additional plugs • Make bulletin board space available for small business advertising • Create a customer referral program
Employees	**Costs** • Offer to continue working at café while in management training or exercising part-time option	• Create employee recognition award • Offer free, still-fresh pastries at the end of morning • Create management training program with landlord • Create part-time option for education • Provide sales training that also serves to sell higher-margin foods
Suppliers	**Revenue** • Pay to sublease space **Costs** • Offer volume discounts	• Provide access to subleased space • Agree to guaranteed purchase levels • Agree to purchase higher-margin ingredients
Landlord	**Revenue** • Approve subleasing **Costs** • Provide rent relief • Help retain employees by providing them with management training	• Propose current employees as source of management talent in training • Sign on to longer-term lease • Offer to pay at the beginning of the month
Movie theater	**Revenue** • Reach new customers through on-screen advertising or referrals	• Distribute fliers about current showings
Grocery store	**Revenue** • Sell café's pastries to reach new customers • Install sign advertising the café in the store window	• Provide pastries • Print a coupon for grocery store on receipts

(Continued)

Table 5.1 (Continued)

	How to fulfill my needs with their offerings	How to fulfill their needs with my offerings
Radio station	**Revenue** • Offer paid advertising • Offer free advertising during fund drive by mentioning café on-air	• Pay for advertising • Provide food for fund drive • Play their music in the café exclusively
Farmers	**Revenue** • Provide fresh, organic ingredients at a low cost • Allow café to publicize local sourcing	• Source ingredients from them • Put up sign in café about the local farms from which ingredients are sourced (thereby advertising)
Politicians	**Revenue** • Make more purchases at the café **Costs** • Provide tax- or fee-relief plan **Community** • Create an economic opportunity zone	• Create a public servant discount program • Support one of their initiatives in a public forum • Put up a supportive sign in the main street window at election time
Artists	**Revenue** • Pay a nominal fee to display art • Agree to display art for a certain period • Agree to host regular art shows and encourage visitors to purchase food and drink • Allow café to publicize support of local artists **Community** • Sell art to customers	• Allow them to display work and signage about themselves • Allow them to host art shows
Soup kitchen	**Revenue** • Allow café to publicize support of soup kitchen **Costs** • Track and acknowledge donations for tax purposes **Community** • Pre-screen clients for jobs • Combat homelessness through increased capacity	• Put up signage in café about the soup kitchen's need for donations • Offer free, still-fresh pastries at the end of the morning • Make monetary donations • Create hire-local program giving preference to their clients • Make referrals to soup kitchen

	How to fulfill my needs with their offerings	How to fulfill their needs with my offerings
Police officers	**Revenue** • Make more purchases at the café **Community** • Informally agree to watch café	• Create a public servant discount program
Neighboring towns	**Revenue** • New spending via food truck	• Lease and operate a daily food truck
Farmers' market	**Revenue** • Reach new customers by selling café's pastries • Agree to install signage advertising the café	• Provide coffee and pastries • Hand out fliers in café about the fact the pastries are now sold in the market (thus advertising for market)
Homeless individuals	**Community** • Work at the café	• Offer free, still-fresh pastries at the end of the morning • Create hire-local program giving them preference • Make referrals to soup kitchen
Real estate agent	**Revenue** • Pay to sublease space • Agree to conduct a certain number of client meetings at the café and encourage clients to buy food and drink	• Provide access to subleased space
Residents who leave early	**Revenue** • Reach new customers through holiday dishes and/or catering	• Offer holiday dishes and/or catering
AA group	**Revenue** • Buy discounted food during meetings at the café **Community** • Host meetings at the café	• Offer meeting space and food

Identifying Power Partnerships

We've said throughout the chapter that power partnerships fulfill both parties' needs extensively and inexpensively, but what do those terms actually mean? Trades that fulfill both parties' needs "extensively" satisfy as many of both parties' needs as completely as possible. In other words, "extensively" refers to the overall benefits of a trade. "Inexpensive" trades, in turn, require minimal investments of money or time from either side – minimal overall costs. To state the semi-obvious, each time a transaction partner fulfills your own needs with their offerings (left column of the table above), that tends to create benefits for you and costs for them – and vice-versa when you fulfill their needs with your own offerings. Since we're striving to identify partners who promise a power partnership, we now want to locate the partners in the table above whose bundle of trades promise the greatest mutual benefit at lowest mutual cost.

You could do that in many ways. But since you know more about your own outcomes, I'd suggest starting with your own benefits and costs. As you'll see, this process doesn't ignore your partners' outcomes – far from it! But it does anchor the analysis in your own. So how do you think you'd identify the costs and benefits lurking behind the table above?

Well, I'd suggest starting with the left column of the table above and asking how well the entries in each cell would meet your three needs. For example, "How well would the grocery store's food sales and sign meet my need for increased revenue, reduced costs, and a healthier community?" If you start asking such questions – and I hope you'll try – you'll probably find that answering them accurately requires you to consider two factors: First, how many of your three needs does this partner address? The food sales and sign address only one – revenue – but other partners like the soup kitchen address several (in this case, all three). Second, how completely does this partner address each need? Returning to the grocery store, how well would additional food sales and a sign meet your need for additional revenue – how much additional revenue would you actually earn? Will your tasty pastries tempt harried shoppers as readily as they tempt caffeine-starved coffee-sippers? Will drivers or pedestrians even see a sign? Using this framework, I'd suggest asking and answering these additional "how" questions for several partners in the table.

If you asked the "how" question for each partner in the table, as you would if the café problem were your own, you'd begin to understand which partners could fulfill many of your needs and/or a few needs really well. Certain partners would "stick out" as particularly promising (for example, the soup kitchen), and you'd obviously retain them for further analysis. If that doesn't sound very precise, I must admit it's not. While partners who could fulfill many of your needs completely should obviously make the list, and those who fulfill a single need marginally should not, there is no mathematical formula for deciding on the parties in the middle – partners who'd fulfill many needs poorly or a single need, sort of. Indeed, the situation becomes even more complicated when you realize that your partners – being human beings in their own right – may not comply with your plans. What if the grocery store refuses to put up a sign? Assessing the benefits sounds hopeless until you realize that your goal at this stage is simply to separate the wheat from the chaff – the promising from the marginal partners. Given that goal, I'd suggest asking yourself which partners seem at least somewhat promising for satisfying your deep need, then retaining them. To indicate which partners you wish to retain, you can simply take the prior table and draw a big outline around the relevant cells in the left column.

In addition to understanding the benefits associated with each partner's trades, and without belaboring the point, you'd also want to understand the costs. At this point you can probably guess the procedure: just take the right column of table 5.1 and ask how much it would cost you to provide each bundle of offerings. For example, "How much money and time would it cost me to supply pastries to and print coupons for the grocery store?" Pretty simple, right? But again, there's the pesky complication that your partners are fickle humans. Perhaps the grocery store will agree to sell your pastries without any discussion of coupons. Great! Or perhaps you'll offer coupons, but they'll show no interest. Not so good. Again the prospect of assessing costs seems hopeless until you realize that your goal is simply to separate the affordable from the cost-prohibitive partners. In asking the above "how" question of all the partners in the chart, trades with certain partners will seem feasible, whereas others (for example, suppliers) will "stick out" for the wrong reason: because they would require a huge outlay of cash or time. Given your goal, I'd recommend asking yourself which trades seem moderately feasible, then retaining those partners. To indicate which partners you wish to retain, you can simply take table 5.1 and draw a big outline around the relevant cells in the right column. At this point, please give it a try, thinking about the boxes in the table that you would outline.

There's no "right" answer, but my updated table might look something like table 5.2.

In making this table, your goal was simply to make the world tractable, to find a way of focusing on neither a single partner nor the whole wide world. Thus while it may seem premature to determine costs and benefits, remember that you're not ruling anyone out – you're just trying to come to grips with the external world. You can always return to your table if the world proves you wrong. And making some educated guess about potential partnerships is so much better than focusing on either a lone partnership or all of them. With those caveats in mind, the table has effectively allowed you to categorize your partners into four groups:

1 High benefit / low cost to me (both columns outlined; for example, employees)
2 High benefit / high cost to me (left column outlined only; for example, customers)

Table 5.2 Your Costs and Benefits from Trades

	How to fulfill my needs with their offerings	How to fulfill their needs with my offerings
Customers	**Revenue** • Spend more money as a result of customer loyalty program • Spend more money on holiday dishes and/or catering • Spend more money on higher-margin foods • Pay more in fees for services (e.g., Wi-Fi, bottomless coffee) • Pay to advertise their small businesses • Refer new customers through customer referral program	• Create a customer loyalty program • Offer holiday dishes and/or catering • Offer more diverse menu with higher-margin foods • Provide a high-speed Wi-Fi option • Provide bottomless coffees for a charge • Create study area with additional plugs • Make bulletin board space available for small business advertising • Create a customer referral program
Employees	**Costs** • Offer to continue working at café while in management training or exercising part-time option	• Create employee recognition award • Offer free, still-fresh pastries at the end of morning • Create management training program with landlord • Create part-time option for education • Provide sales training that also serves to sell higher-margin foods
Suppliers	**Revenue** • Pay to sublease space **Costs** • Offer volume discounts	• Provide access to subleased space • Agree to guaranteed purchase levels • Agree to purchase higher-margin ingredients
Landlord	**Revenue** • Approve subleasing **Costs** • Provide rent relief • Help retain employees by providing them with management training	• Propose current employees as source of management talent in training • Sign on to longer-term lease • Offer to pay at the beginning of the month

(Continued)

Table 5.2 (Continued)

	How to fulfill my needs with their offerings	How to fulfill their needs with my offerings
Movie theater	**Revenue** • Reach new customers through on-screen advertising or referrals	• Distribute fliers about current showings
Grocery store	**Revenue** • Sell café's pastries to reach new customers • Install sign advertising the café in the store window	• Provide pastries • Print a coupon for grocery store on receipts
Radio station	**Revenue** • Offer paid advertising • Offer free advertising during fund drive by mentioning café on-air	• Pay for advertising • Provide food for fund drive • Play their music in the café exclusively
Farmers	**Revenue** • Provide fresh, organic ingredients at a low cost • Allow café to publicize local sourcing	• Source ingredients from them • Put up sign in café about the local farms from which ingredients are sourced (thereby advertising)
Politicians	**Revenue** • Make more purchases at the café **Costs** • Provide tax- or fee-relief plan **Community** • Create an economic opportunity zone	• Create a public servant discount program • Support one of their initiatives in a public forum • Put up a supportive sign in the main street window at election time
Artists	**Revenue** • Pay a nominal fee to display art • Agree to display art for a certain period • Agree to host regular art shows and encourage visitors to purchase food and drink • Allow café to publicize support of local artists **Community** • Sell art to customers	• Allow them to display work and signage about themselves • Allow them to host art shows

	How to fulfill my needs with their offerings	How to fulfill their needs with my offerings
Soup kitchen	**Revenue** • Allow café to publicize support of soup kitchen **Costs** • Track and acknowledge donations for tax purposes **Community** • Pre-screen clients for jobs • Combat homelessness through increased capacity	• Put up signage in café about the soup kitchen's need for donations • Offer free, still-fresh pastries at the end of the morning • Make monetary donations • Create hire-local program giving preference to their clients • Make referrals to soup kitchen
Police officers	**Revenue** • Make more purchases at the café **Community** • Informally agree to watch café	• Create a public servant discount program
Neighboring towns	**Revenue** • New spending via food truck	• Lease and operate a daily food truck
Farmers' market	**Revenue** • Reach new customers by selling café's pastries • Agree to install signage advertising the café	• Provide coffee and pastries • Hand out fliers in café about the fact the pastries are now sold in the market (thus advertising for market)
Homeless individuals	**Community** • Work at the café	• Offer free, still-fresh pastries at the end of the morning • Create hire-local program giving them preference • Make referrals to soup kitchen
Real estate agent	**Revenue** • Pay to sublease space • Agree to conduct a certain number of client meetings at the café and encourage clients to buy food and drink	• Provide access to subleased space
Residents who leave early	**Revenue** • Reach new customers through holiday dishes and/or catering	• Offer holiday dishes and/or catering
AA group	**Revenue** • Buy discounted food during meetings at the café **Community** • Host meetings at the café	• Offer meeting space and food

3 Low benefit / low cost to me (right column outlined only; for
   example, radio station)
4 Low benefit / high cost to me (neither column outlined; for
   example, suppliers)

Partners in the first category may offer power partnerships and
are clearly worth pursuing, while partners in the last will not offer
power partnerships and are probably worth dropping. Partners in
the middle two categories are harder, as they offer trades that are
truly beneficial but costly and/or marginally beneficial but cheap.
Since this slice of economic reality can be hard to swallow, and just
in case our initial thinking about power partnerships was mistaken,
let's keep these partners on the back burner.

You've almost but not quite arrived at a list of potential power
partnerships. In considering the world from your own perspective, you've essentially identified trades that meet your own needs
extensively and your partners' needs inexpensively. But what about
your partners? What about the world from their perspective? Which
of your offerings could meet their needs extensively, and which of
your needs could they meet inexpensively? It's important to care, if
only for the self-interested reason that partners who benefit greatly
at little expense will probably be more motivated to work with you.
Consider the NFL's eagerness to approve the St Louis Rams' relocation, which probably related to the Rams' ability to satisfy the NFL's
goals extensively and with little disruption. Of course, since you – in
the café story – know a lot more about yourself than your partners,
you can assess your partners' benefits and costs only tentatively and
coarsely. Still, tentative and coarse answers are much better than no
answers, as any educated guess will focus you on the most promising partners and avoid wasting time – yours or anyone else's.

So how would you evaluate the benefits and costs from your
partners' perspectives? Well, despite knowing relatively less about
your partners, evaluating the trades through their eyes is quicker
since you only have to consider the trades you've already deemed

high benefit / low cost to yourself (both columns outlined above). In addition, for these trades, your goal is merely to identify any partners who would clearly be unmoved by your offerings or unable to afford the satisfaction of your needs. Thus this final stage in the identification of power partnerships is considerably more efficient than the previous stages. What would you specifically do?

I'd recommend going back to the table directly above, focusing on the partners with both columns outlined, and asking the inverse of the "how" questions you've already asked. Starting with the right column (the part of the trades that fulfill their needs), you might ask, "How well would my food and coupons meet any of the grocery store's needs?" You don't really know but could probably guess on the basis of your own visits to the store. Don't they seem distinctly short on fresh pastries? Or even customers? If it seems your offerings would meet a given partner's needs reasonably well, I'd suggest shading the relevant cell in the right column.

Having asked these questions of all relevant partners in the right column, you might switch to the left column (the part of the trades that fulfill your needs), asking questions like "How much money and time would it cost the grocery store to sell my pastries and install a sign?" Again, you don't really know but could probably guess. Is the store full to the hilt with food or can you think of a space where your fresh pastries would easily fit? When you drive by, do you see any windows without a sign? If it seems a particular partner could meet your needs pretty inexpensively, I'd suggest shading the relevant cell in the left column. Having gone through this process, you'll have a much clearer sense of the trades your partners are likely to consider beneficial and affordable, versus marginal or cost-prohibitive. At this point, you might try asking a few such "how" questions and thinking about which boxes in the table you would personally shade.

Again, there's no "right" answer, but my table might look something like table 5.3.

In shading the table you've decided that only seven of the original nine trades you considered high benefit / low cost are likely

Table 5.3 Everyone's Costs and Benefits from Trades

	How to fulfill my needs with their offerings	How to fulfill their needs with my offerings
Customers	**Revenue** • Spend more money as a result of customer loyalty program • Spend more money on holiday dishes and/or catering • Spend more money on higher-margin foods • Pay more in fees for services (e.g., Wi-Fi, bottomless coffee) • Pay to advertise their small businesses • Refer new customers through customer referral program	• Create a customer loyalty program • Offer holiday dishes and/or catering • Offer more diverse menu with higher-margin foods • Provide a high-speed Wi-Fi option • Provide bottomless coffees for a charge • Create study area with additional plugs • Make bulletin board space available for small business advertising • Create a customer referral program
Employees	**Costs** • Offer to continue working at café while in management training or exercising part-time option	• Create employee recognition award • Offer free, still-fresh pastries at the end of morning • Create management training program with landlord • Create part-time option for education • Provide sales training that also serves to sell higher-margin foods
Suppliers	**Revenue** • Pay to sublease space **Costs** • Offer volume discounts	• Provide access to subleased space • Agree to guaranteed purchase levels • Agree to purchase higher-margin ingredients
Landlord	**Revenue** • Approve subleasing **Costs** • Provide rent relief • Help retain employees by providing them with management training	• Propose current employees as source of management talent in training • Sign on to longer-term lease • Offer to pay at the beginning of the month

	How to fulfill my needs with their offerings	How to fulfill their needs with my offerings
Movie theater	**Revenue** • Reach new customers through on-screen advertising or referrals	• Distribute fliers about current showings
Grocery store	**Revenue** • Sell café's pastries to reach new customers • Install sign advertising the café in the store window	• Provide pastries • Print a coupon for grocery store on receipts
Radio station	**Revenue** • Offer paid advertising • Offer free advertising during fund drive by mentioning café on-air	• Pay for advertising • Provide food for fund drive • Play their music in the café exclusively
Farmers	**Revenue** • Provide fresh, organic ingredients at a low cost • Allow café to publicize local sourcing	• Source ingredients from them • Put up sign in café about the local farms from which ingredients are sourced (thereby advertising)
Politicians	**Revenue** • Make more purchases at the café **Costs** • Provide tax- or fee-relief plan **Community** • Create an economic opportunity zone	• Create a public servant discount program • Support one of their initiatives in a public forum • Put up a supportive sign in the main street window at election time
Artists	**Revenue** • Pay a nominal fee to display art • Agree to display art for a certain period • Agree to host regular art shows and encourage visitors to purchase food and drink • Allow café to publicize support of local artists **Community** • Sell art to customers	• Allow them to display work and signage about themselves • Allow them to host art shows

(Continued)

Table 5.3 (Continued)

	How to fulfill my needs with their offerings	How to fulfill their needs with my offerings
Soup kitchen	**Revenue** • Allow café to publicize support of soup kitchen **Costs** • Track and acknowledge donations for tax purposes **Community** • Pre-screen clients for jobs • Combat homelessness through increased capacity	• Put up signage in café about the soup kitchen's need for donations • Offer free, still-fresh pastries at the end of the morning • Make monetary donations • Create hire-local program giving preference to their clients • Make referrals to soup kitchen
Police officers	**Revenue** • Make more purchases at the café **Community** • Informally agree to watch café	• Create a public servant discount program
Neighboring towns	**Revenue** • New spending via food truck	• Lease and operate a daily food truck
Farmers' market	**Revenue** • Reach new customers by selling café's pastries • Agree to install signage advertising the café	• Provide coffee and pastries • Hand out fliers in café about the fact the pastries are now sold in the market (thus advertising for market)
Homeless individuals	**Community** • Work at the café	• Offer free, still-fresh pastries at the end of the morning • Create hire-local program giving them preference • Make referrals to soup kitchen
Real estate agent	**Revenue** • Pay to sublease space • Agree to conduct a certain number of client meetings at the café and encourage clients to buy food and drink	• Provide access to subleased space
Residents who leave early	**Revenue** • Reach new customers through holiday dishes and/or catering	• Offer holiday dishes and/or catering
AA group	**Revenue** • Buy discounted food during meetings at the café **Community** • Host meetings at the café	• Offer meeting space and food

to strike your partners the same way. Interesting as a deal with the movie theater seemed initially, for example, you're thinking it would cost them quite a lot in opportunity costs to offer on-screen advertising (high costs). And, much as you truly want to assist the town's homeless residents directly, you're now realizing that many of them are far away and have no way of learning about the café's offerings (low benefits for them). Thus you've decided that partnering with the soup kitchen offers an alternative and better hope of helping the homeless.

The Café Story: Sets of Power Partnerships

Time to negotiate with your seven potential power partners? Not quite. Step 4 of the bartering mindset calls on you to refine your list of partners just a bit further. Thinking back to Keith plotting out his negotiations or the NFL deliberating about various relocation options, can you guess how? Step 4 ultimately involves considering your potential power partnerships *as a set*. In other words, you should now seek to identify the *set* of trades that meets your own and your partners' needs most exhaustively and inexpensively, not just the individual trades. In other words, and just as both Keith and the NFL implicitly did before negotiating specific terms, you should take a step back and evaluate the *relationships* between trades, focusing on six types of relationships:

1 *Prerequisites*: trades that must occur for another trade to occur. You can't sublet the extra space to the real estate agent, for example, unless your landlord approves. Thus you'll probably want to talk to both parties.
2 *Complements*: trades that become more valuable when another trade is included. A deal with the artists might become more valuable alongside a deal with the grocery store, as the sign in the grocery store could drive a larger audience to the artists' work. You might want to talk to both parties.

3 *Economies*: trades that become less expensive when another
   trade is included. If you prepare a few extra pastries for the
   soup kitchen, would it cost you less to prepare a few more for
   your employees? You might want to include both parties in your
   subsequent discussions.
4 *Essentials*: trades that must be included to meet all of your core
   needs. Without including the soup kitchen or artists, for example, your trades would not contribute to a healthier community,
   at least not directly. You'd probably want to talk to at least one
   of them.
5 *Substitutes*: trades that lose much of their value or become
   impossible when another trade is included. Do trades with the
   grocery store and farmers' market accomplish essentially the
   same thing? If nearly all of the customers at the farmers' market
   would already buy your pastries at the grocery store, you might
   want to cut one or the other – whichever one seems less beneficial or more costly.
6 *Diminishing returns*: trades that lose some of their value if
   another trade is included. If you thought only a small portion of
   the farmers' market's customers also shop at the grocery store,
   you might or might not want to talk to the farmers' market,
   depending on how much you value your time.

Applying these considerations to your existing trades, you might
decide to talk to most of your potential power partners, as the above
relationships suggest they are more valuable and less costly together
than apart. Supposing you saw the grocery store and farmers' market as substitutes, though, you might exclude the farmers' market
since it reaches fewer people and requires you to get up and bake
pastries early on the weekends.

Taking a step back, this process highlights why it's so valuable
to consider multiple partners and evaluate them as a set: only by
doing so can you develop a comprehensive understanding of the

most promising possibilities but also avoid wasting anyone's time or burning a bunch of bridges. Put differently, only by understanding the full set of power partnerships and evaluating the relationships between them can you anticipate how the market could meet your needs to the fullest (and vice-versa), maximizing the opportunities while minimizing the costs – including the social costs – of capitalizing upon them.

Moving forward, we'll assume you've decided to drop the farmers' market but proceed with the other six partners that are both outlined and shaded, indicating that the underlying trades are likely to fulfill both your own and your partners' needs, both extensively and inexpensively. These six parties – employees, landlord, grocery store, artists, soup kitchen, and real estate agent – represent your best guess at the most powerful set of partners across the market. So let's move on to negotiations with these six parties in something like the traditional sense, at which point our thinking will finally start to converge with Getty's. Onward and upward!

Step 4 of the Bartering Mindset: Key Questions to Ask Yourself

- How could [transaction partners' offerings] satisfy my needs?
  o Answer refines transaction partners' offerings.
- How could I satisfy [transaction partners' needs]?
  o Answer refines my offerings.
- How well would [transaction partners' refined offerings] satisfy my needs? How many of my needs do [transaction partners] address? How completely do [transaction partners] address these needs?
  o Answers indicate how extensively transaction partners satisfy my needs.

- How much would it cost me to provide [my refined offerings]?
  - Answer indicates how expensive it is for me to satisfy transaction partners' needs.
- How well would [my refined offerings] meet [transaction partners' needs]?
  - Answer indicates how extensively I satisfy transaction partners' needs.
- How much would it cost [transaction partners] to satisfy my needs?
  - Answer indicates how expensive it is for transaction partners to satisfy my needs.
- What is the best set of partnerships?
  - Answer indicates the most powerful set of partnerships across the market.

Summary of Key Points from This Chapter

1 Step 4 of the bartering mindset involves using your prior thinking to anticipate the most powerful set of partnerships across the market – the set that will meet both your own and your partners' needs most extensively and inexpensively.
2 The first stage in identifying power partnerships is to translate the needs and offerings you identified previously into specific trades.
3 The second stage is to assess the costs and benefits of these trades to yourself and your partners.
4 Finally, you should assess the trades holistically, understanding the relationships between them and thus anticipating the most powerful set of partnerships.
5 Having anticipated the most powerful set of partnerships, you're finally ready to engage with the external world.

Exercise: Job Negotiation and Step 4
of the Bartering Mindset

By now you're well acquainted with our attempt to apply the bartering mindset to your realistic need for additional income. By the end of the last chapter we had plotted out the full set of partners who could help to meet your needs if only you met theirs – parties ranging from the heads of other departments in your organization to a friend who lives close to your employer. Next you used your own needs and offerings to get a handle on theirs. By the end of the last chapter you understood, in the context of your own life and needs, who the relevant partners might be and how you might interact with them. At this point you might want to review your thinking, which we'll now use to identify power partnerships.

Ready? OK, so step 4 of the bartering mindset involves translating the information you've already gathered into specific trades, assessing whether these trades form the basis of power partnerships, and anticipating the most powerful set of partnerships across the market. Remember how to do that? Test your understanding by pausing to recall.

I hope you'll remember that you can identify specific trades by asking a set of "how" questions – namely, how your partners' offerings can fulfill your own needs and how your own offerings can fulfill theirs. For example, you previously wondered whether your boss might offer you some sort of a virtual work arrangement, but how would such an arrangement work? Perhaps you could work from home three days a week and in the office the other two, except for important meetings. And you determined that your boss doesn't want to travel so much, but how could you turn that into an offering? By expressing a willingness to take some additional trips each month? Whomever the partners you've identified in the previous chapter and whatever their needs and offerings, I hope you'll try to identify specific trades by asking some "how" questions like these.

What next? Well, you've identified specific trades but also need to assess whether they form the basis of a power partnership. Remember how to do that? Again please test your understanding by pausing to recall.

Perhaps you'll remember that you would take the trades identified in the last stage and evaluate their benefits and costs from your own perspective, asking a few more "how" questions to do that. How well would a virtual work arrangement reduce your commuting costs? Presumably quite well. How much would it cost you to travel more? Depends how much you like airports. Whatever the trades you identified in the last stage, I hope you'll try to assess their costs and benefits from your own perspective, with the assistance of some "how" questions like these.

And then I hope you'll use a similar set of "how" questions to take at least an initial stab at your partners' costs and benefits. Switching examples for the sake of variety, what if you offered to move in with the friend who lives closer to work? How well would your split rent help to address any monetary challenges your friend is facing? How much would it cost the friend, perhaps as measured in frustration, to share an already cozy apartment? Supposing a cohabitation arrangement would extensively benefit both sides at a low cost, you've effectively identified a power partnership.

Having analyzed the costs and benefits of multiple trades with multiple partners, you'd then want to complete one more stage. Remember what it is? Evaluating the full set of power partnerships by considering the relationships between them, ultimately to anticipate the most powerful set of partnerships across the market. If your boss could offer virtual work, you'd probably want to accept it, since other solutions would then have diminishing returns for the particular problem you're facing: commuting costs. And wouldn't this arrangement substitute for cohabitation, since working from "home" might be difficult if home was a cramped apartment? Regardless, you might want to pursue complementary possibilities like the bank loan and Costco membership, which (in combination with virtual work or cohabitation) could stabilize your finances in the short term and reduce your commuting costs in the long term.

These are just examples. But again I hope you'll see that power partnerships offer at least the hope of solving the biggest and most important problems in your own life in a variety of innovative ways. Having anticipated the most powerful set of partnerships across the market, you're finally ready to negotiate in something like the traditional sense. Let's get started!

6

STEP 5: CULTIVATE THE MOST POWERFUL SET OF PARTNERSHIPS ACROSS THE MARKET

The year 2016 saw the third-largest acquisition in history: Anheuser-Busch (AB) InBev's purchase of SABMiller for more than $100 billion.[1] The deal between the Belgian and British brewers, already the world's largest and second-largest, created a "super mega brewery" controlling about 30 per cent of the world's beer – including ubiquitous brands like Budweiser, Beck's, Blue Moon, Foster's, and Leinenkugel's.

When the acquisition was floated, many assumed the brewers were seeking to corner the market. Both AB InBev and SABMiller were already the product of massive global consolidations – the former a combination of Interbrew (Belgium), AmBev (Brazil), and Anheuser-Busch (United States), and the latter a combination of South African Breweries and the American company Miller. The two consolidated firms competed in at least sixty-seven nations, battling for beer markets valued at more than $20 billion. In the United States, for example, AB InBev had about a 45 per cent, and SABMiller about a 25 per cent market share, the latter through its controlling interest in MillerCoors. Furthermore, AB InBev had already sought to aggressively purchase craft breweries and privilege its own beers among distributors. Was the proposed combination yet another attempt to control the world's beer?

Surprisingly, that explanation looked increasingly unlikely or at least incomplete as the deal unfolded and the brewers proactively curtailed their own market power. SABMiller, for example, voluntarily announced the sale of its stake in MillerCoors, relinquishing its right to sell Miller and other leading products in the United States or anywhere else – and effectively ensuring that the new firm would not reduce competition in the United States. AB InBev, in turn, raised the idea of eventually selling some of SABMiller's premier European brands, including Peroni and Grolsch, should the deal receive regulatory approval. In addition AB InBev offered to stop privileging its own beers and start letting regulators review all future acquisitions of craft breweries. The fact that the two brewers remained enthusiastic about the partnership despite proactive limitations of their market power suggested alternative or at least additional motives.

Watching these developments unfold, commentators surmised that AB InBev was primarily pursuing the partnership to gain a foothold in emerging markets. With revenues stagnating and competing products (such as craft beers) threatening their position in developed markets, the company was apparently seeking to build a presence in places like Africa, where SABMiller held a 34 per cent market share and revenues were projected to increase 44 per cent over the next decade. SABMiller's interest in the deal, in turn, apparently had a lot to do with the interests of a major shareholder: Altria, best known as a leading manufacturer of cigarettes. As part of the brewery deal, Altria had indicated they would need a major financial stake and set of board seats in the new firm – possibilities offering diversification in the context of flat-lining cigarette sales and increasing disapproval of smoking in developed markets. These needs, it seemed, lay closer to the heart of the emerging power partnership.

While the details of the real-world brewery deal are complex and partially shrouded in secrecy, and the prospects of the super mega-brewery remain to be seen, this example nicely illustrates step 5 of the bartering mindset. This step focuses on engaging with our partners to confirm and refine our understanding of the anticipated power partnerships. Apparently that is just what the two brewers were doing. Through prolonged discussion they probably reviewed the details of SABMiller's portfolio in emerging markets, confirming whether and how a partnership could fulfill AB InBev's need to gain a foothold. Months of meetings also seemed to surface the primary steps AB InBev had to take to win the approval of SABMiller's major stakeholder, Altria: give them a big enough financial and governing stake in the new entity to balance their reliance on cigarettes. In exchange, both firms would have to accept divestures, charges, and changes – far from trivial costs in absolute terms but negligible in comparison to the anticipated benefits.

With the beer example as a backdrop, this chapter will consider how to engage with our potential power partners for the first time, guiding them through a conversation that confirms and refines our understanding of the underlying trades, and thus the underlying power of the partnership. Indeed we'll consider how you can use these conversations to craft partnerships that are even more powerful than anticipated – just as Keith did toward the end of his trip to the market, and just as the breweries appeared to do through prolonged discussion. In other words, and in the context of the café story, we'll finally get down to the business of "negotiating" in something like the traditional sense.

Negotiations with Potential Partners: Setting the Stage

Phew! We've done an awful lot of work in our own brains. On the one hand, that's great, as it suggests that those of us who despise "negotiating" can still excel in many aspects of negotiation. On the other, there's a limit to our solitary efforts, as we can never confirm the existence of power partnerships, let alone secure the underlying deals, without talking to the partners involved. Seeing you about to do that, and sensing a golden opportunity to put you into the right mindset, Monty would probably reappear. And what would Monty say now?

"I've got nothing," Monty might say, prompting immediate looks of confusion from you. "For multiple chapters, I've been encouraging you to focus on a single counterpart, preparing yourself to tussle or at least compromise over a single confrontational issue. You just haven't listened! And now you've found far too much mutual gain to tussle or compromise. So I give up!" Thinking the argument lost and case closed, a dejected Monty might prepare to depart. So imagine Monty's redoubled surprise at your next statement: "Monty," you might say, "I actually agree with you. I get that I might sometimes want the opposite of something somebody else wants. And I expect that at least some of my preferences will eventually be at least partially opposed to some of my partners' preferences. But if I adopted your monetary mindset before now, there's no way I would've discovered all these exciting possibilities. And I can't even adopt it now because I haven't yet confirmed the existence of the underlying deals. So hold tight, Monty," you might say, "I'll come back to you in the next chapter – promise!" With that, you'd shoo distributive-minded Monty off your shoulder, only to find Getty beaming proudly on your other shoulder. And what would Getty probably say?

"So you've finally come around to the idea that my brand of negotiating is better, *and* you're ready to negotiate? Well, fantastic!" And what would you say? At this point, you might agree that it's time to negotiate, thanking Getty for the patience while you developed at least an educated guess about the most promising set of partners. Taking that as encouragement, Getty would probably charge ahead enthusiastically: "Great, well then pick a partner from your list and get going! Separate the problem from the person, and exchange enough information about your mutual interests to find a win-win trade-off that gets you to yes!"

Thinking the argument won and case closed, imagine Getty's surprise at your response: "Now, Getty," you might say, "I agreed to negotiate, and I get the need to create value through win-win trade-offs. In fact, I'll generally follow your guidance in this chapter, revealing some information about my needs and offerings, asking my partners to reciprocate, and finding ways to make everyone happy. But I won't pick a partner – I'll actually pick six. And I won't be getting to yes with anyone right now. I'll seek only to confirm and refine my understanding of the trades I've been considering throughout. Indeed I won't get to yes until I've accepted at least a portion of Monty's advice in the next chapter." With that, integrative go-getter Getty's smile might wane a bit. "So come along on my shoulder and whisper in my ear," you might say. "But make some room for my friend Bart, who will share the same shoulder."

With that, Bart might reappear next to Getty, to everyone's surprise. Following some awkward pleasantries, the two of them would prepare to accompany you into the current chapter. "Come along, you two," you might explain. "In this chapter I'll start to adopt Getty's suggestions. Under the guidance of Bart, though, I'll adopt them in conversations with several people rather than one, and adopt them for a critically different purpose: surfacing possibilities rather than sealing deals."

The Café Story: Negotiations with Potential Partners

The last chapter left you with a set of six partners who promise the possibility of a power partnership. While incredibly useful for focusing your efforts, your assessment of the power partnerships themselves remains an educated guess. Without talking to the six parties, you can't be sure whether these partnerships might work, what exactly they might look like, or whether you might devise an even better way of meeting anyone's needs. These realities underlie your three specific goals for the upcoming conversations:

1 Confirm, revise, or refute the specific trades you already devised
2 Identify new trades you hadn't yet considered
3 Determine how powerful a partnership with each partner is likely to be

It's also important to note some obvious omissions from your list of goals: persuading your partners of anything, making any specific offers, or sealing any actual deals.[2] Indeed, you will not seek to seal a deal with anyone or even pave the way for one per se. Despite Getty's persistent whispers urging integrative agreements, you (like Keith in the market and the brewers through prolonged discussion) know that understanding the situation holistically comes first. The obvious question, then, is how to structure the six conversations. Let's venture through a five-stage discussion guide.

Stage 1: Introducing

Suppose you wanted to start a conversation with one of the six parties on your list, say the grocer. What would Getty suggest? Possibly opening up a discussion of your mutual needs and offerings and how to bridge them. But since you're approaching the grocer out of the blue and asking him to open up about some fairly private topics without any obvious benefits, that approach may come off as too abrupt. You need to prepare the grocer for the discussion, particularly by winning his trust and honestly informing him of its purpose: to explore whether you and he could devise a partnership that benefits both businesses at the same time. Since people are generally reluctant to explore open-ended possibilities with strangers in the absence of trust,[3] the two topics – building trust and establishing a common goal – go hand-in-hand. So Bart, under step 5 of the bartering mindset, would urge you to start by making an overt effort to establish trust.

How could you possibly do that? You have many possible tools at your disposal.[4] But two emerge directly from the bartering mindset. First, and just like Keith, you can consciously assume that your partners will act in a trustworthy fashion. Keith could make that assumption because he knew many of the people in the market. Even when he didn't, he knew that the community comprising the market would punish people who displayed deviant behavior, either formally (for example, by excluding them) or informally (for example, by gossiping about them).[5] And even if they wouldn't, he knew that trust was essential for surfacing the parties' needs, and also that establishing trust would require him to take the lead. In dealing with local residents like the grocer, you should be able to assume trustworthiness for the same reasons. If the grocer was a devious knave, wouldn't he already be the talk of the café? Even in dealing with strangers from faraway places, though, it's critical to assume trustworthiness, since that assumption often leads to a self-fulfilling prophecy described below.[6] And, interestingly, you can assume your partners are trustworthy without even thinking about it consciously: simply considering other people you trust (for example, your mother) can put you in a trusting mindset.[7]

Second, and just as Keith did at the start of his conversations, you can actually build trust from the outset. Since Keith knew many of his potential partners, he probably did that implicitly, for example, by referencing a prior meeting or common friend. Again, in dealing with people from the community, you can probably do the same. But even in dealing with strangers, you can easily build trust by referencing a common interest or acquaintance. Seeing some pictures of sailboats on the walls of the grocer's office, for example, you could ask whether he sails as often as you or knows your friends at the marina. Even if he doesn't or hasn't, your attempt to humanize him tends to build trust.[8] Indeed this second method of trust-building may be particularly important in non-Western cultures, where people sometimes find it less natural to assume trustworthiness without an extended period of relationship-building (see chapter 8 for more information).[9] Of course any attempt to reference commonalities must be genuine, lest it backfire.

However you establish trust, these efforts should enable you to easily transition into a discussion of the meeting's purpose. Again, Keith probably didn't have to do that explicitly, the whole purpose of the market being to help everyone meet everyone else's needs – and the mere initiation of a conversation suggesting the possibility of a partnership. Without the benefit of an existing market, though, you'll have to work harder to convey the purpose of the conversation. For example, "Thanks for meeting me today, Mr Grocer. I asked to meet because I'm thinking the two of us might be able to form a partnership that benefits us both. I came here today to explore the possibilities together." In addition to establishing the conversation's purpose – and in the spirit of trustworthiness (but to the possible consternation of Getty) – you should also consider conveying what you're *not* here to do: reach any deals. Since both of you are considering the possibilities for the first time, you'll probably both need some time to think them over and explore some alternatives. "I'm not expecting that we'll make any decisions today – I just thought it would be good to start a conversation."

Will all this trust-building and openness convince the grocer to open up about his needs and offerings? Research suggests it should, largely because your trust begets your trustworthy behavior, which should beget trust and trustworthy behavior from him – especially when you couple these steps with the open-information sharing described below.[10] And if it doesn't work – if the grocer or any of your other partners remain guarded or downright devious in the face of your efforts – well, you can always move on to someone else. Yet another reason why it was so smart to compile such a long list of potentially promising partners!

Stage 2: Surfacing Needs

Assuming you've successfully established trust and a common goal with the grocer, it's time to get down to business, openly exploring a partnership that could meet both parties' needs. To do so you need to start putting your own needs on the table. Now, I can hear what you're saying. Either "Why tell a stranger my needs?" or "Sure, I'll mention my needs, but what's to say he will tell me his?" And I'd respond by saying there's simply no substitute. Not having the benefit of the café's balance sheet nor really any idea what the conversation is about, the grocer is unlikely to understand your needs or lay his own needs bare unless you do.

Once you've put your own needs on the table, though, there's a better-than-average chance he'll reciprocate. While human interactions come with few guarantees and I can offer none here, many cultures around the world have a norm of reciprocity,[11] meaning that people often feel psychologically compelled to treat others however they were just treated. So when you openly share your needs in the context of a trusting environment, how will the grocer feel? Probably compelled to tell you his. And here's the amazing part: you assumed the grocer was trustworthy, which led you to openly share your needs, which led him to openly share his. And what will you think about him when he does? This guy's trustworthy! Trust assumptions can become self-fulfilling prophecies.[12]

Assuming you're sold on the importance of revealing your needs, how would you actually do that? I'd initiate the process shortly after establishing the common goal by saying something like "My business is currently facing challenges with X," where X stands for the fundamental need(s) that this particular partner could actually stand to meet (left column of table 5.3). For the grocer, this would be revenue. Since your need for revenue is so general and disconnected from any of the grocer's concerns, though, you should quickly elaborate by hinting at whatever you might need the grocer to do, and the fact it might benefit him too. For example, "I'm having trouble reaching new customers, and I thought that perhaps we could explore how to solve this problem and help with some of your own business challenges at the same time." A statement like that begins to outline the broad contours of the potential power partnership.

To engage the norm of reciprocity, you'd then want to transition quickly from your own needs to his: "What kind of challenges is your business facing?" Although you already have an initial sense of the grocery store's challenges, you should still ask an open-ended question in case you got it wrong or missed something critical. In addition, an open-ended question (as opposed to spotlighting problems with big box stores or insufficient pastries) prevents him from becoming defensive. And answering such a question starts to motivate him to deal with you. If you did your homework and he's being honest, the grocer's answer to your open-ended question will probably confirm many of your suspicions. "Well, that big box store is really eating into my customers!" the grocer might say. Voila! You got that one right. And he might even mention some needs you never considered, which you should note in case they eventually make the partnership even more powerful.

But what if the other party doesn't mention one of the needs you suspected – nothing about pastries, for example. Or what if you think he's holding something back? Then, in the most indirect and polite way possible, I'd suggest hinting at his needs yourself. "You know, I often shop at the store in the morning, and I've wondered what it would be like to leave with a freshly baked pastry. Have you ever thought of offering something like that?" Alluding to another party's shortcomings is never risk-free, and no exception here. The owner may take offense at your commentary on his breakfast offerings or simply express disinterest. But since you've phrased your constructive feedback as a question, offering it in the context of a trusting environment, chances are he'll furrow his brow, scratch his head, and think, "Gee, fresh pastries … interesting!" In addition to paving the way for a power partnership, this thought should continue to build trust.

Stage 3: Meeting the Other Party's Needs

Supposing the prior stage confirmed the grocer's need to defend against the big box store and piqued his interest in fresh pastries, what should you do next? Having established and focused the grocer's attention on his needs – and before returning to any of your own – you should explore how to satisfy your partner's in more detail. In particular, I'd suggest homing in on whichever of your own offerings could satisfy your partner's needs. "You know, my café is renowned for our freshly baked pastries, and I've often toyed with the idea of selling them outside the café. And, come to think of it, we interact with so many local customers every day – I wonder whether there's something we could do to drive them to your store instead of the big box?" Since these ideas come in response to two needs the grocer just recognized, he'll probably react favorably. That's great because you already know you could provide the underlying offerings easily.

But you need more than general, positive reactions to understand the nature of a potential power partnership with the grocer: you need to understand what the offering might be, how well it might fulfill his needs, and whether the two of you could devise anything better. Thus I'd immediately follow your ideas with some direct questions. First, to understand the offering, you could ask questions like "Is there a way my [pastries could help with your breakfast selection / customer interactions could help with your sales erosion]?" Having discussed some specific possibilities, you could then ask a follow-up about how well they meet his needs – something like "How well would [my pastries help with your breakfast selection / coupons on the bottom of my receipts help with your sales erosion]?" Finally, and especially if the grocer expresses any hesitation, you could ask,

"Can you think of any other or different ways the café might help with your breakfast selection or sales erosion?"

In asking such questions you're effectively confirming half of a power partnership (the part that meets your partners' needs), as well as exploring new trades and attempting to identify the most powerful partnership possible. In addition asking such questions before returning to your own needs continues to build trust. Finally, and because of the norm of reciprocity, you'll probably find your partner growing increasingly excited about the possibilities – and thus increasingly motivated to meet your own needs, which is precisely where you're going.

Stage 4: Meeting Your Needs

Having identified some promising ways to meet your partner's needs, you've primed the pump for him to meet yours. Indeed, to re-engage the norm of reciprocity, I'd now transition directly to a discussion of your own situation. Something like "I'm glad we've come up with some ways that I could address your business challenges. Is it OK if we talk about mine now?" You'd then reiterate the challenge with revenue, and particularly with attracting new customers. In this case, the owner's agreement to sell your pastries has already started to meet your revenue need – it's a win-win – and you might mention as much. But you decided earlier that you'd also love for the grocer to place a sign about the café in the window. You'll have to find a way to raise that too.

How do you think you'd do that? First, I'd suggest asking another open-ended question: "Can you think of any other creative ways that we might address my challenges with revenue and reaching new customers?" Perhaps he'll come up with some creative ideas that never crossed your mind. If not, or if you'd simply like to redirect the conversation to the sign, I'd suggest going back and referencing whichever of the grocery store's offerings led you to come up with this idea in the first place. You might say something like "I've noticed that I often read the signs in your windows while I'm stopped in the horrendous traffic on Route 40." You'd then transition to the specific offering you have in mind, reiterating what you're offering the grocer and thus reviving the norm of reciprocity: "If I offered my pastries and printed a coupon for the grocery store on my receipts, as we discussed, what do you think about putting a sign about the café in your window?" You might even soften the ask by explaining how the sign could reference the new pastry sales at the grocery store, thus selling more pastries and tempting customers away from the big box store.

No guarantees about his response, but you've now done everything you can to pave the way for a positive response, especially by making the mutual benefits clear and the owner's benefits prominent among them. Although you're starting to strongly suspect a power partnership, detecting such a partnership with confidence still requires you to understand one more piece of information: the owner's costs in meeting your needs. He probably won't volunteer (or know) the exact cost structure associated with selling your pastries or posting your sign, nor do you need it. But I'd recommend a very general question that could surface some useful information about costs. Something like "What are your reactions to these ideas?" If the owner has any cost concerns with the pastry sales or sign, he'll probably air them without hesitation (since the grocer, like most others, generally follows Monty's guidance).

Assuming the grocer reacts receptively and surfaces no major cost concerns, you've effectively confirmed the other half of a power partnership (the part that meets your needs), explored other trades, and attempted to identify the most powerful partnership possible. Indeed, having explored both parties' needs, you're now in a position to assess the overall power of a partnership with the grocer. How exhaustively and inexpensively do the trades you've discussed meet both parties' needs? Pretty well, it seems.

Stage 5: Concluding

If all goes well, the prior discussion should confirm that the grocery store can inexpensively meet your revenue need by selling your pastries and installing a sign in the store window. And you can inexpensively prevent the grocery store's sales erosion and enhance the store's breakfast offerings by printing a coupon on your receipts and providing your pastries. You've thus identified a specific power partnership. Congratulations! While this intriguing trade may tempt you to lock in an immediate agreement – and Getty would probably suggest as much – Bart would call on you to strategically to resist the temptation. You haven't talked to the other five partners and achieved a bird's-eye view of the market, without which you could overlook the important considerations below. So your final goal for the conversation with the grocer should be to summarize, ensure you haven't missed anything, and reiterate what you said at the beginning: that you're interested but want to give both parties some time to think it over.

To do so, I'd simply review the terms of the trade described above, being as specific as possible. Does the grocer have the same understanding? Did you miss anything? In the absence of confirmation, it's amazing how often people walk away from the same discussion with entirely different conclusions. Next, I'd ask some general questions to make sure nothing was missed – questions like "Can you think of any other ways we can help each other?" And "Overall, how interested are you in the deal we just discussed?" The last question naturally leads to the final point you need to make: that you yourself are interested (assuming you are) but need to think things over. Since you said so at the beginning, the grocer should not be particularly surprised. And since you approached him out of the blue, he could probably use some time to contemplate and consider the alternatives too.

Walking out of the meeting, you should compile some clear notes immediately. Stop by the library next door if you need to. In

Table 6.1 Terms Discussed

		Me		Partner	
Partner	Trade	Costs	Benefits	Costs	Benefits
Grocery store	• I provide pastries and print a coupon for grocery store on my receipts	Low	High	Low	High
	• The grocery store sells my pastries and puts up a sign for the café in the store window				

particular, you want to capture the specific terms discussed and also your impressions about how much these terms would cost and benefit both parties. If you're inclined to create another chart, it might look like table 6.1 for the grocer.

Congratulations! It looks as if you, like Keith in the market and the brewers at the beginning of the chapter, have identified and confirmed the contours of a true power partnership. And in so doing, you've gone well beyond the possibilities presented by either Monty or Getty. Thanks Bart!

Concluding Thoughts and Moving Forward

Reflecting on the process you've just followed with the grocer, I think you'll recognize that it represents the ideal structure of the conversation. People being people, yours may be messier. But it should cover the same topics! And you'll recognize that the language above is a guide to adapt to your own style and circumstances. For example, you could easily make the statements less direct, change "business" to "organization" for a non-profit or government entity, etc. In sum, the stages and language above serve as a guide for unpacking the anticipated power partnerships. I hope you'll adopt the spirit but adapt the content to match your own situation.

Of course step 5 of the bartering mindset indicates that this is but the first of six conversations. You'd now want to follow the same model with the other five partners promising the possibility of a power partnership (for example, artists, soup kitchen). If all goes according to plan, you'll confirm the existence of the six power partnerships you anticipated and probably devise some ways to make them even more powerful. Since life rarely goes according to plan, however, it's possible you'll discover that at least one of the partnerships is less powerful than expected. And that's one reason you stepped away from your partners before sealing any deals. You might need to follow up with such partners, politely declining to pursue the partnership – that being easier once you've stepped away and taken the time to consider.[13] In addition to following up with the less-than-powerful partners, you might need to replace the offerings lost in the process of doing so by engaging with someone who previously dropped off the list. If the grocery store wasn't moved by your pastries or coupons, for example, maybe you'd want to meet with the farmers' market after all. Or if the real estate agent already leased a space down the street, maybe you'd want to re-explore a subleasing arrangement with your suppliers (even while encouraging the real estate agent to conduct her client meetings in the café anyway).

In addition to surfacing less-than-powerful partners, your conversations might reveal new and unexpected interdependencies. Although you talked to the artists in good faith, what if a later conversation with the landlord surfaced her discomfort with puncturing walls to hang paintings? This unexpected "prerequisite" (to use chapter 5's terminology) might require you to re-examine a deal with the artists or at least enlist their assistance in identifying creative adhesives. Alternatively, what if the soup kitchen told you they were looking for some volunteer opportunities for their clients? You previously decided not to engage with the radio station, but maybe you're now seeing that the radio station would appreciate volunteers. Could you act as a broker between the two organizations in light of this "complementarity?"[14] Finally, what if the grocer called you unexpectedly and offered to place your pastries next to the checkout lines to increase the probability of an impulse buy? Would this increase your revenue enough to render other partnerships unnecessary ("diminishing returns")?

It is precisely such possibilities that led you to pause your conversations with each partner, resisting Getty's encouragement to reach deals until you re-evaluated the full set of partnerships. Since negotiations with multiple parties almost inevitably turn up unexpected interdependencies – both positive and negative – it's essential to step away from your six conversations. And once you do, it's essential to revisit the six categories of interdependency from the previous chapter (prerequisites, complements, etc.), determining whether you've detected any new relationships between partners. Discovering new interdependencies, you'd then meet with any new partners (for example, the radio station) or tie up any loose ends with existing partners (for example, by asking the artists about adhesives). By doing all of that, you will confirm and cultivate a truly powerful set of partnerships.

Going forward, we'll presume you confirmed the possibility of power partnerships with five of the six original partners and, in some cases, discovered even more powerful possibilities (for example, placing your pastries near the grocery store's checkout lines). But you've learned that the real estate agent already leased a space down the street. In light of the other opportunities, particularly the new development at the grocery store, you've decided to drop the subleasing possibility for now.

Bart's bartering mindset has taken you a long way toward solutions – far from Monty's advice to construe a single counterpart in competitive terms. And far from Getty's advice to cooperate with someone in search of a win-win solution. Indeed, despite your essential reconciliation with Getty in this chapter, you've also moved far beyond the possibilities that Getty – operating alone – would've brought to your attention. You're now poised to negotiate the very best solutions to your most fundamental problems. And you'll go about securing those solutions in the next chapter.

Step 5 of the Bartering Mindset: Key Questions to Ask Your Transaction Partners

- What kind of challenges are you facing? Do you have any interest in [my refined offerings]?
  - o Answers confirm and clarify the transaction partner's needs.
- How could [my refined offerings] help with your needs? Can you think of any other ways I could help with your needs?
  - o Answers confirm and clarify the portion of the power partnership that benefits the transaction partner.
- Can you think of any ways that we might address my challenges with [my deep and broad needs]? Would you be open to offering [transaction partner's refined offerings]?
  - o Answers confirm and clarify the portion of the power partnership that benefits me.
- Can you think of any other ways we can help each other?
- Overall, how interested are you in the partnership we just discussed?
  - o Answers confirm and clarify the overall power partnership.

Summary of Key Points from This Chapter

1 Step 5 of the bartering mindset involves talking to the parties who could offer power partnerships to cultivate the most powerful set of partnerships across the market.

2 At this stage, the purpose of your negotiations is not to persuade, make offers, or reach deals – it's to exchange information that helps you understand each partner and ultimately the whole market holistically.

3 Negotiations with partners follow a five-stage process: introducing, surfacing needs, meeting the other party's needs, meeting your needs, and concluding.

4 You should conduct such negotiations with all partners who
   could offer power partnerships, using the resulting information
   to refine your understanding of the partnerships.
5 Having understood the full set of partnerships, you should re-
   examine the relationships between partnerships to confirm the
   most powerful set of partnerships across the market.

Exercise: Job Negotiation and Step 5 of the Bartering Mindset

Ready to apply step 5 to your realistic need for additional income?
The previous chapters produced a few partnerships that you considered potentially powerful – a partnership with your boss whereby
you'd travel more in exchange for a virtual work arrangement when
not travelling, for example. Remember? And you probably identified other partnerships that apply more directly to your own circumstances. You may wish to review your thinking from the last
chapter, which we'll now use to start negotiating.

OK, so on to step 5 of the bartering mindset, which involves negotiating with all parties who promise a potential power partnership.
Remember the purpose of these initial negotiations? Please assess
your understanding by trying to recall.

These initial negotiations are not intended to persuade our counterparts or lock down the specifics of any particular deal. They're
not even intended to pave the way for a specific deal per se. They're
meant to surface as much information as possible on the potential
power partnerships you previously identified – information you'll
eventually use to negotiate a mutually beneficial set of deals. So it's
time to negotiate – say with your boss about the possibility above.
What would you do first?

You'd initiate the process by setting up an environment con-
ducive to trust. Since we're talking about your boss, hopefully

the relationship already benefits from some level of trust (if not, you might want to reconsider a deal with another department!). Even with a known boss, though, you can still make the conscious assumption that he or she will be trustworthy for the purpose of this discussion, raise topics of common interest, and frame the conversation as an exploration of mutually beneficial possibilities. At this point I'd encourage you to consider the partners you've identified in your own life and consider how you'd go about establishing a trusting environment and common goal. Having done that, then what?

Let's imagine you're talking to your boss. First you'd want to surface the needs under consideration, mentioning your escalating commuting costs. And you'd raise your boss's needs, first through some relatively open-ended questions and then perhaps by referencing the boss's frequent comments about the frustrations of travel. These issues might seem unrelated, you could say. But you think you've devised a way to "kill two birds with one stone." Again, I'd suggest relating these examples to your own life.

Having surfaced the relevant needs, you're well positioned to meet them. Perhaps the previous discussion confirmed that your boss has an upcoming business trip to the other side of the country – a trip that interferes mightily with family responsibilities. Could you propose to take the trip instead? Could you ask how feasible that might be, what exactly you'd have to do on the trip, and whether your boss would appreciate it? Could you even mention that you've actually been hoping to travel and might be willing to do this kind of thing more often, assuming the first trip is successful?

If the boss sees promise, could you then return to your own need for reduced commuting costs? Spending some of your time on a plane would certainly reduce your local driving expenses, but could you propose to reduce them further by working from home on some of the days you're not travelling (especially as this would allow you to devote your lunch break to necessities like unpacking your bags and opening your mail)? Would your boss consider it? How feasible would it be to offer that benefit? Please consider the analogues in your own life: what would you do to meet your partners' needs, and what could they do to meet yours? How would you phrase the proposal and subsequent discussion to ensure you understand the partnership and its power?

Next you'd want to conclude the discussion. Given the marked changes in responsibilities and benefits that you and your boss have discussed, the boss would probably appreciate some time to consider – and possibly to check with HR. That's perfect, because you need some time to consider the other potential power partnerships in your own life: moving in with a friend or applying to a different department that pays more, for example. So, after summarizing and probing your boss's general reactions and ideas once more, you'd politely schedule a time to discuss the matter further. What would this look like in the context of your own partners and negotiations?

Finally, you'd conduct the other relevant negotiations, then take another step back to evaluate the full landscape of potential partnerships. Does considering all the partnerships together reveal any new interdependencies or relationships? Since the travel and virtual work arrangement would probably not transfer to another department, this possibility and another job are probably substitutes. Since the virtual work arrangement would probably be even more powerful if you also signed up for a Costco membership and bought discount gas, these possibilities might be complementary. Again, these are just examples – and perhaps a bit tongue-in-cheek. But I hope you'll see the point that engaging with multiple partners offering potentially powerful partnerships, then evaluating the landscape of power partnerships you surfaced, sets you up for an excellent set of solutions to a pressing problem. Having done that, and essentially reconciled with Getty in the process, you now need to seal the deal with the relevant partners. Sealing these deals, in turn, will entail a reconciliation with Monty. And that's where we're going.

7

INTEGRATING THE BARTERING
AND MONETARY MINDSETS

In May 2010 a British election produced the first hung Parliament in decades.[1] The ruling Labor party lost ninety-one seats, while the Conservative (Tory) party picked up ninety-seven, for the largest overall share. But no party won a majority, necessitating the first coalition government since the Second World War. Which coalition would form?

On the surface, a coalition between Labor and the country's third-largest party, the Liberal Democrats (Lib Dems), seemed natural: the "unwritten rules" allowed the sitting prime minister, Labor's Gordon Brown, to try and form a government first. And the two parties were both broadly progressive. But a Labor–Lib Dem coalition would still fall short of a majority in Parliament, and Nick Clegg, the leader of the Lib Dems, quickly called the unwritten rules into question by announcing his intention to negotiate with the Tories. Accordingly, Clegg and the Tories' David Cameron initiated negotiations to explore a Tory–Lib Dem coalition, notwithstanding ideological differences and Brown's repeated efforts to negotiate with Clegg at the same time.

Over five days, Clegg, Cameron, and their teams worked through what must've been an exceptionally intense negotiation. The talks unfolded in private, but two critical details percolated into public view. First, both sides saw the discussion as a multi-issue negotiation in which they had to tackle many topics at the same time. Any hope of reaching a deal rested on achieving just the right balance across issues. Second, both sides expressed an aversion to either strong-arming or compromising with the other, recognizing that any deal resting on pressure tactics or dissatisfactory compromises would not long endure.

In recognition of the first point, the Tories came into negotiations focusing on numerous issues including deficit reduction, immigration, and the EU relationship. Their platform called for specific measures like selling off parts of the Royal Mail, capping non-EU immigration, and preventing any loss of national sovereignty to the EU. While none of these positions was particularly attractive to the Lib Dems, they were more focused on issues like school tuition, care for the elderly, and voting system reform. The details that emerged suggested that Cameron and Clegg treated many of these issues as fluid, exchanging many multi-issue proposals that sought to balance the parties' respective priorities as a whole. In other words, they didn't nail down any one issue until they nailed down all the issues.

Ultimately the leaders agreed to a program in which neither party achieved all of their demands on all issues, but both got most of what they wanted on their most important issues. On immigration, for example, the Tories got an annual limit on immigration from non-EU countries, and the Lib Dems dropped their intention to chart a path to citizenship for illegal immigrants. Likewise, on Europe, the Tories won an agreement that the United Kingdom would not adopt the euro nor cede power to the EU without a referendum. In accordance with the Lib Dems' priorities, however, the Tories agreed to call a referendum on voting reform and support fixed terms for members of Parliament. In these and many other ways, the parties figured out how to satisfy each other's most critical demands, even while ceding ground on less important issues.

In retrospect both the leaders and public commentators emphasized how the two parties had worked together to produce a deal that was greater than the sum of the parts, neither strong-arming each other nor compromising. The document the leaders compiled, for example, said, "In every part of this agreement we have gone further than simply adopting those policies where we previously overlapped. We have found that a combination of our parties' best ideas and attitudes has produced a programme for government that is more radical and comprehensive than our individual manifestos." Likewise, *The Economist* noted the distinct lack of compromise in the agreement, saying that "giving each governing party most of what it wants on its pet causes is better than endless compromise ... Sure enough, the Tories have retained the bulk of their policy on immigration and Europe, while the Lib Dems can claim a victory on voting reform."[2]

Collectively these measures probably contributed to the durability of the coalition, which was widely expected to crumble quickly but lasted five years and produced notable achievements. This story is obviously more complicated, especially in retrospect. For example, the lack of an initial deal on school tuition eventually came back to bite the Lib Dems, who backtracked with severe political consequences. Clearly the story is also more complicated than the bartering or monetary mindsets. Still, it nicely illustrates the integration of the two mindsets, which is the topic of the current chapter.

By exchanging a series of multi-issue proposals that held firm on multiple core priorities, even while ceding on less important issues, the parties found a way to capitalize on their complementary interests but insist on their most important demands. Consistent with the bartering mindset, these offers continued to implicitly communicate information about the parties' most important needs, allowing them to identify mutually beneficial trades. Consistent with the monetary mindset, though, the offers also allowed the parties to state aggressive goals and achieve advantageous outcomes on (most of) their critical issues. In this chapter we'll show you how to use multi-issue proposals to effect an integration of the bartering and monetary mindsets in your own life.

Why would you need to do that? Well, the bartering mindset was probably sufficient in bartering economies, leaving people like Keith with a beneficial set of trades that they could execute without much haggling – that being inappropriate or simply impossible for indivisible goods.[3] But our monetary world is populated by people with monetary mindsets. And people with monetary mindsets know they need to do more than make advantageous trades without much bargaining. They need to seal the best possible deals for themselves – to identify and walk away with advantageous terms, monetary or otherwise.

Put differently and more formally, people in the modern monetary world expect (and are expected) to do more than create the maximum amount of value through integrative negotiation – as the last four chapters have enabled you to do. They expect (and are expected) to claim the maximum amount of value through distributive negotiation. And doing so requires you to transition from the bartering mindset back to the monetary mindset – that is, to integrate the two mindsets, thereby reconciling with Monty. In the context of the café story, and with the British coalition as a backdrop, this chapter will show you how to do that.

Integrating Two Mindsets: Setting the Stage

You left the last chapter with an impressive set of power partnerships, specifically the ones shown in table 7.1.

What a powerful set of possibilities – congratulations! In addition to these opportunities, you left the last chapter with Getty and Bart on the same shoulder, watching you implement and integrate their advice. In particular, you followed Getty's recommendation to act integratively. At Bart's urging, however, you followed that recommendation with many more partners and a markedly different purpose: surfacing possibilities rather than sealing deals.

Table 7.1 Power Partnerships

	How to fulfill my needs with their offerings	How to fulfill their needs with my offerings
Employees	**Costs** • Agree to continue working at café while in management training or exercising part-time option	• Create employee recognition award • Offer free, still-fresh pastries at the end of morning • Create management training program with landlord • Create part-time option for education • Provide sales training that also serves to sell higher-margin foods
Landlord	**Revenue** • Pre-approve subleasing (when café eventually exercises that option) **Costs** • Freeze rent • Help retain employees by providing them with management training	• Most promising café employees assist with landlord's managerial role as part of training program • Sign on to longer-term lease • Pay at the beginning of the month
Artists	**Revenue** • Pay a nominal fee to display art • Agree to display art for a certain period • Agree to host regular art shows and encourage visitors to purchase food and drink • Allow café to publicize support of local artists **Community** • Sell art to customers	• Allow them to display work and signage about themselves • Allow them to host art shows • Keep café open late during art shows
Grocery store	**Revenue** • Sell café's pastries near checkout lines to reach new customers • Install sign advertising the café in the store window	• Provide pastries • Print a coupon for grocery store on receipts
Soup kitchen	**Revenue** • Allow café to publicize support of soup kitchen **Costs** • Track and acknowledge donations for tax purposes **Community** • Pre-screen clients for jobs • Combat homelessness through increased capacity	• Put up signage in café about the soup kitchen's need for donations • Offer free, still-fresh pastries at the end of the morning • Make monetary donations • Create hire-local program giving preference to their clients • Make referrals to soup kitchen

Looking toward the occupied shoulder now, you'd probably see Getty smiling, reclining, and sipping a margarita. But you'd also find Bart looking pensive and possibly a bit concerned. "What's got your goat, Bart? Lighten up!" Getty might say. And how would Bart respond?

"I can't put my finger on it," Bart might say, "but something doesn't feel right. We implemented and integrated our two approaches in the last chapter, and the process produced some interesting possibilities. But possibilities are not deals: they're possibilities. Doesn't getting to a set of deals necessitate hammering out the specifics – and specifics that are sufficiently valuable to the owner of the café?"

"But the café owner already *knows* what to do," Getty might protest. "In a deal with the grocery store, the owner would offer pastries and print some coupons, while the store would sell the pastries and put up a sign. What's more to discuss?"

"Well, again, I'm not entirely sure," Bart might say, "but it seems like the owner and grocer still have to work out some critical details. For example, how many pastries will the store stock, where exactly will the sign go, and who will pay the cost of the coupons? I know they need to sort through the details for the deal to work, but my bartering mindset doesn't explain how to do that – at least not on its own. I think we need to hear from Monty." In response to this monologue, integrative go-getter Getty would probably look quite confused. Overhearing the invitation from Bart, though, Monty might suddenly reappear on the other shoulder. And what would Monty probably say?

"I told you so!" an exasperated Monty might say, looking directly at you, the café owner. "I told you Getty wouldn't get you where you wanted. I've been telling you since chapter 3 to adopt a distributive, fixed-sum view of negotiation – the monetary mindset – a view that would've prompted you to go out and claim some value. Why haven't you been listening?" a frustrated Monty might ask. And how would you, the café owner, reply?

Chances are you'd let Monty cool off, then calmly explain why you couldn't listen until now. "In chapter 3, Monty," you might say, "I didn't even know who my partners were, let alone what to say to them. In chapter 4, I mapped out a whole bunch of partners and issues but didn't know which ones formed the basis of a power partnership. So I would've probably tried to claim value from the wrong parties (probably on the wrong issues), engaging the movie theater or farmers' market in a protracted and contentious negotiation without any real benefits for anyone. Can you see the bridges burning? In chapter 5, I identified some possible power partnerships but hadn't yet confirmed them, so even if I had the parties right, there's a chance I'd still have the issues wrong. For example, I'd be shooting for a high pastry price before realizing that I could earn comparable revenue by simply placing my pastries near the checkout line. And in the last chapter, well, I could've started claiming some value, except I hadn't confirmed the full set of power partnerships. So I wouldn't be in a position to offer art shows until I knew the landlord would allow it (for example)."

"If I listened to you before now, Monty," you might continue, "I'd almost definitely be talking to the wrong parties about the wrong issues. In so doing, I'd be wasting a lot of time – my own and everyone else's. I'd be driving to far-flung farms or lobbying the politicians for a tax break or waking up early on Sundays to bake some pastries for the farmers' market, only to sell a few. At best, all this legwork would produce some mediocre deals that solved everyone's problems poorly. At worst, I'd poison my relationships in the community – a community whose help I'll need to solve my future if not my current problems. To conclude, Monty, your advice would've been consistently counterproductive if I adopted it before now."

Taken aback, Monty might need a few moments to respond. Before long, though, a humbled yet still distributive-minded Monty might offer a feeble question: "Would you at least adopt my advice now?"

And your answer might well leave the humbled Monty speech-less: "Yes, Monty," you might say, "I'm finally ready. Bart's bartering mindset helped me identify the most promising set of deals, and Getty's integrative advice helped me cultivate them in the last chapter. But neither Bart's nor Getty's advice will take me much further. We live in a monetary world, and I need some help getting back to it. In other words, I'm finally ready to hammer out some deals and make sure they're sufficiently valuable to me, as you've been urging me throughout. Before you get too excited, though, let me warn you that I won't be able to adopt all your advice – at least not literally. So come along on my shoulder – the one across from Bart and Getty – and whisper your advice in my ear. Along the way, I think you'll see why that advice needs some tempering, even at this late stage of the game."

Single-Issue Offers (SIOs)

So you're finally ready to adopt Monty's advice, but the obvious question is how – how to revive a monetary mindset you've been actively suppressing. Does that seem easy in a monetary world? Maybe it will be. Having immersed yourself in the bartering mindset for at least four chapters, though, I bet it you'll find yourself having some difficulty.

In particular, you the café owner have now spent a great deal of time and effort seeing the world in non-monetary terms. You've been thinking about yourself not narrowly but holistically, as someone who brings value to the world in addition to placing demands on the world. You've been thinking about more than one partner with one opposing need – indeed, you've come to realize the world contains many potential partners with many needs and offerings. And you've been seeking out deals that don't just claim value from one party but meet the needs of many parties extensively and inexpensively – power partnerships. Finally, you've now spent considerable time confirming and cultivating those partnerships, producing a variety of intriguing possibilities. Since you've now gone to great lengths to see the world broadly rather than narrowly, creatively rather than combatively, shifting to Monty's much narrower perspective will take some serious work.

"So where should I start?" you might ask Monty. In response, Monty would probably advise you to define a clear target – an aggressive yet attainable goal[4] – for each issue with each partner. In other words, Monty would tell you to identify the best-case scenario for each partner – the most pastries, highest pastry price, best possible sign placement, and largest possible coupon printing reimbursement that you could reasonably extract from the grocer. Though potentially jarring in the context of your still-fresh bartering mindset, doing so would probably remind you of the monetary mindset – particularly its assumptions that you *may now be* on one side of a transaction with one other party who has opposing preferences, at least when talking to the grocer about each specific issue.

With the grocer, for example, you might determine that you'd really like him to stock 500 pastries a day at $0.50 each, place your sign in the biggest possible window, and reimburse you $500 a month for the cost of printing coupons. You've decided that these numbers will probably seem aggressive to the grocer, given the approximately 350 people who shop at the store each day and low-margin nature of the business. In other words, the grocer will probably regard these numbers as pretty close to his bottom line. Still, you consider them attainable insofar as each customer buys several pastries, which the grocer could mark up substantially. And they certainly support your overall need to ensure business viability through increased revenue. If you've identified a set of terms for a particular issue that seem aggressive, attainable, and capable of meeting your own needs – as well as close to the other side's bottom line – you've probably identified a reasonable target.

Plotting out a set of targets for each partner initiates the process of shifting yourself back into the monetary mindset, but here comes the hard part: meeting with each of your partners again and moving *them* back to the monetary mindset. If that seems easy, given their daily immersion in the monetary mindset, think again. In particular, think back to your open, honest, and exploratory conversation in the last chapter. Given your previous meeting, how would each of your partners feel if you suddenly adopted Monty's next piece of advice: pick a partner and issue, then formulate an aggressive offer based on the target just defined?

Well, imagine you did just that, then re-approached the grocer to put the offer on the table. "Good to see you again, Mr Grocer," you might say. "How about stocking 500 pastries a day at $0.50 each?" Seeing as you spent the last chapter planting the seeds of trust, discussing multiple issues, and establishing a relationship grounded in open-information sharing and a mutual eagerness to help, how would the grocer react? At best, with surprise over the abrupt change in tactics – at worst, with shock or annoyance. And what would he probably do? Counteroffer both reciprocally and aggressively. "I don't think that's gonna work!" he might say, taken aback. "How about we start with 300 at $0.30 and see what happens?" Faced with such disparate offers, how would the discussion unfold? You'd probably battle it out until you reached some sort of mutually dissatisfactory compromise on the one issue of pastries, or at least agreed to disagree and dissolve the relationship.

Assuming you reached a compromise on pastries, what would happen next? Already fatigued and irritated, the two of you would probably duke it out over the next issue, say signage. Maybe you'd propose the biggest window, or maybe he'd propose the smallest. Either way, you'd probably follow the same aggressive and exhausting back-and-forth. Maybe you'd make it to coupons, or maybe the conversation would end acrimoniously beforehand. Assuming you made it to coupons, you'd probably follow the same process ("Huh?

Try a $100 reimbursement!"), walking away drained and settling for three dissatisfying deals if you're lucky.

But wait: it was easy enough to move yourself back to the monetary mindset by adopting Monty's first piece of advice – focusing on your targets. What happened to your budding and promising relationship with the grocer when you adopted Monty's second piece of advice? Your Monty-inspired strategy to abruptly switch the grocer back to the monetary mindset by making and exchanging a series of aggressive single-issue offers (SIOs) – offers that focus on each issue in succession[5] – left the grocer shocked and annoyed. Given this tactic's complete and immediate departure from the integrative climate of the last discussion, it ultimately left both parties drained and dissatisfied at best, fuming and deal-less at worst. As this example shows, simply abandoning the bartering mindset and replacing it with the definitional distributive behavior – SIOs – doesn't really work.[6]

Moving your partners toward the monetary mindset requires a more graceful transition. In particular you'll have to push back on Monty's suggestion to think and ultimately act in terms of SIOs, easing your partners into the monetary mindset without startling them into forgetting your integrative overtures. Luckily SIOs are far from the only way forward. Indeed, even if you hadn't started with the bartering mindset and knew nothing about it, SIOs represent a pretty poor way of approaching a multi-issue negotiation.[7] The following sections will discuss two alternatives that can help any negotiator resolve multiple issues better – but especially negotiators trying to transition from the bartering to the monetary mindset.

Multi-Issue Offers (MIOs)

Your negotiation with the grocer is focused on several fundamental issues, and Monty's line of thinking prompted you to discuss them in succession – but why? Which law of nature compels us to take the world one issue at a time? None that I know. In fact, making a smoother transition between mindsets requires you to deal with multiple issues together. Accordingly, I'd suggest you consider some alternative types of offers that incorporate several issues, the simplest being a multi-issue offer (MIO): a single offer involving all negotiable issues.[8] A MIO in the café story, for example, would mention pastries, signage, and coupons, all at the same time.

Perhaps this strikes you as a mere stylistic difference. Why would one offer with three issues have an impact that's any different from three offers with one issue each? But the impact is dramatically different: using MIOs rather than SIOs holds major consequences, both for the seamlessness of the transition between mindsets and for the attractiveness of the ultimate deals.[9] To see why, let's reset the example. Suppose you had never made the ill-fated SIOs inspired by Monty and instead approached the grocer with a MIO. How would you do that?

Well, you'd first want to frame the offer as a continuation of last week's integrative conversation. For example, you might say something like "Mr Grocer, it was a pleasure to meet you last week. I feel like we got a good understanding of our respective business challenges and explored some interesting ways to resolve them. Today I thought we could dive into the details and discuss what an actual deal might look like. Sound good?" Note that you've explicitly reiterated and re-established the integrative tone from last week, rather than diving right into an offer and associated distributive behavior.

But then, having received his assent, you'd directly transition into an offer. "OK, well in the interest of moving the conversation forward, I prepared a proposal for you. What it does is lists the issues we discussed last week and attaches some numbers to them. These are just my initial thoughts, and I'd like to ask for your initial reactions. OK?" Note how you've positioned the upcoming MIO as a means of continuing the conversation – a mere discussion document

Table 7.2 Your First MIO

Café owner to grocer	Grocer to café owner
• 500 tasty pastries per day	• $0.50 per pastry (wholesale price)
• Coupon printed on each receipt (approximately 100 per day)	• Sign in largest window
	• $500 per month printing fee

with some numbers attached, not an aggressive and unexpected single-issue ultimatum.

And just like that, you'd slide your MIO across the table. Based on the targets mentioned above, it might look like table 7.2.

This is a MIO. Like all MIOs, it lists all the issues you've discussed and attaches some specific (and rather aggressive) terms to those issues. But it's also a special kind of MIO – one that builds from the bartering mindset and transitions everyone into the monetary mindset and associated distributive behavior. To see why, consider some additional features of your MIO. First, it lists not just your demands but also what you're offering to the grocery store; indeed, it lists your offerings *first* (on the left), before your demands. Second, it doesn't shy away from the monetary issues but does separate the monetary terms from whatever they're buying. For example, it lists the 500 pastries and $0.50 as separate items in separate columns rather than saying, "500 pastries at $0.50 each."

The benefits become apparent when you consider the grocer's likely response. Having taken a few minutes to review the MIO, how will he likely respond? Well, since your offer still involves a series of aggressive demands, he won't necessarily love it. But note some critical differences of your MIO – versus the ill-fated SIOs – that suggest he probably won't hate it or walk away.

First, since you listed all the issues recently discussed, he's likely to see the offer just the way you described it: as a continuation of last week's multi-issue conversation rather than an unexpected and aggressive demand on just one issue. Second, since you listed what he's getting in addition to what he's giving (the former first) he's likely to recall the mutual benefits rather than fixating on the costs, experiencing at least a surge of excitement amidst his irritation. Third, since you separated the monetary terms from whatever they're buying – in this case, the pastries – he's likely to see the money itself in a very different light: as one of several traded items rather than an annoying feature of the pastries.[10]

Collectively these features of the MIO will likely prompt a very different response. Rather than aggressively counteroffering on one and only one issue, the grocer, having considered the offer, will likely respond in one of two ways. First, he might respond by telling you which parts of the offer he really doesn't like, saying something like "Well, I don't love any of the terms in this offer, but the 500 pastries really won't work. I mean, we only get 350 customers a day, so I can't sell 500 pastries." Put differently, he might respond to your MIO with an implicit MIO of his own – one that subtly counter-anchors on pastries but also expresses more openness to your other ideas. Alternatively, and after taking some time to consider your offer, he might respond with an *explicit* MIO of his own. For example, he might say he'd prepared a counteroffer, presenting you with something like table 7.3 (differences underlined).

Whether the grocer responds with an implicit or explicit MIO, you've just made tremendous progress – huge strides toward integrating the two mindsets and thereby resolving the three fundamental issues! Why? By building from the bartering mindset, you've kept the tone cordial and focused on mutual benefit, positioning even the monetary issues as part of the win-win calculus. In addition you've continued to learn about the grocer's preferences, with either response telling you something about those preferences – namely, that he's most concerned about the number of pastries. In other words, the grocer has signaled the relative importance of the issues, indicating that the number of pastries is relatively more important than the other issues. So you've continued to act

Table 7.3 Grocer's MIO

Café owner to grocer	Grocer to café owner
• <u>300</u> tasty pastries per day	• <u>$0.45</u> per pastry (wholesale price)
• Coupon printed on each receipt (approximately 100 per day)	• Sign in largest window <u>except special sales periods (approximately one per quarter)</u>
	• <u>$450</u> per month printing fee

consistently with the bartering mindset by exchanging some critically important information.

At the same time you've subtly but undoubtedly transitioned into the monetary mindset and associated distributive behavior. Perhaps Monty, still perched on your shoulder, would admire the fact that you've dropped a strong anchor on all the relevant issues, making a first-offer that strongly benefits yourself – a move that will likely lead to a final agreement in your own favor (according to the well-known "first-offer effect").[11] Second, by emphasizing the benefits to the other side (even accentuating them by saying things like "tasty" pastries), you've started to persuade the grocer of the need to accept your offer or something very much like it – persuasion being a critical step in distributively claiming value.[12] Finally, although you exchanged more information through a MIO than a SIO, you exchanged less information than in the prior meeting – the move from information-sharing to offers often signaling a transition to the value-claiming phase of a negotiation.[13]

In short, your MIO offered a vehicle for transitioning seamlessly between the bartering and monetary mindsets. Indeed the transition will probably continue, as you'll likely respond to the grocer's implicit or explicit MIO with yet another MIO of your own (differences relative to his MIO underlined), as shown in table 7.4.

With this MIO you've suggested that you're open to the 300-pastry counteroffer if he accepts a much higher per-pastry price and intermediate printing fee. In other words, while you've continued the implicit information exchange, consistent with the bartering mindset, you've

Table 7.4 Your Second MIO

Café owner to grocer	Grocer to café owner
• 300 tasty pastries per day • Coupon printed on each receipt (approximately 100 per day)	• $0.80 per pastry (wholesale price) • Sign in largest window except special sales periods (approximately one per quarter) • $475 per month printing fee

also re-anchored aggressively on the other issues, consistent with the monetary mindset. And ultimately, if he accepts the most recent MIO or anything like it – and chances are growing he will – you've just secured a tremendous deal. To see for yourself, compare this MIO to the most optimistic outcome of a SIO, a 50:50 compromise on each issue, which would've probably resulted in something like this:

• 400 pastries per day at $0.40 each ($160 versus $240 in daily revenue)
• Signage in medium-sized window
• $300 printing fee

The economics don't lie. MIOs offer a vehicle for transitioning between the bartering and monetary mindsets, resolving multiple issues not only amicably but advantageously for yourself. Indeed, in the opening example, both Cameron and Clegg must've observed the advantages of MIOs as they hammered out a multi-issue coalition deal. But MIOs represent only one way of dealing with multiple issues. Let's consider another, potentially more potent approach.

Multiple Equivalent Simultaneous Offers (MESOs)

Given the benefits of MIOs, wouldn't more MIOs be better? Such is the logic of multiple equivalent simultaneous offers (MESOs): multiple MIOs, equivalent in value to you and made at the same time.[14]

A MESO in the café story, for example, would mention several different configurations of the three fundamental issues: pastries, signage, and coupons. MESOs are far from simple in the abstract. Having mastered MIOs, though, you'll probably find MESOs quite intuitive.

To see for yourself, let's reset the story again. Suppose you had made neither the ill-fated SIO inspired by Monty nor the advantageous MIO just described. Instead, you approached the second meeting seeking to make a MESO. To do so you'd start the conversation with the same preamble, reiterating the integrative tone of the last meeting and requesting the grocer's approval to get specific. Receiving said approval, you'd then transition into your MESO a bit differently: "OK, well in the interest of moving the conversation forward, I prepared a couple different proposals for you. What they do is list out a few different ways we could work through the various issues we discussed last week, attaching some numbers to them. These are just a couple of options, and I'd like to ask for your initial reactions. OK? Which of these options do you like best?" Again, you've positioned the offer as a discussion document, but you've now laid the groundwork for a MESO.

And just like that, you'd slide your printed MESO across the table. Although MESOs can include any number of MIOs greater than or equal to two, I'd generally advise two or three in the interest of keeping things manageable. If you chose to make a MESO containing three MIOs, it might look something like table 7.5.

This MESO, like all MESOs, lays out multiple MIOs at the same time, all of which you value about the same. In this case, as you ask the store to stock more or fewer pastries each day, you tweak the window size or per-pastry price – the requirement being that you truly see all three options as comparably attractive. Since MESOs consist of MIOs, they have all the same benefits. Building from the bartering mindset, they promote the perception that you're continuing

Table 7.5 Your MESO

	Option A	
Café owner to grocer		Grocer to café owner
• 500 tasty pastries per day • Coupon printed on each receipt (approximately 100 per day)		• $0.50 per pastry (wholesale price) • Sign in largest window • $500 per month printing fee

	Option B	
Café owner to grocer		Grocer to café owner
• 525 tasty pastries per day • Coupon printed on each receipt (approximately 100 per day)		• $0.50 per pastry (wholesale price) • Sign in medium-sized window • $500 per month printing fee

	Option C	
Café owner to grocer		Grocer to café owner
• 400 tasty pastries per day • Coupon printed on each receipt (approximately 100 per day)		• $0.625 per pastry (wholesale price) • Sign in largest window • $500 per month printing fee

last week's conversation, remind both parties they benefit (despite the monetary issues), and continue the flow of information. And, transitioning to the monetary mindset and associated distributive behavior, they again allow you to anchor, persuade, and transition to the value-claiming phase of the negotiation.

For three reasons, though, properly constructed MESOs may go beyond the benefits of MIOs. First, since MESOs contain multiple MIOs, they probably magnify the benefits of MIOs simply by including several. Second, since your MESO holds at least one issue constant across all the underlying MIOs (the $500 printing fee), it sends the strong signal that you consider this particular fee important. Third, since each of the underlying MIOs varies as few issues as possible relative to the others, your MESO says something about the absolute value you attach to the issues. By offering up MIOs A and B in tandem, for example, you've implicitly informed the grocer of the actual value you attach to a larger window. Option B suggests you're willing to accept a smaller window in exchange for an additional (25 pastries x $0.50) = $12.50 per day (~$375 per month), so chances are you value a larger window about that much.

And it's not just *you* who will probably share more information through a MESO. Consider the grocer's likely reaction. Although he probably won't make an explicit MESO of his own, that being complicated for untrained negotiators, he may well make an implicit MESO analogous to the implicit MIO above. In particular, and in response to your MESO, he may offer his reactions to the individual MIOs within the MESO. "Well, I don't love any of the options you're presenting," he might say, "but option B is definitely the worst. There's no way I can hope to sell that many pastries, so that option really won't work."

Again, with that reaction, you've made tremendous progress. You've learned that the grocer is open to a large window, printing fee, and per-pastry price in exchange for stocking fewer pastries (for example, option A or C). Indeed, if the grocer accepts anything like option A or C (and chances are growing he will), you will once again walk away with a tremendous deal. Both options may still require some modifications (for example, to the window proposal during special sales periods), but anything like these options could well produce a windfall. And that's the beauty of making multiple, equally attractive offers. To see for yourself, compare option C to the outcome of the SIOs, or even the outcome of a MIO.

In sum, MESOs offer another useful bridge between the bartering and monetary mindsets. Compared to MIOs, they reveal more information and also probably anchor the other side more strongly. Thus they offer a high-octane version of MIOs. Still it's not always easy to calculate or convincingly make a MESO, let alone elicit a counterpart's honest reactions.[15] "I hate all of these offers!" the grocer might say, walking off in a flurry of frustration. Alternatively, he might start cherry-picking his favorite terms from the three MIOs: "Hmm, well, 400 pastries (option C) at $0.50 (options A and B) and a medium-sized window (option B) sounds good." Since you definitely don't want him to do that, you'll have to nip that reaction in the bud, reiterating that you're merely trying to ascertain which MIO in the MESO he likes best (not which specific terms). In sum, MESOs may offer a higher-reward but also a higher-risk way of bridging the two mindsets – a potentially impactful strategy to nevertheless choose carefully.

The Café Story: Deciding Whether to Accept

Whether you use MESOs or MIOs, such are the steps you'd follow to transition between mindsets – with the grocer, but also with the other four partners remaining on your list. And what would you do when the potential agreements with each partner start to solidify? At that point you'd obviously need to decide whether to accept them. Now, since all five relationships are grounded in power partnerships, all should probably produce highly favorable agreements of some sort or another. Still you'll need a concrete standard of comparison – a precise criterion for deciding whether to accept or reject a particular deal.

You've already developed one such standard – the targets defined at the beginning. And if your agreements look anything like your targets, you should definitely accept them. But what if they don't? What if your agreements look much less attractive? Here you'd want to define and compare them against some sort of a bottom line – a numerical point of indifference between the current partner and your next-best alternative.[16] Luckily the bartering mindset has probably equipped you with a clear alternative, and thus the means to calculate your bottom line.

In particular, by taking the time throughout this process to consider the world broadly, identifying numerous parties who could meet your needs if only you met theirs, you probably identified an alternative to many of your partners already. What if the grocer plays hardball? Well, you initially set aside the farmers' market in favor of the grocer, but the former is probably your next-best alternative if the latter plays hardball. And if you hadn't previously set aside any partners in favor of the grocer? Well, you definitely set aside some partners offering the same thing as the grocer – more revenue – so you could turn to them instead.

In this way you could and probably should identify a next-best alternative for each of your five power partners, preferably *within* the list of partners originally identified. Though far from its main function, the bartering mindset has hopefully and helpfully left you with a wide range of alternatives. And with those alternatives in hand, you can probably estimate a bottom line for each partner. Your bottom line for the grocer? Probably the expected revenue from the farmers' market. Assuming an eventual deal with the grocer promises more than that amount, you should likely move forward. And what if it doesn't? Probably time to revisit the farmers' market or even the movie theater, radio station, or police officers – cycling back through the bartering mindset until you identify the optimal solution to your underlying problem. Good thing you spent all that time identifying so many partners, providing so many alternatives if you need them.

Concluding Thoughts

Throughout this book Getty has urged you to start negotiating integratively with a promising counterpart. You didn't accept that advice until the previous chapter – you couldn't until Bart's bartering mindset helped you understand the most powerful set of partners and right set of issues. And when you did adopt Getty's counsel, you applied it to many more parties than Getty would generally advise, and to a much different end: surfacing possibilities rather than sealing deals. But you didn't stop there.

You turned back to Monty, who had constantly urged you to think of any particular partner and issue in competitive, distributive terms. But you were hesitant to adopt that advice until the current chapter, when you finally started thinking competitively and translating that mentality into offers. You couldn't until you had understood yourself, the external world, and the powerful partnerships that might unite you. And when you did adopt Monty's council, you didn't adopt its literal implication to switch immediately to SIOs. Instead, after setting some targets in your own mind, you integrated the bartering and monetary mindsets in your partners' minds through MIOs or MESOs.

In sum neither Monty nor Getty offered the best counsel for meeting your needs and solving your problems, at least not on their own. Monty saw you and the rest of the world as locked in an intractable conflict – a counterproductive viewpoint that would've left you and everyone else unhappy (and generally does). Getty saw your task as negotiating integratively right away – a premature piece of advice that would've prevented you from achieving a clear understanding of yourself, the external world, and the many ways you and the external world could partner. Under Bart's guidance you did just that – and thereby surfaced a truly intriguing set of possibilities. Looking back on your ultimate approach, all three alter egos should feel reasonably satisfied, since you eventually implemented and integrated their essential points of view. But the greatest beneficiary of this approach is you, since you achieved a much better solution to a very important problem – a solution that meets your own and other people's needs extremely well. Here's hoping you retain and apply these lessons to the most important problems in your own life.

Summary of Key Points from This Chapter

1 Having identified a set of power partnerships, you need to transition from the bartering to the monetary mindset.

2 You can start the transition in your own mind by identifying a target for each issue with each partner.

3 But an abrupt shift to the monetary mindset and its associated SIOs would produce an overly distributive response from your partners.

4 MIOs represent a smoother way of making the transition, and MESOs offer a higher-risk / higher-reward version of MIOs.

5 These offers will probably produce advantageous agreements that you'll nevertheless need to compare against your targets and bottom lines.

Exercise: Job Negotiation and Integrating the Two Mindsets

Over the last few chapters you've explored some solutions to your realistic desire for more money, which really reflected your need to cope with commuting costs (we decided). In the last chapter you determined that a power partnership with your boss might be possible: you could offer to assume some additional travel, thereby reducing the boss's time away from home. In exchange the boss could potentially find a way to offer a virtual work arrangement when you're not actually travelling, thereby reducing your commuting costs further. Whatever the analogues in your own life, I'd encourage you to review them now.

Continuing with the example, suppose you now wanted to approach your boss for the second time and hammer out the terms of the deal. According to the guidance in this chapter, what should you do? Ultimately I hope this chapter has convinced you that you now need to transition from the bartering back to the monetary mindset. More specifically, I hope it's provided you with some ideas about how to do that – and not do that. Remember?

First, you'll want to initiate the transition in your own mind by defining some targets. In the example, how much additional travel do you really want to take on? Are two days of virtual work per week sufficient or do you intend to shoot for more? I'd encourage you to define the relevant targets in your own life, according to the real negotiations you'd initiate – identifying aggressive but attainable outcomes that apply to you.

Having defined a set of targets and thus transitioned into the monetary mindset in your own mind, I hope you'll remember that you can't just plop your counterpart into the monetary mindset without warning. You'll need to ease your counterpart into the monetary mindset using some specific offer strategies. Hopefully you remember what they are: MIOs and/or MESOs. What would a MIO look like with your boss? Something like table 7.6 perhaps?

I'll leave it to you to develop a MIO that applies to your own case. In so doing, remember that you'd develop MIOs for all of the other partners you're considering, not just one. Or perhaps you'd be so bold as to try a MESO for each of your partners? Going back to the job example, perhaps it would look something like table 7.7.

Perhaps this looks a little formal or a little pushy for your own case? Perhaps you'd present it informally or verbally instead of in a table? Or push for three days at home if the boss insisted on additional regional travel, without making the trade-off quite so explicit? All of that is just fine. The point here is not to prescribe a specific format for your offers, nor to force a formal method on an informal relationship. It's to suggest that you should go to the effort of tackling all the issues together – formally or informally, through MIOs or MESOs – as any multi-issue approach will help everyone transition between mindsets. Whatever your preferred approach, I'd

Table 7.6 MIO in the Example

Employee to boss	Boss to employee
• One 4-day, domestic long-distance trip per month • Two 2-day, regional train trips per month • One additional international trip per year as requested	• Two days of virtual work each week not on a domestic long-distance or international trip

Table 7.7 MESO in the Example

Option A	
Employee to boss	Boss to employee
• One 4-day, domestic long-distance trip per month • Two 2-day, regional train trips per month • One additional international trip per year as requested	• Two days of virtual work each week not on a domestic long-distance or international trip
Option B	
Employee to boss	Boss to employee
• One 4-day, domestic long-distance trip per month • Three 2-day, regional train trips per month • One additional international trip per year as requested	• Three days of virtual work each week not on a domestic long-distance or international trip

encourage you to apply it to your own, real-life problems – even those that have nothing to do with money, travel, or virtual work. If you take away nothing other than the idea that identifying the best solutions to your most important problems requires you to use and transition gracefully between two mindsets, I'll consider the book a success.

8

OBJECTIONS TO THE
BARTERING MINDSET

Herb Sukenik was once an acclaimed scientist.[1] After earning advanced degrees in medicine and physics, he conducted groundbreaking research on nuclear magnetic resonance, then made foundational contributions to the field of space medicine. By his early thirties, he enjoyed considerable prominence and prosperity.

Yet he was also growing increasingly embittered. In grad school his father was convicted of a felony and died. In his late thirties he abandoned his career for a surprisingly menial job. In his forties he disappeared into a tiny New York apartment – there to complete crossword puzzles and avoid social contact for the next three decades. By 2004, his thirtieth year in seclusion, few people knew of Sukenik or cared about his accomplishments.

But his story was about to take another turn, as a group of developers bought his apartment building for $400 million, then announced their intention to transform it into the city's fanciest residential property. To do that, they just had to convince the four tenants in rent-controlled apartments to move. Of the four, three quickly accepted million-dollar checks and left. But the fourth, a seventy-three-year-old Sukenik, had other plans. The developers realized as much as soon as the others left, at which point Sukenik started making outrageous demands. A new apartment with sweeping park vistas? Free meals by world-renowned chefs? Figures many multiples of a million? Nothing was off the table.

But why, wondered the developers, who were well aware of his backstory? Why, after three decades of stock-piling rent-controlled cash, would a man in seventies – with no close relatives nor charitable tendencies – make such outrageous demands? Greed? The developers had no other explanation until Sukenik himself suggested an alternative motive, saying, "I wasted my life. I could have been at the heart of research into CAT scans and MRIs. I should have invented something like that. Instead, I've been up here thirty years doing crossword puzzles." His stated demands apparently masked a deeper need for one final accomplishment to counterbalance if not compensate for his wasted life.

Consistent with step 1 of the bartering mindset, then, Sukenik appeared to understand one of his deep needs. And he also understood his offerings: fully conscious of the building's worthlessness while he lived there – coupled with the enormous price of insurance, taxes, and carrying costs on an unused 52,000 square-foot building in New York City – Sukenik understood the immense value of his lone apartment. Seeing that he was offering the developers nothing short of an escape from bankruptcy, he mustered the confidence to stall even as wrecking balls destroyed the surrounding structure. "Oh, I love to watch construction," he said.

And shortly after his intransigence drove the project to a screeching halt, Sukenik walked away with the city's largest-ever relocation package: $17 million, in addition to a $2 million apartment with the requested park vistas, for which he would pay a mere $1 a month. At least in his own mind, then, Sukenik probably succeeded in satisfying his deep need for one final accomplishment – and he did so by acutely understanding his offerings. Seems pretty consistent with the first step of the bartering mindset, doesn't it?

But something also seems amiss. The story raises new and potentially difficult questions about the bartering mindset – questions like: Can the bartering mindset enable seemingly petty and narcissistic objectives like Sukenik's in addition to respectable objectives like the café owner's? To what extent does the bartering mindset still apply when others like the developers bring a problem *to you*? Does the bartering mindset help when you employ it with just a few partners, or employ just a subset of its steps – both of which Sukenik seemed to do?

This chapter will seek to answer these and other questions you might still might have about the bartering mindset. Acknowledging that I won't be able to answer every conceivable question, especially on issues that require additional research, I will earnestly seek to answer ten common questions that others have asked *me* about the bartering mindset (with my thanks to the questioners). And even if you don't agree with my answers, I hope you'll walk away with an appreciation for the bartering mindset's credibility and applicability, along with an eagerness to apply it to your own life. So here goes!

1. What If There's Only One Person on the Other Side of the Table?

Taken literally, Sukenik's story involved only two "parties": Sukenik and the developers. What if a real-life problem involved only you and one other party? Going back to the café story, what if you thought a negotiation with the landlord would probably solve your problem? Should you still consider other partners, as suggested throughout the book?

In response to the last question, and in my humble opinion, the clear answer is yes. Think back to the first chapter, where we noted that most of us think our problems are best solved by dealing with one other party. Then recall that we diagnosed this belief as a symptom of the monetary mindset. Remember? Hopefully so, and hopefully you then realize that the perception of a single counterpart is not a good reason to avoid the bartering mindset. It's one of the primary reasons to adopt the bartering mindset in the first place. Put differently and simply, the assumption that each problem involves one counterpart often reflects an encroaching monetary mindset. It's the sound of Monty's persistent whispers. For most of us and most of our important problems, the perception of a lone counterpart should raise a red flag that we haven't yet embraced the bartering mindset, particularly steps 2–3 (chapter 4).

And what if you have? What if, in real life, you've read and reread chapter 4 and still can't seem to devise another party in your own situation? Unlikely as that may be, you could still apply the principles from chapters 3 and 5–7. Why not, with this one pesky party, consider not just what you need but what you can offer (chapter 3)? And why not anticipate the most powerful set of trades with this one party, if not the most powerful set of partnerships across the market (chapter 5)? And why not try to cultivate these powerful trades (chapter 6), then perhaps make some MIOs or MESOs (chapter 7)? Even if the world presents you with one lone partner, much of the bartering mindset still applies.

With all of that said – and yes, I really believe it – I would hasten to note a special type of negotiation that often does emphasize a single partner: disputes. A dispute occurs when one person makes a claim and another person rejects it.[2] Common examples include lawsuits, divorces, and breaches of contract. Beyond the rejected claim, disputes differ from normal (deal-making) negotiations in several respects, particularly the fact that both parties often face the same poor outcome if talks break down (for example, going to court if a couple cannot dissolve their marriage amicably). In contrast to normal negotiations, where the parties can walk away and exercise their separate alternatives, the parties to a dispute often share the same poor alternative if they can't "get to yes."

The fact that a dispute originates in a claim made by one party and rejected by another – and could result in the same adverse outcome for both – means that disputants may have a harder time devising any other relevant parties or considering their needs and offerings (chapter 4). Still the potentially high stakes and heavy emotional toll mean that disputants probably have even more of an incentive to understand their own needs and offerings thoroughly (chapter 3), find powerful trades with the other disputant (chapter 5), do what they can to cultivate these trades (chapter 6), and ease into the monetary mindset with finesse (chapter 7). None of this will be easy, at least until the disputants can manage their anger and move beyond matters of rights and power.[3] But these steps take on a special importance in the face of a collectively poor alternative.

2. What If I or My Counterpart Cares Only about Money?

Sukenik's story was pretty focused on money – namely, the amount of money required to get him out. Similarly, the café story at least initially focused on money and money alone – namely, the perceived need to cut costs. At least in the café story, though, you quickly saw that the issues stretched far beyond money. In particular, you saw that your perceived need to cut costs actually reflected a deeper need to ensure business viability, which in turn highlighted three broad needs involving costs but also revenue and the community. In other words, engaging the bartering mindset led you to discover that the story was substantially more complicated than a single monetary need. But what if you were negotiating with a critical supplier about just one issue: the cost of ingredients? And what about real life? What if you, in the real world, were dealing with a contractor, employer, or real estate agent, for example, and couldn't see the relevance of a single non-monetary issue?

Much like the intuition that a negotiation involves only one counterpart, negotiations focused on one monetary issue tend to represent hidden manifestations of the monetary mindset – Monty's persistent whispers – rather than exceptions to the bartering mindset. Why do our negotiations seem to focus exclusively on money? Typically because we and our counterparts see them through the lens of the monetary mindset. Thus a money-focused negotiation should not cue us to abandon the bartering mindset but embrace it – especially by asking ourselves whether we've really defined all our needs and offerings, our counterparts and theirs, and the full range of power partnerships that become apparent when we do. Is money really the only thing in the whole wide world that you care about? By extension, is it the only thing everyone else cares about? Probably not. In sum, we can be confident about the existence or non-existence of non-monetary issues only if we've fully embraced the bartering mindset.

With that said, it's worth reiterating what the bartering mindset is intended to do: help you prepare to solve problems before you go about solving them. So if your problem is a need to get home and you've already implemented the solution of hopping on the bus, it's probably too late to apply the bartering mindset. With the bus driver and busload of passengers waiting for you to pay, the problem is truly about money: it's time to apply the monetary mindset or rapidly exit the bus.

In addition it's worth considering the types of negotiations in which money looms largest: one-issue transactions with one partner whom you need now but will never encounter again. In my negotiations classes I often give the following example: You and your significant other decide to take a road trip in your beloved but beat-up pickup truck, and you now find yourself in the middle of a steaming-hot desert. Considering the location, your pickup picks a heck of a time to break down. The last time you saw a town? A hundred miles back. But the last time you saw a person? Luckily about a mile ago. Indeed, as luck would have it, the last person you saw was an unkempt guy leaning against an unkempt shack housing a couple of heavily used cars. Strange place for a car dealer, you thought at the time, but you're now counting your blessings.

Having walked the hot mile back to the shack, you and your significant other now need a car. Although you'd prefer any of his vehicles to no vehicle at all, only one of the vehicles – a large SUV – would hold all of your possessions. The major point of contention, of course, is price. This decades-old behemoth must've scaled every mountain in the region and tumbled down others. But he's asking a whopping $30,000!

At this point, consider your situation carefully: you're negotiating over one commodity, the SUV, with one party whom you'll probably never encounter again: the used car guy. In this situation, when it's hard to spot any issue but money or any reason to think outside the box, you might be tempted to apply the monetary mindset.

Unfortunately, the single issue, lack of relationship, and extreme heat don't change the fact that the monetary mindset, for all the reasons listed in chapter 1, will probably lead to a poor solution. Indeed, given your extreme dependence on the dealer, it will probably lead to an *exceptionally* poor solution. Even in these trying circumstances, then, I'd advise you to give the bartering mindset a try. For starters, you might consider whether you have anything else to offer. Could you rent the SUV and return it on your way back, with your significant other driving the nicer and more appropriately priced car you intend to purchase from a legitimate dealer in a proper municipality? Could you sell him your stalled clunker for scrap metal? In addition, you might consider what else you need. Could the dealer repair your pickup? Would you pay his price if he at least changed the oil, filled it with gas, and fixed the rickety bumper? These are just examples, but they illustrate the extension of the bartering mindset to extreme, money-focused situations, suggesting that most problems do (or could) involve non-monetary issues if you look hard enough.

3. What If Someone Else Initiated the Discussion?

Sukenik's story started when the developers presented him with a problem. What if your own story, in your own life, was more like Sukenik's than the café owner's? What if another person or

organization brought a problem to you: would the bartering mindset still apply? To answer, let's dive back into the café story. Imagine
the story had not started with your own need to cut costs; rather, it
started with a critical supplier asking for a big and unexpected price
hike. Would the principles in the previous chapters still work?

Since the café story followed such a specific progression, it's reasonable to ask. At the risk of sounding dismissive, though, it doesn't
really matter who initiates the discussion. To the extent you have
unmet needs and unclaimed offerings at the time someone else
approaches you (and who doesn't?), most of the principles in the
book still apply. What if the supplier requested a price hike? Sounds
like she just surfaced an important and unmet need of her own.
Although it might be tempting to follow Monty's counsel and react
to the supplier's request competitively, why not take the request
as an opportunity to understand her situation better? In particular,
why not ask the supplier why she suddenly needs a price hike? And
is there anything else she needs? With her responses, and thus a
deeper and broader understanding of her needs in hand, you could
then offer to consider the request and respond soon.

Stepping away from the supplier, you could then ask yourself a
critical question: how easily can I fulfill the underlying needs just
described? If the supplier's underlying needs are really beyond
your purview – perhaps she's adjusting to market agglomeration
among corporate farms – then you've just identified a big need of
your own: managing your own costs in light of rapidly rising prices.
In other words, you're right back where you started the café story,
and you could certainly engage the bartering mindset through the
preceding principles. Could you identify some alternative suppliers
or alternative sources of wheat (for example, local farmers) who are
somewhat insulated from global trends?

But what if you could easily meet the needs she just surfaced?
What if the supplier was trying to protect against the unexpected
price spikes that weather-logged farmers occasionally impose on

her, and you could absorb some of the price risk yourself if she oth-erwise held the price constant (or even gave you a slight discount)? If you could easily meet her needs, you could then be more selective about the aspects of the bartering mindset to apply. You'd certainly want to understand which of your own offerings could fill the sup-plier's needs – in this case, your ability to offer insurance out of your cash reserves. And since this amounts to a big concession, you'd also want to consider which of your needs the supplier might meet in return (chapter 3). If she could meet some of your own needs (for example, by offering a slight discount or premium product), then you might've surfaced a power partnership. Particularly if she rejected such ideas, though, you'd probably want to anticipate at least a couple of alternative wheat sources as well as those parties' needs and offerings (chapter 4). With the alternative suppliers you might want to anticipate any potential power partnerships (chapter 5), though you could choose whether to cultivate them (chapter 6) on the basis of the original supplier's response. And with any of these suppliers, you could readily present your ideas in MIOs or MESOs (chapter 7).

Bottom line: the bartering mindset and most of its underlying principles still apply in spades, particularly if the other person's problem surfaces a problem for you. But if it doesn't – if the problem is purely someone else's – you can choose how extensively to apply the bartering mindset. Realistically you can't go around implement-ing all five steps of the mindset every time someone else presents you with a problem: otherwise, the mindset would consume all your waking hours and brain cells. But you can and should apply the bar-tering mindset anytime another person's problem surfaces a prob-lem for you, or you simply wish to treat the other person's problem as an opportunity to improve your own lot at the same time.

The challenge, then, is motivating yourself to take the problems presented by others seriously enough. Consider another example: a call from a headhunter. Someone else has a serious problem – an open position requiring an expensive headhunter. Having received the headhunter's call, should you take the problem seriously, treating it as an opportunity to advance your own career via the bartering mindset? Or should you treat it as an interesting if unnecessary distraction? The choice about what to do and how extensively to apply the bartering mindset in a given situation is ultimately up to you.

4. Couldn't the Bartering Mindset Be Used for Questionable Purposes?

Sukenik seemingly used at least one piece of the bartering mindset for petty and narcissistic ends, employing its first step to squeeze the maximum value out of some developers and nearly bankrupt their project. Surely you, the reader, don't have petty or narcissistic designs, but perhaps you wonder whether the bartering mindset could enable other people's questionable objectives? For example, could the café owner use the mindset to make the café so viable that it devours the local competition, thereby creating a local monopoly to gouge local diners?

The short and potentially surprising answer is yes. The bartering mindset is a strategy – a way of thinking about the world that ultimately leads you to take a certain set of actions, actions that help you meet the particular needs underlying a specific problem. But it has nothing to say about the problem or needs themselves – particularly whether the problem is worth solving or the needs are worth satisfying. If the underlying "problem" is not really a problem from society's perspective (for example, competition among local cafés), or if fulfilling the needs is going to harm other people (for example, by driving up local coffee prices), then the bartering mindset would probably aid in the satisfaction of a questionable objective. Thus it is the responsibility of all who apply the bartering mindset – like the monetary mindset and the integrative behaviors espoused by Getty – to apply it to appropriate ends.

5. Won't My Transaction Partners Feel Used?

In real life we hold loyalty in high regard. We think well of people who devote themselves to one spouse rather than several, commit themselves to one organization rather than jumping among them continuously, and follow the tenets of one religion or belief system rather than dabbling haphazardly among viewpoints. Something about loyalty appears to hold intuitive appeal. So it may have surprised you to learn that the bartering mindset involves the pursuit of multiple, promising partners. Won't that approach cast you as disloyal at best and manipulative at worst? In other words, won't your partners feel used when they learn that they are but one of many nodes in your multi-partner solution?

Since the bartering mindset prompts you to go against your single-partner instincts, it's a valid question. But if you're adopting the bartering mindset in the manner described here, the straightforward answer is no. As described here, the bartering mindset directs you to do everything in your power to avoid approaching anyone who doesn't offer at least the promise of a power partnership – which, remember, is beneficial to both sides. Indeed it was not the bartering mindset but Monty and Getty who encouraged you to start negotiating early, before you really knew whom to talk to or what to say. Had you taken their advice and started negotiating right away, rather than systematically distilling the world down to a list of mutually beneficial partners, you probably would've talked to someone or even multiple people and then abandoned them – either because you couldn't help them or the reverse. Either way, the abandoned parties probably would've felt annoyed or even used as you left them in the dust for someone better.

Instead, the bartering mindset urged you get the list of counterparts and issues right before engaging with anyone else (chapters 3–5). And when the bartering mindset finally prompted you to engage with your partners (chapter 6), it also urged you to transparently admit that, while you suspect and want to realize the possibility of mutual gain, neither you nor your partners will be able to reach a deal until both consider the possibilities further. And your actions matched your words, as chapter 6–7 led you to re-approach the great majority of your partners, contacting the others immediately. Overall the bartering mindset built from the economic reality that it's hard to solve anyone's problem very well unless many parties talk to many other parties. But it tried to mitigate any relational costs and probably did so better than Monty or Getty, focusing your attention on partners who promise the greatest probability of mutual gain.

6. What If My Counterpart Is Unreceptive to the Bartering Mindset?

In chapter 6 you approached the grocer with an implicit proposition: you sell my pastries and hang my sign, and I'll supply my pastries and print your coupon. Collectively that should attract some customers to your store. Of course you didn't say it that way – you systematically cultivated a trusting environment and posed a series of open-ended questions about your respective needs and offerings. But such was the basic proposition. The question is this: what if the grocer wasn't interested? What if he expressed absolutely no interest in your pastries and even less in your coupons? What if he had no other ideas and simply wanted to return to the store to attend to the morning rush? Or, as a very different example, what if you approached the first of several co-workers with a creative way to lighten everyone's workloads, tried all the fancy tactics in this book, and found the colleague completely uninterested (that is, unreceptive to the bartering mindset)?

The short answer: if you've really done your homework and carefully considered all the relevant parties and their possible needs and offerings, that shouldn't happen too often. Who wouldn't appreciate another person appearing out of the blue, expressing genuine concern about a problem of acute concern, and earnestly trying to solve it? I don't know many. Indeed, even if you initially got their problem wrong, most people I know would be happy to solicit your help in solving others. Humans being human beings, however, you're bound to encounter a few grumpy souls who would rather deal with their own problems, hold their cards close, or attribute every honest overture to something sinister. Thus the question: how to deal with unreceptive partners?

The longer but still-simple answer: you don't really have to. One of the real side-benefits of the bartering mindset, as mentioned in chapter 7, is that considering many partners (chapter 4) tends to afford many alternatives. If the grocer comes off as a stick-in-the-mud while exploring opportunities (chapter 6) or exploring your MESO (chapter 7), you still have the farmers' market. Didn't you previously decide that the market could satisfy your need for pastry sales just about as well? Even if you haven't identified an a priori alternative for every possible stick-in-the-mud, hasn't the process of thinking through all the parties put you way ahead of Monty or Getty, who essentially urged you to consider just one? The bartering mindset may not win the entire world to your side. But it should give you enough options to solve your problem despite the occasional curmudgeon.

7. Does the Bartering Mindset Apply across Cultures?

Although I never mentioned the café's location, you probably imagined it in your own country. Hopefully you considered the story and bartering mindset valid in your own cultural setting, but perhaps you wondered whether it would apply in others.

While we need much more research to judge the cultural generality of the bartering mindset per se, researchers have already studied the cultural generality of many of the negotiation principles on which it's based. Thus some general comments on culture seem warranted. In general the research suggests that negotiators around the world have a surprising amount in common.[4] Negotiators everywhere seek to advance their own interests and build relationships with others, suggesting that many of the principles in this book are not specific to any one culture. But negotiators do vary on several dimensions, including the amount of emphasis they put on achieving interests versus building relationships at the outset, as well as the nature of their interests and the behaviors they tend to display.[5]

Particularly relevant to the bartering mindset are the cultural differences in relationship-building, trust, and information-sharing. Certain cultures (for example, in Latin America) seem to emphasize the need to build a relationship before "getting down to business."[6] Thus in those cultures you might want to consider pausing the information-sharing components of chapter 6 to engage in an extended period of relationship-building.[7] Other cultures (for example, in South Asia) appear to place a heavy reliance on social information when deciding whether to trust their negotiation counterparts.[8] In these cultures you might need to bolster the trust-building strategies in chapter 6 with some personal references or the mention of some common friends or family. Finally, a third set of cultures (for example, in East Asia) appear to avoid much overt information-sharing early in a negotiation.[9] Instead they jump right into the offer-making strategies described in chapter 7. Although efforts to build trust and share information in these cultures are still worthwhile, you might need to shift to the offer-making strategies sooner than expected, embedding some information about your respective needs and offerings in MIOs or MESOs. In other words, in East Asian cultures, you might want to merge chapters 6 and 7.

Based on the existing cross-cultural negotiation research, these are some of the biggest cultural differences you may encounter when applying the bartering mindset. While they don't exhaust the universe of cultural differences – far from it! – we'll need additional research before saying much more.

8. What If I Don't Care about Anyone Else's Needs and Offerings?

Somewhere in the middle of the café story – perhaps in chapter 4 when you were compiling your long list of partners and seeking to understand their situations – you might've wondered whether and why you care about the needs of local farmers and artists. "Why am I spending so much time listing out all these random parties and their problems," you might have thought, "when all I really care about is the café?" Or, to state it more generally, "Do I really need to consider other parties and their needs and offerings when I'm ultimately just concerned about my own problem?" Or, more bluntly, "Do I really have to care other people?"

The answer to all these interrelated questions is the same: you don't have time *not* to consider other people's needs and offerings. You can't systematically and routinely avoid thinking about other people and their situations and still solve your own problems reasonably well. Sure, you didn't have to develop a list of partners quite as long as chapter 4's. Sure, you might've omitted some parties like the radio station who seemed tangential. But you simply can't solve your own problems particularly well without embracing the needs and offerings of at least a portion of the external world. Otherwise you'll come to other people (and probably the wrong people) focusing exclusively on yourself and your sad story. You'll have nothing obvious to offer them, nor will you seem particularly concerned about their welfare. Have you ever encountered a person who acts like that? If so, you know how it feels. And you probably weren't overly motivated to help.

But let's be really clear on what this means: the bartering mindset is not an act of charity. Although the rest of the world will probably appreciate your earnest desire to solve their problems, the bartering mindset is fundamentally intended to help you identify the best solutions to your own problems, not theirs. Think about it: With the onset of winter and some serious problems back home, Keith didn't travel to market hoping to benefit humanity writ large, nor did anyone else. He came to market hoping to help himself and his family. The fact that he cared about other members of the market and their needs, and authentically so, was both the right thing to do and the only real means of achieving the best solutions to his most pressing problems. In sum the bartering mindset highlights a good and benevolent way of treating other people. But it's not fundamentally an act of charity – it's a tool for achieving your enlightened self-interest.

9. But What If I Really Don't Have the Time?

So perhaps you understand the need to care about other people but are still concerned about the time required to do so. Doesn't it take a lot of time to engage with multiple parties, as chapters 6–7 advised? In the real world, won't the bartering mindset require you to dedicate even more of your precious time to negotiation? The short answer is yes. It does take more time to talk to several partners than one, and we all know time is money. Missing from the equation, though, is a consideration of the benefits – or, if you like, the opportunity costs of *not* talking to multiple parties. Multiple partners are almost guaranteed to generate multiple possibilities, which will typically be preferable to one. The real issue, then, is whether the benefits of these additional possibilities outweigh the time costs associated with engaging in additional negotiations.

As indicated in the first chapter, a key reason for our frequent use of the monetary mindset is time: for our mundane problems, engaging in highly sophisticated negotiations often takes more time than it's worth. Does your car need gas? A series of innovative and open-ended negotiations with various fuel providers will take a lot of time but probably produce middling benefits. Do you need a car to consume the gas, though? The benefits of innovative and open-ended negotiations with various transportation providers will probably far outweigh the costs. As with other questions about the bartering mindset, then, the choice about whether it will pay in a particular situation is ultimately yours to make. But I'd encourage you to choose the bartering mindset in the face of any serious or even mildly serious problem, in which the benefits will almost assuredly outweigh the costs.

And what if you want to engage the bartering mindset but can't afford to engage it fully? Is there a way to scale it down? Should you engage in just some of the steps (as Sukenik did), or is there another way to reduce its burden? Well, you could certainly pull a Sukenik if you like, but a better way to down-scale the bartering mindset is to limit the number of transaction partners. In other words, try to follow all five steps, but use a more stringent criterion to decide which parties to consider (chapters 4–5) and engage (chapters 6–7). Since most of the time costs come from talking to other people, reducing the number of partners should substantially reduce the costs.

In sum a really big problem, involving really serious needs, deserves a really earnest attempt to devise the best solution. The bartering mindset is a relatively high-cost/high-benefit way of solving problems. Its time costs may well predominate for small problems, in which excellent solutions afford only modest benefits. But its benefits are likely to predominate for even mildly serious problems and certainly for serious problems, in which the benefits of excellent solutions will far outweigh the cost of time spent devising them. How much does it really cost to prepare a few lists? A lot in comparison to a tank of gas – but not much in comparison to a car, or even a car repair. In short, the bartering mindset pays in direct proportion to the gravity of the problem. And you can make it pay for fairly minor problems by reducing the number of transaction partners you consider.

10. Doesn't the Bartering Mindset Make Me Look Weak?

Somewhere in the midst of the café story – maybe in chapter 6 when you approached your prospective partners and tried to foster a trusting and open environment – you might've concluded that the bartering mindset is just too weak for the "real world." "Sounds good on paper," you might've decided, "but what about the jackals sitting across my own bargaining tables? Wouldn't they eat me for lunch if I started opining on their needs and offerings?"

The world undoubtedly contains many jackals, and any claim to the contrary would be silly. But a close reading of this book (and discussion above) should remind you that, far from making you look weak, the bartering mindset makes you look strong. Think about it: Had you never embraced the bartering mindset in the café story, what would you have done? Gone to your landlord, hat in hand, meekly requesting a rent freeze. Gone to your loyal customers, meekly mentioning your price increase, or your employees, sheepishly summarizing your reasons for withholding a raise. Strong as we might imagine ourselves under the monetary mindset and its behavioral implications – aggressively offering, steeply demanding, and boldly proclaiming – it's the monetary mindset that makes us look weak, leading us to offer nothing and ask everything of everyone else.

And it's the bartering mindset that makes us look strong. Think about it: by showing us how to satisfy other people's needs, the bartering mindset gives us the keys to other people's happiness. Having engaged the bartering mindset, we now know what we're offering in addition to what we're demanding – as well as the parties who might want our offerings and why. Thus it's the bartering mindset that leads us to command the right people's attention, raising the right possibilities – ideas they actually find exciting rather than annoying. Will others see us as weak when we offer to satisfy their most cherished needs? Since controlling other people's outcomes is the very definition of power, it's not especially likely.[10] In sum, whatever objections you might level at the bartering mindset, a fear of weakness should not be among them. Implemented thoughtfully, the bartering mindset will substantially strengthen your hand.

Concluding Thoughts

These are just some of the questions that might have occurred to you while learning about the bartering mindset. But even if I haven't answered *your* question, I hope my answers have established the bartering mindset's credibility – as well as its applicability to a wide range of problems. And I hope the preceding chapters have motivated you to apply the bartering mindset to your own life – a task we'll practice in the next and last chapter.

CONCLUSIONS AND APPLICATIONS

In 2017 the North Face introduced an innovative product: the Apex Flex GTX, a comfortable and fashionable yet completely waterproof jacket.[1] Behind the jacket lay an interesting idea: The weather shouldn't dictate our fashion. We should have the right to feel both fashionable and comfortable, even when the forecast calls for rain. Indeed, with the benefit of an attractive yet waterproof jacket, we should even look forward to the occasional storm!

Coupled with the product was an innovative marketing campaign: the North Face enlisted the help of White Denim (an Austin-based rock band) to write a song for the jacket's commercials, as well as Spotify (an online music streaming service) to limit the song's availability to locations where it was raining. If it wasn't raining where you were, you couldn't stream the song. Could this campaign build a sense of excitement for the rain and, by extension, the jacket?

Regardless, it offers an interesting bird's-eye view of the bartering mindset. Consistent with step 1, the North Face probably understood its need for publicity and demand, particularly among young, sophisticated White Denim followers or Spotify users who might not otherwise consider its apparel. But the company also understood its offerings – probably the ability to offer its partners some corporate-sized revenue. And, consistent with steps 2–3, the North Face identified the band and streaming service as out-of-the-box transaction partners with out-of-the-box needs and offerings. For example, the company probably recognized that both potential partners would benefit from the buzz and opportunity to experiment at the cutting edge of music, in the process of offering to help advertise the jacket. But critically, and consistent with steps 4–5, the North Face recognized that a power partnership required a mutually beneficial deal with both (and presumably not with others).

The North Face probably never heard of the bartering mindset, but its marketing campaign nicely illustrates the mindset anyway. Much like this story, the current chapter will first seek to review the bartering mindset at a bird's-eye level, reiterating the key messages briefly. Then it will seek to solidify the bartering mindset at a hands-on level, prompting you to apply the mindset to three realistic scenarios. These scenarios will help you practice the steps involved in understanding yourself (step 1, example 1), understanding the market (steps 2–3, example 2), and understanding the partnerships that can connect you with the market (steps 4–5, example 3).

A Brief Review

Money is not the only solution to our daily problems. But it's a common solution. We can easily remedy most of our mundane problems and meet our mundane needs by paying or receiving money – paper, plastic, or electronic. But the ease and utility of money also inject monetary thinking into our psychology in ways that few of us fully appreciate. In particular, our use of money immerses us in the monetary mindset: a fixed-pie view of the world that fixes our attention on one of our needs and portrays it as utterly opposed to the one need of the one person we engage to solve the problem. This approach works well enough for our mundane problems, in which the benefits of a more sophisticated approach are negligible.

But the ease and utility of money also lead us to apply the monetary mindset to our biggest and most important problems – personal, organizational, and societal. Unlike mundane problems, big problems often necessitate negotiations. Since the monetary mindset prompts a fixed-pie view of the world that inevitably elicits distributive (competitive) negotiation behaviors, and since negotiators cannot perform particularly well without balancing distributive against integrative ("win-win") behaviors, the monetary mindset leaves us ill-equipped to handle our biggest problems. Thus chapter 1 concluded that most of us continue to labor under the weight of the simmering conflicts or disappointing compromises that follow from a single-minded focus on distributive negotiation.

And "single-minded" is just the right term, as the monetary world leaves us with no obvious mindset to support integrative negotiation behavior. Most of us have no mode of thinking that would facilitate integrative negotiation. But by stepping into a full-blown bartering economy and the mind of one of its occupants, chapter 2 sought to remind modern readers of a mindset that people with pressing needs adopted more routinely in the past: the bartering mindset. Having to trade whatever they could offer for whatever they might need, the members of bartering economies faced a much harder task than we do with our money: to somehow overcome a double coincidence of wants – a potentially rare situation in which whatever they needed was exactly what someone else happened to have, and vice-versa.

Because of the very real economic difficulties imposed by such a system, the members of bartering economies probably had little choice but to adopt a sophisticated psychological response: a more flexible, open-ended, and creative way of seeing the world that I called the bartering mindset. And just as the bartering mindset allowed them to surmount a double coincidence of wants then, it can elicit the integrative negotiation behaviors needed to solve our most pressing problems today. Born of the difficulty inherent in bartering, the bartering mindset leads the problem-solver to a better and more productive set of behaviors in any age and economic system. Fundamentally I hope this book has made you mindful of that mindset.

With a basic sense of the bartering mindset in hand, chapters 3–7 transitioned to translating the mindset for the negotiations that most of us face today, in a world where bartering persists but is less prevalent and money necessarily enters into many if not most negotiations. Using the extended example of a struggling café, an analogy for anyone grappling with the realities of resource constraints, these chapters sought to train you in the modern application of the bartering mindset. Even if your own problems have nothing to do with cafés, I hope these chapters provided a model – a template for devising better solutions to your own problems. And if the café story didn't entirely accomplish that, I hope the job exercise at the end of the chapters did.

Despite all of this application and practice, though, a nettlesome fact remains: most of us still live in a monetary economy. Since the monetary mindset and its accompanying distributive behaviors will always come more naturally in a monetary economy, this final chapter will provide you with a few more opportunities to apply and practice the bartering mindset in the modern world. In particular we'll consider three additional real-life scenarios you could easily face, which map onto an abbreviated version of the bartering mindset's five-step process. The first scenario reiterates the need to understand yourself (step 1, chapter 3); the second focuses on understanding the market (steps 2–3, chapter 4); and the third focuses on understanding the partnerships that can connect you with the market (steps 4–5, chapters 5–6).

Shortly after presenting each scenario, I'll ask you to indicate how Monty and Getty would encourage you to respond. The point in this chapter is not to evaluate their recommendations – I hope we've already accomplished that. The point is to develop the habit of contrasting Monty and Getty's recommendations with Bart's, which I'll

Figure 9.1 Alter Egos, Mindsets, and Negotiation Behaviors

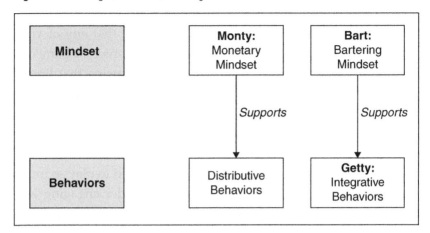

ask you to consider right after. To aid in the process, you might want to review figure 9.1, which is a reiteration of the first figure you encountered in chapter 3. This figure identifies the three alter egos and their fundamental viewpoints.

By applying Bart's bartering mindset to a few more real-world scenarios and actively contrasting its suggestions with Monty and Getty's, you should feel confident deploying the bartering mindset in the modern world, and cognizant of the everyday problems it can help to solve. So please consider the following three scenarios carefully, trying to answer the questions actively and thoughtfully. I promise it'll be worth this last bit of effort.

1. Understanding Yourself (Step 1, Chapter 3): Dwindling Savings

One morning you wake to the reality that your family's expenses are outstripping your income. Continue on the current path and you'll find yourself constantly dipping into savings, which will dry up your bank account in a hurry. What would Monty urge you to do? Please consider that question before moving on.

First and foremost, Monty would remind you that any of your attempts to reduce expenses probably runs counter to someone else's desire to make and/or spend money. Following that line of thinking, Monty might urge you to think about cutting the expenses imposed by others, perhaps by cancelling your Netflix subscription or buying generic products. Under Monty's guidance you might also consider instructing your family members to cut *their* expenses or offer to do it for them. Does your son really need to play so much soccer? Finally, Monty might urge you to consider engaging in a distributive negotiation with some of your more expensive yet still-necessary service providers. Can Comcast bring down that escalating cable bill? Now please reset and reconsider the original problem: what would Getty urge you to do? Again, please consider before proceeding.

Getty would probably urge you to pick a transaction partner with whom you see some opportunities for mutual gain, say Comcast. You'd then engage that partner in an integrative negotiation immediately, doing things like anticipating and asking about their interests, sharing information about your own, separating the increasingly insistent person on the other end of the phone from the problem, and using objective standards. For example you might ask whether they have any promotions available for loyal customers like you, convey your interest in remaining a Comcast customer over the long term, enlist the representative's help in solving your budget problems, or mention the prevailing rates at alternative providers. Finally, please reconsider the original problem and ask yourself what Bart would suggest.

At this early stage of the process, having just identified a problem, Bart would essentially suggest that you're not ready to listen to Monty or Getty. While none of their advice is inherently bad or wrong, the bartering mindset (step 1) would urge you to apply the brakes and then back up. Before thinking about anyone or anything

in competitive terms – or engaging anyone in an integrative negotiation – you need to understand the problem a whole lot better: what
is your real need, and what else might you need to do to solve it?
Having asked those questions, you might realize your problem is
not costs or savings per se but salary. And it's not even the amount
of your salary – it's the timing. A large portion of your salary comes
in the form of a once-a-year bonus, which you obviously can't use
until you receive it (and can't rely on until you know its amount).
In the meantime, your accumulating bills create a big hole in your
bank account. Might you eventually ask your employer to consider
issuing the bonus in two instalments, or at least preview (and ideally commit to) its amount?

Beyond whatever you might need, the bartering mindset would
also urge you to consider what you are offering and could offer the
world. Since your employer is certainly relevant to the problem, what
value do you now or could you eventually deliver to your employer
if only the company helped with your cash flow? A willingness to
take on additional responsibilities, transfer to a new office that is
currently ramping up, or receive an even larger portion of your salary as a bonus if it could be issued in instalments? Just examples,
of course, but the point is that Monty's advice is not particularly
helpful for the fundamental problem, at least not now, and Getty's
potentially valuable advice is premature. Monty (and, to a lesser
extent, Getty) essentially takes the perceived problem and potential solution as given rather than matters to consider. In contrast,
the bartering mindset prompts you to actively consider whether the
stated problem is the real problem – or the obvious solution the right
solution. In the process you typically realize you're not quite ready
to negotiate – at least not until you understand your own needs
and offerings a whole lot better. In sum, the first step of the bartering mindset encourages you to file away Monty and Getty's advice
but first seek to understand yourself and the problem you're really
facing.

2. Understanding the Market (Steps 2–3, Chapter 4): Getting to Work

Your beloved car, a throwback to the Reagan administration, just decided to take its last breath. Since you work a few suburbs away, this amounts to a tremendous problem. Following step 1 of the bartering mindset, you dug behind the need for a car to discover the need to get to work in both the short and longer term (along with several measures you might need to take to do so), then gave some initial thought to what you might offer potential transaction partners in exchange. Having already defined your needs and offerings, what would Monty advise you to do? Please consider.

Monty would first remind you that your desire for a low-priced, fuel-efficient car (for example) conflicts with any salesperson's desire for a high price, particularly at the one dealer you plan to visit. Accordingly Monty might prompt you to plot out some distributive behaviors like lowballing the dealer, paying particular attention to the desired car's shortcomings, or demanding some concessions. Most likely Monty would also prepare you to haggle back and forth until you received an acceptable price. And now let's re-examine what Getty might suggest.

Most likely Getty would prompt you to visit a dealer and focus on a car that serves your interests particularly well. At the dealer, however, Getty would encourage you to take a different tack – namely to display many of the same behaviors that you did with Comcast in the example above. With respect to the car dealer, you might explore whether the salesperson wants to offer dealer financing, then suggest you could accept it if he gave you a price break. In other words, you'd exchange some information on your respective interests and priorities, finding a way to integrate your preferences, potentially through mutually beneficial trade-offs. And what would Bart suggest?

At this stage of the process Bart would again suggest that you're still not ready to negotiate – that you still need to do some thinking, particularly about the people who might solve your problem if only you solved theirs. Before engaging anyone in a negotiation, and after understanding your fundamental need to get to work in both the short and longer term, step 2 of the bartering mindset would suggest that you need to identify all the relevant parties who might help you, even if they don't involve a car. This would include your preferred car dealer but also all other dealers in the area, as well as anyone selling a car online or in person. And at least in the short term it might include some creative options for getting to work like carpooling, public transportation, Uber, car rental, or biking (coupled with an Airbnb close to the office).

Then step 3 of the bartering mindset would advise you to take the most realistic subset of these options and determine what the associated partners might need and be willing to offer. For example, didn't your co-worker recently complain about the morning traffic, saying she wishes she could work instead of wasting time driving? Crazy idea, but would she ever share her car if you offered to drive it while she works? Assuming she likes you, she'd probably agree to that in the short term. And didn't your HR representative recently mention that the company is about to pilot an eco-friendly transit program that provides monetary incentives to people who take public transportation? Could you sign up for the pilot, take the train, and perhaps earn some money toward the down payment on a car? Oh, and come to think of it, didn't you sign up for a special program at the insurance company that provides free rentals for two weeks after a breakdown? Should you give it a try in the short term? Insofar as this benefit increases your allegiance to the insurance company, they would probably be happy if you did.

In conclusion the bartering mindset does not assume you should see the world through a competitive lens or engage with any one party immediately in the spirit of cooperation. It assumes that you should first understand the landscape of individuals and organizations with whom you could partner, as well as their associated landscape of needs and offerings. While this certainly requires more work, it will almost certainly lead to better solutions – solutions well worth the effort for a big problem like the lack of a car.

3. Understanding Partnerships (Steps 4–5, Chapters 5–6): Kitchen Remodel

You and your spouse have slowly come to regard your kitchen as a disaster. Cabinet doors frequently break, there's barely enough counter space for a glass of milk, and your appliances are ancient. Following steps 1–3 of the bartering mindset, you've identified your need: to obtain a functional but not an extravagant new kitchen, and to participate in its design and possibly its construction without eating up all your time. You've given some initial thought to what you can offer: money as well as a bit of your own elbow grease and home repair expertise. You've also considered the various individuals and entities who might help, as well as what they might need and offer. For example you've identified two independent contractors as well as one full-service remodeling company who could coordinate the various subcontractors needed to complete the job. You've also considered coordinating the subcontractors yourself and doing most of the job yourself, with a little help from the local DIY. At this point what would Monty urge you to do? Please consider.

By now you probably see that Monty would urge you to think about the lowest-priced option and figure out how to lowball them further, potentially by making aggressive offers, mentioning your various alternatives, or electing to downgrade the quality of the cabinets. With one of the independent contractors, for example, Monty might encourage you to consider haggling down their commission rate or asking them to use the lowest grade of wood. And what would Getty suggest?

By now you can probably predict Getty's advice too: to select and start negotiating with whichever of the providers offers the most win-win potential. But unlike Monty, and as in the examples above, Getty would suggest being more open about your needs and ascertaining theirs. If you decided to talk to one of the contractors, perhaps you could explore whether they'd give you a deal if you did the work in a slower part of the year? Or if you talked to the full-service remodeling company, maybe you could explore the possibility of obtaining your dream cabinets for a markdown if you went with a preferred supplier? And for one final time, what would Bart suggest?

At this stage of the process (step 4), Bart would urge you to be much more systematic in deciding whom you approach, before negotiating with them. In particular, the bartering mindset would urge you to identify power partnerships. Among the five options, which would meet your needs most extensively and inexpensively? Either of the contractors or the coordinate-the-subcontractor strategies, perhaps, since all would result in a functional but non-extravagant kitchen and allow you to participate without consuming your every waking hour. And, among these options, which would allow you to satisfy your partners' needs most extensively and inexpensively? Perhaps the second contractor since he, unlike the first, expressed a keen interest in jobs costing less than $40,000 (like yours). Or the coordinate-the-subcontractors approach, as you would probably pay them more and be more flexible than a contractor. Following step 4 of the bartering mindset, you might decide that the second contractor and "coordination" approach offer the best prospect of power partnerships (though potentially substitutable power partnerships).

Finally, step 5 of the bartering mindset would prompt you to approach the relevant partners and cultivate the associated partnerships. For example, you might meet with the second contractor, as well as the set of subcontractors you'd engage under the "coordination" approach. In all meetings the conversation would go much as

Getty advised, but you'd now have a better sense that you're talking to the right people. In addition the conversations would benefit from a clearer structure focused on establishing trust, identifying the outlines of a power partnership, and devising the most powerful partnerships possible – along with an understanding that all parties have to "think it over" before deciding. In sum, Bart's bartering mindset would now show signs of convergence with Getty's advice. But Bart would also encourage you to apply Getty's advice to the right conversations, more conversations, and conversations focused on identifying power partnerships rather than "getting to yes" right away.

Concluding Thoughts

The bartering mindset, grounded in an old economic idea, offers a new and better way of thinking about our critical problems today. How can you start applying it to your own life? Since we've covered a lot of ground, I'll leave you with one final tool – a reminder of the key questions to ask while implementing each of the five steps. While far from a substitute for the preceding chapters (and far from exhaustive), I hope the list helps you remember the steps as you apply the bartering mindset to your own life:

Step 1 (Chapter 3): Deeply and Broadly Define Your Needs and Offerings

- Why do I need [my perceived need]?
  - o Answer(s) indicate my deep need.
- How do people like me generally satisfy [my deep need]? How could I, specifically, satisfy [my deep need]?
  - o Answers indicate my broader set of needs.
- What value do I provide to my current transaction partners?
  - o Answer indicates my deep offerings.

- What value could I provide to my current transaction partners?
  - o Answer indicates my broader set of offerings.

Steps 2–3 (Chapter 4): Map Out the Full Range of Transaction Partners and the Full Range of Their Possible Needs and Offerings

- Who else might help me satisfy my [deep and broad needs]? Who else might value my [deep and broad offerings]? Who else might help me to satisfy any of my needs or value any of my offerings?
  - o Answers indicate transaction partners.
- What value do [transaction partners] provide to me? What value could [transaction partners] provide to me?
  - o Answers indicate transaction partners' offerings.
- What do [transaction partners] generally need from people like me? What do these specific [transaction partners] need from me?
  - o Answers indicate transaction partners' needs.

Step 4 (Chapter 5): Anticipate the Most Powerful Set of Partnerships across the Market

- How could [transaction partners' offerings] satisfy my needs?
  - o Answer refines transaction partners' offerings.
- How could I satisfy [transaction partners' needs]?
  - o Answer refines my offerings.
- How well would [transaction partners' refined offerings] satisfy my needs? How many of my needs do [transaction partners] address? How completely do [transaction partners] address these needs?
  - o Answers indicate how extensively transaction partners satisfy my needs.

- How much would it cost me to provide [my refined offerings]?
  - o Answer indicates how expensive it is for me to satisfy transaction partners' needs.
- How well would [my refined offerings] meet [transaction partners' needs]?
  - o Answer indicates how extensively I satisfy transaction partners' needs.
- How much would it cost [transaction partners] to satisfy my needs?
  - o Answer indicates how expensive it is for transaction partners to satisfy my needs.
- What is the best set of partnerships?
  - o Answer indicates the most powerful set of partnerships across the market.

Step 5 (Chapter 6): Cultivate the Most Powerful Set of Partnerships across the Market

- What kind of challenges are you facing? Do you have any interest in [my refined offerings]?
  - o Answers confirm and clarify the transaction partner's needs.
- How could [my refined offerings] help with your needs? Can you think of any other ways I could help with your needs?
  - o Answers confirm and clarify the portion of the power partnership that benefits the transaction partner.
- Can you think of any ways that we might address my challenges with [my deep and broad needs]? Would you be open to offering [transaction partner's refined offerings]?
  - o Answers confirm and clarify the portion of the power partnership that benefits me.
- Can you think of any other ways we can help each other? Overall, how interested are you in the partnership we just discussed?
  - o Answers confirm and clarify the overall power partnership.

With that we've come to the end of the book. But for you I hope it's actually the beginning. I hope you're now mindful of the monetary mindset's risks, the bartering mindset's benefits, and the steps you can take to apply the bartering mindset to the monetary world. In particular I hope you see that solving big problems requires you to comprehensively understand your own needs and offerings, your many potential partners and theirs, and the partnerships that can powerfully unite you. If so, then I know you'll agree that a mostly forgotten mindset – the bartering mindset – promises better solutions to your most pressing problems. And now, happy trades to you.

NOTES

1. The Limits of the Monetary Mindset

1 J. Horowitz, "The United Fiasco: What We Know Now," CNN Money, 11 April 2017, https://money.cnn.com/2017/04/11/news/companies/united-48-hours-passenger/index.html; CBS/Reuters, "United Says It Won't Use Police with Bumped Passengers," CBSNews, 12 April 2017, https://www.cbsnews.com/news/united-man-dragged-off-plane-reviews-booking-police-policy/.

2 K.D. Vohs, M.L. Mead, and M.R. Goode, "The Psychological Consequences of Money," *Science* 314 (2006): 1154–6.

3 E.M. Caruso, K.D. Vohs, B. Baxter, and A. Waytz, "Mere Exposure to Money Increases Endorsement of Free-Market Systems and Social Inequality," *Journal of Experimental Social Psychology* 142 (2013): 301–16.

4 C. Humphrey, "Barter and Economic Disintegration," *Man* 20 (1985): 48–72.

5 R.E. Nisbett, K. Peng, I. Choi, and A. Norenzayan, "Culture and Systems of Thought: Holistic versus Analytic Cognition," *Psychological Review* 108 (2001): 291–310.

6 D.D. Rucker and A.D. Galinsky, "Growing beyond Growth: Why Multiple Mindsets Matter for Consumer Behavior," *Journal of Consumer Psychology* 26 (2016): 161.

7 C. Dweck, *Mindset: The New Psychology of Success* (New York: Random House, 2006).

8 F. Harinck and C.K.W. De Dreu, "Take a Break! Or Not? The Impact of Mindsets during Breaks on Negotiation Processes and Outcomes," *Journal of Experimental Social Psychology* 44 (2008): 397–404.

9 K.D. Vohs, M.L. Mead, and M.R. Goode, "The Psychological Consequences of Money," *Science* 314 (2006): 1154–6; K.D. Vohs, M.L. Mead, and M.R. Goode, "Merely Activating the Concept of Money Changes Personal and Interpersonal Behavior," *Current Directions in Psychological Science* 17 (2006): 208–12; F. Gino and L. Pierce, "The Abundance Effect: Unethical Behavior in the Presence of Wealth," *Organizational Behavior and Human Decision Processes* 109 (2009): 142–55; E. Sharma, N. Mazar, A.L. Alter, and D. Ariely, "Financial Deprivation Selectively Shifts Moral Standards and Compromises Moral Decisions," *Organizational Behavior and Human Decision Processes* 123 (2014): 90–100.

10 A. Gasiorowska, L.N. Chaplin, T. Zaleskiewicz, S. Wygrab, and K.D. Vohs, "Money Cues Increase Agency and Decrease Prosociality among Children: Early Signs of Market-Mode Behaviors," *Psychological Science* 27 (2016): 331–44.

11 R.H. Frank, T. Gilovich, and D.T. Regan, "Does Studying Economics Inhibit Cooperation?," *Journal of Economic Perspectives* 7 (1993): 159–71.

12 A.P. Fiske, "The Four Elementary Forms of Sociality: Framework for a Unified Theory of Social Relations," *Psychological Review 99*, no. 4 (1992): 689–723; K. Vohs, M.L. Mead, and M.R. Goode, "Merely Activating the Concept of Money Changes Personal and Interpersonal Behavior," *Current Directions in Psychological Science 17* (2006): 209.

13 Caruso et al., "Mere Exposure to Money"; S.E. DeVoe and S.S. Iyengar, "The Medium of Exchange Matters: What's Fair for Goods Is Unfair for Money," *Psychological Science* 21 (2010): 159–62.

14 B.C. Gunia, "On the Fiscal Cliff, Neither Side Should Compromise," *Baltimore Sun*, 5 December 2012, http://www.baltimoresun.com/news/opinion/oped/bs-ed-against-compromise-20121205-story.html.

15 D. Diaz, "Mexican President Cancels Meeting with Trump," CNN, 27 January 2017, https://www.cnn.com/2017/01/25/politics/mexico-president-donald-trump-enrique-pena-nieto-border-wall/.

16 B.C. Gunia, "On the Fiscal Cliff, Neither Side Should Compromise, *Baltimore Sun*, 5 December 2012, http://www.baltimoresun.com/news/opinion/oped/bs-ed-against-compromise-20121205-story.html.

17 L.L. Thompson, J. Wang, and B.C. Gunia, "Negotiation," *Annual Review of Psychology* 61 (2010): 491–515.

18 R. Fisher and W. Ury, *Getting to Yes: Negotiating Agreement without Giving In* (Boston: Houghton Mifflin, 1981); B.C. Gunia, J.M. Brett, A.

Nandkeolyar, and D. Kamdar, "Paying a Price: Culture, Trust, and Negotiation Consequences," *Journal of Applied Psychology* 96 (2011): 774–89; M.J. Kimmel, D.G. Pruitt, J.M. Magenau, E. Konar-Goldband, and P.J.D. Carnevale, "Effects of Trust, Aspiration, and Gender on Negotiation Tactics," *Journal of Personality and Social Psychology* 38 (1980): 9–22; D.G. Pruitt, *Negotiation Behavior* (New York: Academic, 1981); R.E. Walton, and R.B. McKersie, *A Behavioral Theory of Labor Negotiations* (New York: McGraw-Hill, 1965).

19 M. Bazerman and M.A. Neale, *Negotiating Rationally* (New York: Free Press, 1992); M. Bazerman, H.T. Magliozzi, and M.A. Neale, "Integrative Bargaining in a Competitive Market," *Organizational Behavior and Human Decision Processes* 35 (1985): 294–313; L. Thompson and T. DeHarpport, "Social Judgment, Feedback, and Interpersonal Learning in Negotiation," *Organizational Behavior and Human Decision Processes* 58 (1994): 327–45; L. Thompson and R. Hastie, "Social Perception in Negotiation," *Organizational Behavior and Human Decision Processes* 47 (1990): 98–123.

20 B.C. Gunia, R.I. Swaab, N. Sivanathan, and A.D. Galinsky, "The Remarkable Robustness of the First-Offer Effect: Across Culture, Power, and Issues," *Personality and Social Psychology Bulletin* 39 (2013): 1547–58.

21 Bazerman and Neale, *Negotiating Rationally*; Bazerman, Magliozzi, and Neale, "Integrative Bargaining in a Competitive Market"; Thompson and DeHarpport, "Social Judgment, Feedback, and Interpersonal Learning"; Thompson and Hastie, "Social Perception in Negotiation."

22 Gunia et al., "Paying a Price."

23 Kimmel et al., "Effects of Trust, Aspiration, and Gender."

24 Walton and McKersie, *Behavioral Theory of Labor Negotiations*.

25 Bazerman and Neale, *Negotiating Rationally*; Bazerman, Magliozzi, and Neale, "Integrative Bargaining in a Competitive Market"; C.K.W. De Dreu, S.L. Koole, and W. Steinel, "Unfixing the Fixed Pie: A Motivated Information-Processing Approach to Integrative Negotiation," *Journal of Personality and Social Psychology* 79 (2000): 975–87; Gunia et al., "Paying a Price"; Kimmel et al., "Effects of Trust, Aspiration, and Gender"; D.T. Kong, K.T. Dirks, and D.L. Ferrin, "Interpersonal Trust within Negotiations: Meta-analytic Evidence, Critical Contingencies, and Directions for Future Research," *Academy of Management Journal* 57 (2014): 1235–55; Pruitt, *Negotiation Behavior*; Thompson

and DeHarpport, "Social Judgment, Feedback, and Interpersonal
Learning"; Thompson and Hastie, "Social Perception in Negotiation."
26 K. Jensen, "Why Negotiators Still Aren't 'Getting to Yes,'" *Forbes*,
5 February 2013, https://www.forbes.com/sites/keldjensen/2013/02/
05/why-negotiators-still-arent-getting-to-yes/#212a32a92640.
27 G. Gentner, J. Loewenstein, and L. Thompson, "Learning and Transfer:
A General Role for Analogical Reasoning," *Journal of Education
Psychology* 95 (2003): 393–408; B. McAdoo and M. Manwaring,
"Teaching for Implementation: Designing Negotiation Curricula to
Maximize Long-Term Learning," *Negotiation Journal* 25 (2009): 195–215.
28 C.K.W. De Dreu, L.R. Weingart, and S. Kwon, "Influence of Social
Motives on Integrative Negotiations: A Meta-analytic Review and Test
of Two Theories," *Journal of Personality and Social Psychology* 78 (2000):
889–905.
29 L. Anderlini and H. Sabourian, "Some Notes on the Economics of
Barter, Money, and Credit," in *Barter, Exchange, and Value*, ed. C.
Humphrey and S. Hugh-Jones, 75–106 (New York: Cambridge
University Press, 1994).
30 R. Belk, "You Are What You Can Access: Sharing and Collaborative
Consumption Online," *Journal of Business Research* 67 (2014): 1595–1600;
J.B. Schor and C.J. Fitzmaurice, "Collaborating and Connecting:
The Emergence of the Sharing Economy," in *Handbook on Research
on Sustainable Consumption*, ed. L. Reisch and J. Thogersen, 410–35
(Cheltenham, UK: Edward Elgar, 2015).
31 https://www.couchsurfing.com.
32 B.S. Fisher and K.M. Harte, *Barter in the World Economy* (New York:
CBS Educational and Professional Publishing, 1985); G.T. Hammond,
Countertrade, Offsets, and Barter in International Political Economy (New
York: St Martin's, 1990); S.J. Khoury, "Countertrade: Forms, Motives,
Pitfalls, and Negotiation Requisites," *Journal of Business Research*
12 (1984): 257–70; D. Marin and M. Schnitzer, *Contracts in Trade and
Transition* (Cambridge, MA: MIT Press, 2002); also H. Smith, "Euros
Discarded as Impoverished Greeks Resort to Bartering," *Guardian*, 2
January 2013, https://www.theguardian.com/world/2013/jan/02/
euro-greece-barter-poverty-crisis; M. Mir, "In Hard-Hit Spain,
Bartering Becomes a Means of Getting By," *USA Today*, 20 February
2013, https://www.usatoday.com/story/news/world/2013/02/20/
spanish-bartering/1894365/; G. Cerioli, "Argentina: Bartering –

Here to Stay?," Inter Press Service, 9 April 2009, http://www
.ipsnews.net/2009/04/argentina-bartering-ndash-here-to-stay/;
http://www.theguardian.com/commentisfree/2013/jan/04/
barter-exchange-goods-recession.

33 Humphrey, "Barter and Economic Disintegration."
34 K. Roberts, *The Origins of Business, Money, and Markets* (New York: Columbia University Press, 2011).
35 Humphrey, "Barter and Economic Disintegration."
36 Ibid.
37 W. Brough, *The Natural Law of Money* (New York: G.P. Putnam's Sons, 1894).
38 N. Thomas, "Politicized Values: The Cultural Dynamics of Peripheral Exchange," in *Barter, Exchange, and Value*, ed. C. Humphrey and S. Hugh-Jones, 21–41 (New York: Cambridge University Press, 1994).
39 Roberts, *Origins of Business, Money, and Markets*, 21.
40 Humphrey, "Barter and Economic Disintegration," 60.
41 Gasiorowska et al., "Money Cues Increase Agency and Decrease Prosociality"; DeVoe and Iyengar, "Medium of Exchange Matters."
42 D. Wagenvoord and A. Pervez, *No Cash? No Problem! How to Get What You Want in Business and Life, without Using Cash* (New York: Morgan James Publishing, 2013). Also see K.S. Hoffman and S.D. Dalin, *The Art of Barter: How to Trade for Almost Anything* (New York: Skyhorse Publishing, 2010).

2. The Bartering Mindset

1 K. MacDonald, *One Red Paperclip: How to Trade a Red Paperclip for a House* (Austin, TX: River Grove Books, 2007).
2 Humphrey and Hugh-Jones, *Barter, Exchange, and Value*.
3 R.W. Clower, ed., *Monetary Theory* (Harmondsworth, UK: Penguin, 1969); P. Einzig, *Primitive Money in Its Ethnological, Historical and Economic Aspects* (London: Eyre & Spottiswoode, 2014); W.S. Jevons, *Money and the Mechanism of Exchange* (London: Appleton, 1885).
4 Humphrey, "Barter and Economic Disintegration."
5 Humphrey and Hugh-Jones, *Barter, Exchange, and Value*; G.O. Faure, "Dumb Barter: A Seminal Form of Negotiation," *Negotiation Journal* 27 (2011): 403–18.

6 N. Thomas, "Politicized Values: The Cultural Dynamics of Peripheral Exchange," in Humphrey and Hugh-Jones, *Barter, Exchange, and Value*, 21–41.
7 Jevons, *Money and the Mechanism of Exchange*, 3.
8 R.A. Jones, "The Origin and Development of Media of Exchange," *Journal of Political Economy* 84 (1976): 757–76.
9 Jevons, *Money and the Mechanism of Exchange*; Jones, "Origin and Development of Media of Exchange."
10 Anderlini and Sabourian, "Some Notes on the Economics of Barter, Money, and Credit."
11 Jones, "Origin and Development of Media of Exchange."
12 Humphrey and Hugh-Jones, *Barter, Exchange, and Value*.
13 Ibid.
14 Ibid.
15 Humphrey, "Barter and Economic Disintegration"; Khoury, "Countertrade."
16 Anderlini and Sabourian, "Some Notes on the Economics of Barter, Money, and Credit.
17 Humphrey, "Barter and Economic Disintegration," 64.
18 Faure, "Dumb Barter."
19 Ibid.; Humphrey, "Barter and Economic Disintegration," 64.
20 Humphrey and Hugh-Jones, *Barter, Exchange, and Value*.
21 Gunia et al., "Paying a Price."
22 Humphrey and Hugh-Jones, *Barter, Exchange, and Value*; T. Yamagishi and M. Yamagishi, "Trust and Commitment in the United States and Japan," *Motivation and Emotion* 18, no. 2 (1994): 129–66.

3. Step 1: Deeply and Broadly Define Your Needs and Offerings

1 M. Farrand, *The Framing of the Constitution of the United States* (New Haven, CT: Yale University Press, 1913).
2 The Connecticut Compromise was not a compromise but an integrative tradeoff. I use the word *compromise* to reflect the name usually applied to this historical event, even though the name is inaccurate from the perspective of negotiation research.
3 Some of many examples: Bazerman, Magliozzi, and Neale, "Integrative Bargaining in a Competitive Market"; Gunia et al.,

"Paying a Price"; Kimmel et al., "Effects of Trust, Aspiration, and Gender"; Pruitt, *Negotiation Behavior*.

4 Some of many examples: Bazerman and Neale, *Negotiating Rationally*; Kimmel et al., "Effects of Trust, Aspiration, and Gender"; D.G. Pruitt and S.A. Lewis, "Development of Integrative Solutions in Bilateral Negotiation," *Journal of Personality and Social Psychology* 31 (1975): 621–33; L.R. Weingart, L.L. Thompson, M.H. Bazerman, and J.S. Carroll, "Tactical Behavior and Negotiation Outcomes," *International Journal of Conflict Management* 1 (1990): 7–31.

5 Fisher and Ury, *Getting to Yes*.

6 Aristotle and L. Brown, *Nichomachean Ethics* (Oxford: Oxford University Press, 2009).

7 Fisher and Ury, *Getting to Yes*.

8 E.M. Rasiel and P.N. Friga, *The McKinsey Mind: Understanding and Implementing the Problem-Solving Tools and Management Techniques of the World's Top Strategic Consulting Firm* (New York: McGraw-Hill, 2002).

9 Ibid.

10 P.H. Kim and A.R. Fragale, "Choosing the Path to Bargaining Power: An Empirical Comparison of BATNAs and Contributions in Negotiation," *Journal of Applied Psychology* 90 (2005): 373–81.

11 A.D. Galinsky, W.M. Maddux, D. Gilin, and J.B. White, "Why It Pays to Get Inside the Head of Your Opponent: The Differential Effects of Perspective-Taking and Empathy in Negotiations," *Psychological Science* 19 (2008): 378–84.

4. Steps 2–3: Map Out the Full Range of Transaction Partners and the Full Range of Their Possible Needs and Offerings

1 N. Casey, "Colombia's Congress Approves Peace Accord with FARC," *New York Times*, 30 November 2016, https://www.nytimes .com/2016/11/30/world/americas/colombia-farc-accord-juan -manuel-santos.html?_r=0; C. Kraul, "Colombia Has a Peace Deal, but Can It Can Be Implemented?," *Los Angeles Times*, 13 March 2017, http://www.latimes.com/world/mexico-americas/ la-fg-colombia-peace-outlook-2017-story.html; A. Vitali, "Trump Welcomes Colombia's President to White House," NBC News, 18 May 2017, http://www.nbcnews.com/politics/white-house/ trump-welcomes-colombia-s-president-white-house-n761606.

2 Fisher and Ury, *Getting to Yes*.
3 D.A. Lax and J.K. Sebenius, *3-D Negotiation: Powerful Tools to Change the Game in Your Most Important Negotiations* (Boston: Harvard Business School Publishing, 2006).
4 Galinsky et al., "Why It Pays to Get Inside the Head of Your Opponent."

5. Step 4: Anticipate the Most Powerful Set of Partnerships across the Market

1 S. Wicersham and D. Van Natta Jr, "The Wow Factor," ESPN, 02/11 2016, www.espn.com/espn/feature/story/_/id/14752649/the-real -story-nfl-owners-battle-bring-football-back-los-angeles; S. Farmer and N. Fenno, "A Behind-the-Scenes Look at a Rams' Proposal the NFL couldn't Refuse," *Los Angeles Times*, 16 January 2016, www.latimes .com/sports/nfl/la-sp-nfl-la-tick-tock-20160117-story.html.
2 Pruitt and Lewis, "Development of Integrative Solutions in Bilateral Negotiation."
3 Brett, *Negotiating Globally*; also M. Rowe, "Negotiating for Jobs, Salaries – and Everything Else) Prepare, Prepare, Prepare" (Ombuds Office, Massachusetts Institute of Technology, 2001), https://ombud .mit.edu/sites/default/files/documents/prepare_prepare_prepare2001 .pdf.
4 R.E. Freeman, *Strategic Management: A Stakeholder Approach* (Boston: Pitman, 1984).
5 Since you don't know as much about your partners' deep needs as you do about your own, though, you wouldn't necessarily have to map each of your offerings onto your partners' deep needs.

6. Step 5: Cultivate the Most Powerful Set of Partnerships across the Market

1 A. Alkhatib, "Advantage of an A-B InBev/SABMiller Merger Lies in Emerging Markets," Euromonitor International, 13 January 2015, https://blog.euromonitor.com/2015/01/advantage-of-an -a-b-inbevsabmiller-merger-lies-in-emerging-markets.html; N. Rossolillo, "How Atria Will Benefit from the AB InBev-SABMiller

Merger," Motley Fool, 7 October 2016, https://www.fool.com/
investing/2016/10/07/how-altria-will-benefit-from-the-abinbev
-sabmiller.aspx; Trefis Team, "How the Potential AB InBev-SABMiller
Deal Focuses on Aftrica," *Forbes*, 15 December 2015, https://www
.forbes.com/sites/greatspeculations/2015/12/15/how-the
-potential-ab-inbev-sabmiller-deal-focuses-on-africa/#5f58aa9d1393;
Trefis Team, "AB InBev and SABMiller Merger Focuses on Markets
outside the U.S.," *Forbes*, 16 November 2015, https://www.forbes
.com/sites/greatspeculations/2015/11/16/ab-inbev-and-sabmiller
-merger-focuses-on-markets-outside-the-u-s/#47ee63bf4713; J. Chew,
"These Are All the Beers Combined ABInBev-SABMiller Would
Brew," *Fortune*, 16 September 2015, http://fortune.com/2015/09/16/
sabmiller-ab-inbev-beer-merger/; J. Cosgrove, "Hold My Beer: An
Analysis of the AB InBev/SABMiller Merger," Juristat, 17 August
2016, https://blog.juristat.com/2016/8/16/hold-my-beer-an
-analysis-of-the-ab-inbevsabmiller-merger.

2 Gunia et al., "Paying a Price."
3 J.K. Butler, "Trust Expectations, Information Sharing, Climate of Trust,
   and Negotiation Effectiveness and Efficiency, *Group & Organization
   Management* 24 (1999): 217–38; Gunia et al., "Paying a Price"; Kong,
   Dirks, and Ferrin, "Interpersonal Trust within Negotiations."
4 B.C. Gunia, J.M. Brett, and A. Nandkeolyar, "In Global Negotiations,
   It's All about Trust," *Harvard Business Review* (December 2012): 4.
5 Humphrey and Hugh-Jones, *Barter, Exchange, and Value.*
6 Gunia et al., "Paying a Price."
7 L. Huang and J.K. Murnighan, "What's in a Name? Subliminally
   Activating Trusting Behavior," *Organizational Behavior and Human
   Decision Processes* 111 (2010): 62–70.
8 M. Morris, J. Nadler, T. Kurtzberg, and L. Thompson, "Schmooze or
   Lose: Social Friction and Lubrication in E-mail Negotiations," *Group
   Dynamics: Theory, Research, and Practice* 6 (2002): 89.
9 E. Meyer, *The Culture Map: Breaking through the Invisible Boundaries of
   Global Business* (Philadelphia: Public Affairs, 2014).
10 Kong, Dirks, and Ferrin, "Interpersonal Trust within Negotiations."
11 A.W. Gouldner, "The Norm of Reciprocity: A Preliminary Statement,"
   American Sociological Review 25 (1960): 161–78.
12 R.K. Merton, "The Self-Fulfilling Prophecy," *Antioch Review* 8 (1948):
   193–210.

13 M. Humphreys, "Strategic Ratification," *Public Choice* 132 (2007): 191–208.
14 R.S. Burt, R*Brokerage and Closure: An Introduction to Social Capital (Clarendon Lectures in Management Studies)* (Oxford: Oxford University Press, 2005).

7. Integrating the Bartering and Monetary Mindsets

1 "Election 2010: First Hung Parliament in UK for Decades," BBC, 7 May 2010, http://news.bbc.co.uk/2/hi/8667071.stm; "Cameron and Clegg Set Out 'Radical' Policy Programme," BBC, 20 May 2010, http://news.bbc.co.uk/2/hi/uk_news/politics/8693535.stm; "Election 2010 Timeline: How Coalition Was Agreed," BBC, 13 May 2010, http://news.bbc.co.uk/2/hi/uk_news/politics/election_2010/8677552.stm; B. Wright, "Election 2015: Manual Sets Out the Rules for a Hung Parliament," BBC, 26 April 2015, https://www.bbc.com/news/election-2015-32475098; "Servants of the People," *Economist*, 27 May 2010, https://www.economist.com/node/16219311; L. Maer, "A Hung Parliament: Key Issues for the 2010 Parliament," n.d., https://www.parliament.uk/business/publications/research/key-issues-for-the-new-parliament/the-new-parliament/a-hung-parliament/.
2 "Servants of the People," *Economist*, 27 May 2010, http://www.economist.com/britain/2010/05/27/servants-of-the-people.
3 Humphrey and Hugh-Jones, *Barter, Exchange, and Value.*
4 Kimmel et al., "Effects of Trust, Aspiration, and Gender."
5 Weingart et al., "Tactical Behavior and Negotiation Outcomes."
6 Ibid.
7 Ibid.
8 Brett, *Negotiating Globally.*
9 Ibid.
10 Treating money in this way also means that any negotiation with a monetary price can be seen as a multi-issue negotiation.
11 A.A. Benton, B. Liebling, and H.H. Kelley, "Effects of Extremity of Offers and Concession Rate on Outcomes of Bargaining," *Journal of Personality and Social Psychology* 24 (1972): 73–83; J.M. Chertkoff and M. Conley, "Opening Offer and Frequency of Concession as Bargaining Strategies," *Journal of Personality and Social Psychology* 7 (1967): 181–5;

A.D. Galinsky and T. Mussweiler, "First Offers as Anchors: The Role of Perspective-Taking and Negotiator Focus," *Journal of Personality and Social Psychology* 81 (2001): 657–69; Gunia et al., "Remarkable Robustness of the First-Offer Effect"; R.M. Liebert, W.P. Smith, and J.H. Hill, "Effects of Information and Magnitude of Initial Offer on Interpersonal Negotiation," *Journal of Experimental Social Psychology* 4 (1968): 431–41; G.A. Yukl, "Effects of Situational Variables and Opponent Concessions on a Bargainer's Perception, Aspirations, and Concessions," *Journal of Personality and Social Psychology* 29 (1974): 227–36.

12 Gunia at al., "Paying a Price."

13 W.L. Adair and J.M. Brett, "The Negotiation Dance: Time, Culture, and Behavioral Sequences in Negotiation," *Organization Science* 16 (2005): 33–51.

14 G.J. Leonardelli, J. Gu, G. McRuer, A.D. Galinsky, and V. Medvec, "Negotiating with a Velvet Hammer: Multiple Equivalent Simultaneous Offers," Working paper, 2016.

15 Ibid.

16 D. Malhotra and M.H. Bazerman, *Negotiation Genius: How to Overcome Obstacles and Achieve Brilliant Results at the Bargaining Table and Beyond* (New York: Bantam, 2008).

8. Objections to the Bartering Mindset

1 M. Gross, *House of Outrageous Fortune: Fifteen Central Park West, the World's Most Powerful Address* (New York: Altria, 2014). Also M. Gross, "Hotel Hermit Got $17M to Make Way for 15 Central Park West," *New York Post*, 2 March 2014, https://nypost.com/2014/03/02/hotel-hermit-got-17m-to-make-way-for-15-central-park-west/.

2 A. Lytle, J.M. Brett, and D. Shapiro, "The Strategic Use of Interests, Rights, and Power to Resolve Disputes," *Negotiation Journal* 15 (1999): 31–52.

3 Ibid.

4 B.C. Gunia, J.M. Brett, and A. Nandkeolyar, "Trust Me, I'm a Negotiator: Using Cultural Universals to Negotiate Effectively, Globally," *Organizational Dynamics* 43 (2014): 27–36.

5 J.M. Brett, *Paying a Price: How to Negotiate Deals, Resolve Disputes, and Make Decisions across Cultural Boundaries*, 3rd ed. (San Francisco: Jossey-Bass, 2014).
6 Meyer, *Culture Map*.
7 M. Morris, J. Nadler, T. Kurtzberg, and L. Thompson, "Schmooze or Lose: Social Friction and Lubrication in E-mail Negotiations," *Group Dynamics: Theory, Research, and Practice* 6 (2002): 89–100.
8 Gunia et al., "Paying a Price."
9 Adair and Brett, "Negotiation Dance."
10 J.C. Magee and A.D. Galinsky, "Social Hierarchy: The Self-Reinforcing Nature of Power and Status," *Academy of Management Annals* 2 (2008): 351–98.

9. Conclusions and Applications

1 A. Jardine, "The North Face Teams with Spotify to Release a Track That You Can Hear Only if It's Raining," AdAge, 13 March 2017, http://creativity-online.com/work/the-north-face-seek-no-shelter/51242; L. Plaugic, "Spotify Will Only Let You Listen to This Song If It's Raining," https://www.theverge.com/platform/amp/2017/3/13/14908236/spotify-rain-geotargeting-white-denim-north-face-song; J. Beer, "Spotify and the North Face Collaborate to Make a Song Only Available in the Rain," Fast Company, 13 March 2017, https://www.fastcompany.com/3068935/spotify-and-the-north-face-collaborate-to-make-a-song-only-available-in-the-rain; L. Westcott, "Spotify Releases White Denim Song to Be Streamed in Rainy Areas Only," *Newsweek*, 13 March 2017, https://www.newsweek.com/spotify-white-denim-rainy-areas-climatune-567305; North Face, "The North Face Invites You to 'Seek No Shelter' with the Launch of Apex Flex GTX Jacket," Cision PR Newswire, 13 March 2017, https://www.prnewswire.com/news-releases/the-north-face-invites-you-to-seek-no-shelter-with-launch-of-apex-flex-gtx-jacket-300422176.html; M. Lewis, "White Denim and North Face Made a Rainy Day Anthem," Fader, 13 March 2017, https://www.thefader.com/2017/03/13/north-face-white-denim-collab-launch-apex-flex-gtx/.

INDEX

AA (Alcoholics Anonymous)
  group, 108–9
Africa, 137
agreements. *See* deals
alter egos. *See* Bart; Getty; Monty
Altria, 137, 138
Anheuser-Busch InBev, acquisition
  of SABMiller, 136–8
anthropological research, bartering,
  34–5
Articles of Confederation (U.S.), 54
assumptions: in distributive and
  integrative behaviors, 14; own
  needs and, 5; trustworthiness,
  142. *See also* five assumptions
  (bartering mindset; monetary
  mindset)

Bart, 58, 62, 178, 205, 206–7; on
  deals, 162; on identifying power
  partnerships, 109, 208–9, 211; on
  understanding partners, 86
bartering: anthropological research
  on/psychological effects of,
  34–5; compared with monetary
  transactions, 33–4; definition

and "sharing economy," 18;
  double coincidence of wants
  and, 34, 50; Kyle MacDonald
  project, 29–31; multi-partner,
  38–9; as "primitive," 19–20,
  34; psychology of, 20, 50;
  settings for, 18–19; societies, 33.
  See also bartering mindset; five
  assumptions (bartering mindset)
bartering economies, 31, 32–5,
  36, 46; critical features of, 40–1;
  double coincidence of wants
  in, 203; own needs in, 43.
  See also bartering mindset; five
  assumptions (bartering mindset)
bartering mindset, 203; benefits,
  198; compared with monetary
  mindset, 45–6, 49; creating value,
  100; integrative negotiation
  behaviors and, 20, 25; money
  and, 187; negotiations and,
  21–2; objections to, 183–200;
  problems as opportunities,
  190–1. *See also* five assumptions
  (bartering mindset); five-step
  process (bartering mindset);

mindsets: integration of; *under*
  job negotiation exercises
beer market, 136–7
benefits, 138; bartering mindset,
  198; high/low of partners, 120,
  124–5, 129; MESOs, 173–5;
  multiple partners, 197, 198;
  mutual, 118, 148, 150, 155, 170,
  193; trade, 111, 114, 121–3, 126–8,
  132, 134. *See also* costs
Bernsen, Corbin, 30
best-case scenarios, 165
border wall, Mexico-U.S., 11–12
bottom lines 176–7, 179
British Parliament, coalition
  negotiations, 157–9
Brown, Gordon, 157
business viability, 63–9, 76, 94, 96,
  165, 186
buyers, 36–8, 45, 49

Cameron, David, 157, 158, 172
case studies: Anheuser-Busch
  InBev acquisition, 136–8;
  Colombian peace deal, 82–4;
  Connecticut Compromise,
  54–5; Kyle MacDonald trading
  project, 29–31; Mexico-U.S.
  border wall conflict, 11–12; NFL
  LA teams relocation agreement,
  104–7; North Face marketing
  campaign, 201–2; Sukenik-NYC
  relocation package, 182–3; Tory–
  Lib Dems coalition negotiations,
  157–9; United Airlines and David
  Dao, 3–4
categories, mutually exclusive,
  66–8. *See also* deductive approach

challenges, 145, 147, 153, 214
cigarette market, 137, 138
Clegg, Nick, 157, 158, 172
coalitions, 157–9
Colombian peace deal, 82–4
community: as market, 19, 142;
  promoting healthier, 67–8, 75–6, 89,
  108–9, 118, 130; relationships, 163
complements, 129. *See also*
  relationships: six types of
compromises, 9, 10, 45, 158; 50:50,
  172; dissatisfactory, 12, 53, 159,
  166–7; double coincidence of
  wants and, 46; Mexico-U.S.
  border wall, 11, 12
concessions, 158
concluding (discussion stage 5),
  149–50, 153
Connecticut Compromise (U.S.), 55
Conservative (Tory) party (U.K.),
  157–9
Constitutional Convention (U.S.),
  54–5, 71
conversations: goals, 141;
  language, 150; multi-issue, 169;
  for partnerships, 138, 211–12;
  purpose of, 143; redirecting,
  147–8; reiteration in, 168. *See also*
  discussions
Cooper, Alice, 30
costs, 66, 138, 161, 170; assessing,
  119–20; high/low of partners,
  120, 124–5, 129, 148; managing,
  189; mutual, 118, 150; opportunity,
  197, 198; of providing offerings,
  214; reducing, 62, 64–5, 67–9,
  75–6, 89, 131; relational, 193;
  time, 197, 198; trade, 111, 114,

121–3, 126–8, 132, 134. *See also* benefits

Couchsurfing (website), 18

counteroffers, 170, 171

counterparts, 61, 180, 193; negotiation, 73–4, 195; single, 184–5; unreceptive, 193–4. *See also* negotiation(s)

cultural differences, 195–6

customers, 72, 75. *See also* partners, transaction

Dao, David, 3–4

deals, 141, 143; advantageous terms, 160, 179; Bart and Getty on, 162; criterion for, 176–7; integrative negotiation behaviors and, 164; MIOs and, 168, 172; mutually beneficial, 154, 202; set of potential, 106, 164; terms, 160

deductive approach, 96; as complementary to inductive approach, 66; MECE categories and, 65, 67–8

defining deeply and broadly. *See under* needs; needs and offerings; offerings

demands, 159; in MIOs, 169; Monty on, 84–5

developers, NYC, 182–3

diminishing returns, 130. *See also* relationships: six types of

discussions: five-stage process, 141–50, 153; limitations, 109; of own situation, 147; as source of information, 111; suppliers initiating, 189–90; terms, 150. *See also* conversations

disputes, negotiation, 185–6

distributive negotiation behaviors, 100, 108, 168, 179, 205, 208; assumptions, 14; claiming value, 160, 162, 171; definition, 13–14; as disadvantageous, 15, 16, 60; encouraged by monetary mindset, 24–5, 69–70, 203; five assumptions (monetary mindset) and, 16; integrative behaviors and, 13–17, 203; MESOs and, 174; MIOs and, 169, 171; rejected, 57; SIOs as, 167. *See also* five assumptions (monetary mindset); monetary mindset; Monty

diversity of commodities, 41–2

double coincidence of wants, 37, 39, 40, 62; bartering and, 34, 50; in bartering economies, 203; compromise and, 46; difficulty of, 38; diversity of commodities and, 41–2; market and, 43; mutually beneficial trades and, 45

drug traffickers (Colombia), 83

East Asia, 195

economies, 130. *See also* relationships: six types of

Economist, 159

educated guesses, 112; needs and offerings, 92–3, 110; offerings, 71; potential partners, 87, 109, 120, 124; power partnerships, 140

empathy, 74

employees, 72, 75. *See also* partners, transaction

essentials, 130. *See also* relationships: six types of

EU (European Union), 158
Europe, 158, 159
exercises. *See* job negotiation exercises
external world, 132; needs
    and offerings, 196; own
    understanding of, 86, 89, 120,
    178; as partners, 97; transaction
    partners' understanding of, 83

FARC (Revolutionary Armed
    Forces of Colombia), 82–4
feedback, constructive, 145
final good, 64
financial outlook, long-term, 64
first offer effect, 171
five assumptions (bartering
    mindset), 23, 35, 36–45, 46,
    47, 50; assumption 1, 36–8,
    51–2; assumption 2, 38–9,
    52; assumption 3, 39–40, 52;
    assumption 4, 40–3, 53;
    assumption 5, 43–5, 53; in context
    of real job, 51. *See also* bartering
    mindset
five assumptions (monetary
    mindset), 5, 7–9, 11, 26–8, 35, 165;
    distributive behaviors and, 16;
    as harmful, 9–10; Mexico-U.S.
    border wall conflict and, 11–12.
    See also distributive negotiation
    behaviors; monetary mindset;
    Monty
five-stage process (discussions)
    141–50, 153
five-step process (bartering
    mindset), 23, 47, 50, 198, 204; key
    questions, 212–14; understanding
    and, 47, 202

fixed-pie view, 202, 203. *See also*
    monetary mindset
free-market competition, 6–7

Getting to Yes (book), 22, 57, 60, 69;
    Forbes's commentary on, 15, 16.
    See also Getty
Getty, 57, 58, 61, 211; on deals,
    162; on mutual interests, 97,
    139–40; integrative negotiation
    behaviors and, 85–6, 108, 178,
    205, 206, 208. *See also* integrative
    negotiation behaviors
goals: aggressive, 159; common,
    141, 144, 155; conversation/
    negotiation, 141
goods and services, 18, 33–4, 37,
    39–40, 71; as payment, 48; values,
    41
guessing. *See* educated guesses

House of Representatives (U.S.),
    55, 71

incentives, monetary, 3, 4
inductive approach, 65, 96; as
    complementary to deductive
    approach/definition, 66
information: exchange, 14, 61, 159,
    208; social, 195; surfacing, 154.
    See also open-information sharing
integration. *See under* mindsets
integrative negotiation behaviors,
    22, 57–8, 61–2, 76, 85–6, 141, 206; as
    advantageous, 15; assumptions/
    definition, 14; bartering mindset
    and, 20, 25; creating value, 160;
    deals and, 164; difficulty of,

16–17; distributive behaviors and, 13–17, 203; MIOs as, 168; for problem solving, 24; trust-building as, 14, 61. *See also* Getty

interaction, multiple partners, 38–9

interdependencies, 151–2, 154, 156; six categories of, 152

interests: common, 142, 159, 214; culture and, 195; Getty on mutual, 97, 139–40; respective, 61

introducing (discussion stage 1), 141–3, 153

job negotiation exercises: bartering mindset and (chap. 2), 50–3; integrating two mindsets and (chap. 7), 179–81; monetary mindset and (chap. 1), 25–8; step 1 and (chap. 3), 78–81; steps 2–3 and (chap. 4), 101–3; step 4 and (chap. 5), 133–5; step 5 and (chap. 6), 154–6

Keith's farm, 35–45

key points summaries: chap. 1, 24–5; chap. 2, 50; chap. 3, 77; chap. 4, 100–1; chap. 5, 132–3; caph. 6, 153–4; chap. 7, 179

key questions: step 1 (chap. 3), 77, 212–13; steps 2–3 (chap. 4), 100, 213; step 4 (chap. 5), 131–2, 213–14; step 5 (chap. 6), 153, 212–14

LA. *See* Los Angeles

Labor party (U.K.), 157

Latin America, 195

Liberal Democrats (Lib Dems; U.K.), 157–9

logic trees, 64–5, 67, 68, 78, 79, 80

Los Angeles (LA), NFL teams relocation, 104–7

loyalty, 192

MacDonald, Kyle, trading project, 29–31

mapping out, 101; transaction partners, 93–5, 96–9, 102, 213

market(s): absence of prices, 40–1; beer, 136–7; broader, 89; cigarette, 137, 138; community as, 19, 142; double coincidence of wants and, 43; as solution, 99, 131; understanding, 40, 43, 208–10

"market-pricing orientation," 6–7

MECE (mutually exclusive, collectively exhaustive) categories, 66–8; definition, 65. *See also* needs: defining own broadly

MESOs (multiple equivalent simultaneous offers), 178, 179, 180–1, 185, 190; benefits, 173–6; definition, 172; disadvantages, 175–6; implicit, 175; method and MIOs within, 173, 174–5; needs and offerings in, 195

Mexico, border wall conflict, 11–12

MillerCoors, 137

mindsets, 205; definition, 6; important needs and, 10; integration of, 159–60, 170, 171–2, 174, 178, 179–81; trusting, 142. *See also* bartering mindset; monetary mindset

MIOs (multi-issue offers), 171–2, 178, 179, 180–1, 185, 190;

definition and features, 168–70; demands and offerings in, 169; within MESOs, 173, 174–5; needs and offerings in, 195; responses to, 170

monetary incentives, 3, 4

monetary mindset, 59–60, 69–70, 205; compared with bartering mindset, 45–6, 49; definition, 4, 202; encouraging distributive behaviors, 17, 162; inadequacy of, 28; job negotiation exercise and, 25–8; link between money and, 47–50; needs and, 8–9, 12, 17; negotiation and, 13; in organizational and political problems, 10–12; politics and, 11–13. *See also* distributive negotiation behaviors; five assumptions (monetary mindset); mindsets: integration of; Monty

monetary transactions, 4–5, 31; benefits/psychological effects, 5; compared with bartering, 33–4; eliciting monetary mindset, 50; with one-time partner, 187–8; satisfying needs and problems, 24

money: bartering mindset and, 187; exposure to and psychological effects of, 6–7; link between monetary mindset and, 47–50; as payment, 48; as solution, 202

Monty, 57, 58, 59–60, 107–8, 210; conflict and, 178; on demands, 84–5; distributive view and, 162, 205, 206, 208; on single-minded counterpart, 97, 139; SIOs and, 167. *See also* distributive negotiation behaviors; five assumptions (monetary mindset); monetary mindset

multi-issue offers. *See* MIOs

multiple equivalent simultaneous offers. *See* MESOs

National Football League. *See* NFL

needs: assumptions and own, 5; bartering economy and own, 43; conveying mutual, 144, 159, 211; deep vs original, 79; defining own broadly, 63, 65, 73; defining own deeply, 63–4; defining own deeply and broadly, 67, 68–70, 76, 84, 88; as impetus for offerings, 94; interrelated, 46; meeting extensively and inexpensively, 111, 114, 118, 124, 131, 149, 211; mindsets and important, 10; monetary mindset and, 8–9, 12, 17; own, 36–8, 41, 52, 62–3, 147–8, 207; partners addressing, 103, 118–19, 124–5, 131–2, 133–5; partners', 90, 98–9, 101, 124–5, 145–7, 153, 190; questions about partners', 96–7; for revenue, 144–5, 147; serving other needs, 68–9; surfacing, 144–5, 155; understanding own, 63, 65, 76, 189; understanding partners', 44. *See also* deductive approach; inductive approach; MECE categories; needs and offerings; questions: "how"; questions: "why"

needs and offerings, 115–18, 121–3, 126–8; defining deeply and broadly, 55, 77, 78–81, 212–13;

diverse, 38, 39, 41–2; own, 102,
75, 83, 140, 183, 208; partners', 47,
102–3, 196–7, 209, 213; potential
partners', 91–100; respective, 43–4,
52–3, 62, 131–2, 161, 193, 213–14;
understanding own, 37, 38
negotiating power, 71–2
New Jersey Plan, 54
New York City (NYC), Sukenik
relocation package, 182–3
NFL (National Football League),
LA teams relocation, 104–7, 124
Nobel Committee, 83
No Cash? No Problem! (book), 21
North Face marketing campaign,
201–2
notes, meeting, 149–50
NYC. *See* New York City

Oakland Raiders, LA relocation,
104–6
Obama, Barack, 83
objectives, questionable, 191–2
offerings: defining own broadly,
73, 81; defining own deeply,
72–3, 77, 80; defining own deeply
and broadly, 71, 73, 76, 77, 84;
educated guesses about, 71;
as impetus for needs, 97; list,
74–5; in MIOs, 169; own, 70, 112,
190, 207; partners', 95–6, 101,
131, 146; to partners, 88, 89–90,
124–5, 133–5; refined, 153, 214;
questions, 94. *See also* needs and
offerings
offers, 14, 171, 178; aggressive,
210; strategies, 180, 195. *See also*
MESOs; MIOs; SIOs

open-information sharing, 144–6,
166, 171; cultural differences, 195.
See also information
outcomes, advantageous, 159, 180

partners, transaction, 37, 46, 71, 74,
163; alternative, 151, 177, 189,
190; best-case scenarios for, 165;
conversation, 43; current, 86,
93; external world as, 97; four
groups of, 120, 124; fulfilling your
needs, 118–19; high/low costs
and benefits of, 120, 124–5, 129,
148; interdependencies, 151–2;
mapping out, 101; multiple,
38–9, 47, 156, 194, 197; mutually
beneficial, 192, 206; needs,
98–9, 153; needs and offerings,
102, 115–18, 121–3, 126–8, 161;
offerings, 95–6; one-issue, one-
time, 187–8; potential, 88–100, 101,
102, 208, 209; preferences, 170;
proper, 87; questions for, 112–13;
reducing number of, 198; targets
for, 165–6, 169; understanding,
101; understanding needs of, 44;
value for/of, 71–3, 77, 80–1, 84,
212–13, 214. *See also* counterparts;
educated guesses: partnerships;
potential partners; power
partnerships; *under* mapping
out; needs; needs and offerings;
offerings
partnerships: associated, 212;
economic and standard, 106;
potential, 120; re-evaluating set
of, 152; understanding, 210–12.
See also power partnerships

Peña Nieto, Enrique, 11
perspective-taking, 87; definition
    and negotiators, 73–4
persuasion, 171
politics, monetary mindset and,
    11–13
possibilities: complementary, 135;
    vs deals, 162; multiple, 197;
    mutually beneficial, 155; open-
    ended, 141; partnerships, 143,
    152; right, 200; surfacing, 44, 140,
    160, 178
power partnerships, 40–1, 192;
    alternative, 177; anticipating,
    47, 106, 109, 148, 213; as benefit
    to transaction partner, 153;
    categories, 124; cultivating, 47,
    214; definition, 42, 106; educated
    guess on, 120; fulfilling mutual
    needs, 117–18, 161; identifying,
    117–18, 124–5, 147, 163, 190, 212,
    214; mutually beneficial deal and,
    202; NFL-LA example, 104–7;
    potential, 130, 138, 145–6, 156,
    179, 190; relationships between,
    130–1, 134–5, 154, 156; as a set,
    43, 45, 53, 129, 130–3; trades as
    basis of, 111, 133; understanding,
    137–8, 178
prerequisites, 129. See also
    relationships: six types of
pressure tactics, 158, 159
price: protection, 61; risk, 190
problem-solving, 34, 194;
    integrative negotiation for, 24
proposals: multi-issue, 158, 159;
    multiple, 173

psychological effects: of bartering,
    34–5; of exposure to money, 6–7;
    of monetary transactions, 5
psychology of bartering, 20, 50

questionable objectives, 191–2
questions: defining offerings
    broadly, 73; direct, 146–7; general,
    148, 149; "how," 65–6, 68–9, 79,
    88, 112–14, 118–20, 125, 133–5;
    about offerings, 94; open-ended,
    145, 147, 155, 193; for partners,
    111; about partners' needs,
    96–7; trust-building through, 147;
    "who," 88, 90, 91; "why," 78, 88.
    See also key questions

reciprocity, 144, 145, 147, 148, 153,
    156
relationships: cultural differences,
    195; six types of, 129–30, 132, 152.
    See also under power partnerships
revenue(s), 66, 85, 161, 163;
    increasing, 65, 67–8, 75–6, 89,
    118–19, 165; need for, 144–5, 147
Revolutionary Armed Forces of
    Colombia (FARC), 82–4
risk, price, 190

SABMiller, Anheuser-Busch InBev's
    acquisition of, 136–8
San Diego Chargers, LA relocation,
    104–6
Santos, Juan Manuel, 82–4
sellers, 36–8, 45, 49
Senate (U.S.), 55
services. See goods and services

shareholders, 137, 138; analysis, 110
sharing economy, 18
Sherman, Roger, 55
single-issue offers. *See* SIOs
SIOs (single-issue offers), 166, 167, 168, 169, 178, 179
social capital, 109
social information, 195
social media, United Airlines, 3
solutions, 62, 69, 101, 156, 178, 207; bartering mindset, 21, 209; limited, 86; market as, 43, 99, 131; money as, 202; resulting from discussions, 28, 53
South Asia, 195
Spotify, 201
stadiums, LA, 104–6
stakeholders, 137, 138; analysis, 110
state sovereignty (U.S.), 54–5
St Louis Rams, LA relocation, 104–6, 124
strength, 199–200
studies. *See* case studies; research
substitutes, 130. *See also* relationships: six types of
Sukenik, Herb, 182–3, 198
suppliers, 72, 75; initiating discussion, 189–90. *See also* partners, transaction

targets, 169; identifying, 165–6, 179, 180
terms: deal, 160; discussion, 150; monetary, 169; trade, 149
"think it over," 212
3-D Negotiation (book), 87
time-banking services, 18

time costs and benefits, 197–9
Tories (U.K.), 157–9
Tory–Lib Dems coalition (U.K.), 157–9
trade-offs, 9, 10, 53, 139–40; mutually beneficial, 208
trade(s), 40, 170; "balanced" and "excess demand reducing," 33; as basis of power partnerships, 111, 114, 133; beneficial, 124–5; costs and benefits, 121–9, 132, 134; "extensive" and "inexpensive," 118; feasible, 119–20; identifying through questions, 133–5; mutually beneficial, 159; mutually beneficial and double coincidence of wants, 45; "pass-through," 37, 89; potential, 110–14, 115–18; reliant on diversity of commodities, 41–2; relationships, six types, 129–30, 132, 152; as a set, 42; terms of, 149. *See also under* benefits; costs; trust
trading, 33–4, 36, 43–5; Kyle MacDonald project, 29–31; multiple partners, 38
transaction partners. *See* partners, transaction
transactions: bartering, 50; both sides of (buyer and seller), 36–8, 45, 47. *See also* monetary transactions
Trump, Donald, 11, 83
trust: building, 141–3, 154–5, 166, 193, 212; building as integrative behavior, 14, 61; building through questions, 147; cultural

differences, 195; as necessary for trade, 43–5, 47, 53, 142; in non-Western cultures, 143

understanding, 50, 77, 100, 178; five-step process and, 47, 202; own needs and offerings, 37, 38; partnerships, 210–12; partners' needs, 44; power partnerships, 137–8, 178; problems, 207; transaction partners, 101; transaction partners'/negotiators' of external world, 83; value, 183; yourself, 205–7. *See also* external world: own understanding of; needs: understanding own; *under* market(s)

United Airlines: David Dao and, 3–4; monetary mindset and, 4
United Nations, 83
United States: Anheuser-Busch and beer market shares, 136–8;

border wall conflict, 11–12; Colombia and, 83; Connecticut Compromise (1787), 54–5, 71; NFL LA teams relocation agreement, 104–7; North Face marketing campaign, 201–2; Sukenik-NYC relocation package, 182–3; United Airlines and David Dao, 3–4

value(s), 30–1, 37, 40, 70, 72, 130; absolute, 174–5; bartering mindset creating, 100; claiming, 163, 171, 174; goods and services, 41; integrative negotiation creating, 160; MIOs, 173; for/of transaction partners, 71–3, 77, 80–1, 84, 94, 212–13; understanding, 183
Virginia Plan, 54

weakness, fear of, 199–200
White Denim, 201

Printed and bound by CPI Group (UK) Ltd, Croydon, CR0 4YY

25/03/2025

14647328-0001